SUPERMARKET WARS

Supermarket
WARS

Global strategies for food retailers

Andrew Seth

and

Geoffrey Randall

palgrave
macmillan

First published 2005 by
PALGRAVE MACMILLAN
Houndmills, Basingstoke, Hampshire RG21 6XS and
175 Fifth Avenue, New York, N.Y. 10010
Companies and representatives throughout the world

PALGRAVE MACMILLAN is the global academic imprint of the Palgrave
Macmillan division of St. Martin's Press, LLC and of Palgrave Macmillan Ltd.
Macmillan® is a registered trademark in the United States, United Kingdom
and other countries. Palgrave is a registered trademark in the European
Union and other countries.

ISBN-13: 978–1–4039–1910–6
ISBN-10: 1–4039–1910–0

This book is printed on paper suitable for recycling and made from fully
managed and sustained forest sources.

A catalogue record for this book is available from the British Library.

Library of Congress Cataloging-in-Publication Data

Seth, Andrew.
    Supermarket wars : global strategies for food retailers / by Andrew Seth
    and Geoffrey Randall.
        p. cm.
    Includes bibliographical references and index.
    ISBN 1–4039–1910–0
      1. Food industry and trade. 2. Grocery trade. 3. International business
    enterprises. 4. Competition, International. I. Randall, Geoffrey. II. Title.
    HD9000.5.S4175 2005
    381'.456413—dc22   2005049805

10 9 8 7 6 5 4 3 2 1
14 13 12 11 10 09 08 07 06 05

Printed and bound in Great Britain by
Creative Print & Design (Wales), Ebbw Vale

Contents

List of Tables and Illustrations

Tables

Illustrations (see plate section)

Preface

In our previous book (Seth and Randall 2001), we started from the proposition that supermarkets are an extremely important part of the lives of all those living in industrialised societies. The statement most quoted from the book by reviewers and commentators was that in these countries, the average adult will spend about 2 per cent of their life in a supermarket: we cannot escape their influence, for good or bad.

We also pointed out that the future of the industry would be international, but that only a few European firms had made any real progress in developing an international strategy (we mentioned specifically Carrefour, Ahold, Metro and Aldi). This book therefore concentrates on the development of international food retailing, which has been proceeding apace in the past few years. While Western Europe, North America and Japan have been stable, many other countries have seen dramatic changes – political, economic and social. One of these is the entry of international food retailers, and the development of a modern retailing system.

Unusually in an emerging world industry, American or Japanese companies do not dominate the field. Wal-Mart, the giant among retailers (and indeed among companies of any sort), is, of course, a major player, but the rest are European – French, German and British. For us, it is a fascinating story, with very different strategies and, as yet, no clear winners – though some spectacular failures. We hope that you find it equally interesting.

Acknowledgements

Particularly warm thanks are due to members of the two world-class contender companies now present in UK – Tesco plc and Asda (Wal-Mart). At Tesco, Sir Terry Leahy was his usual courteous and lucid self, full of ideas with a well-developed global perspective. Several members of his team were readily available and informative – David Reid gave me early guidance after taking over as Chairman. Philip Clarke, who took over the direction of the overseas markets, David Potts and Tim Mason were all helpful about their own key areas. Lucy Nevill-Rolfe read the script of Chapter 4 in draft and was interesting on the subject of culture and people – crucial areas for international companies. Her assistant Deborah Girling was the soul of helpfulness when we were up against publishing deadlines.

At Asda, Tony de Nunzio gave me a highly relevant interview, and Christine Watts and Olivia Gilmore assisted with perspectives and with photographs.

At Sainsbury, Sir Peter Davis gave me interviews in his second period of office. I also talked to Stewart Mitchell who led the trading team. Jeremy Schwartz, Brand Director, became a close contact during a year of working together.

Several city analysts shared their views. David McCarthy at Citibank Smith Barney reviewed the relative performances of Tesco and Asda. Andrew Fowler has a truly excellent worldwide perspective and a wealth of experience, and I was able to check impressions of future challenges in the world stakes with him.

The strategies of the brand owners are a key area for debate and have seen much change in recent years. Gerry Warner, head of retail accounts at Lever Faberge brought me up to date with the Unilever strategies.

The quality of reading material available was increasingly interesting as worldwide competition became a reality. The references at the end of the book list many of these but three specific publications stand out in my mind – Sam Walton's autobiography, an international study by Deutsche Bank *Eat Cheese or Surrender: Global Food Retail* (Rabattu and Botteri, 2003) and a series of good pieces on Wal-Mart often authored by Neil Buckley at the *Financial Times*.

The Institute of Grocery Distribution (IGD) team at Letchworth was well placed to provide articles and quantified information on the key industry players. Its annual publication, *Global Retailing*, is an excellent summary of the industry. Rachel Aggarwal was informative and directed us to good sources in the IGD library.

Wyatt Cameron and Peter Levi, based in Shanghai at Dulwich International College produced a series of exciting photographs of the Chinese retail scene (see plate section).

Peter Law and Susann Jerry at the Media Foundry gave first class industry perspectives and helped with the introduction to the book.

Two of my best professional friends – Mark Sherrington of SAB Miller, an erstwhile colleague at the Added Value company, and Chris Ingram, on two of whose boards I have been privileged to serve as a non-executive director – were constantly offering ideas and guidance and I count myself lucky to have worked so closely with them in two-top class marketing environments.

I would like to make two final acknowledgements. First to my co-author, who, since our first meeting at Oxford in 1957, I have grown to know very well. He is a genuine pleasure to work with, an eminent teacher and a cool and objective scholar who knows how to evaluate my often inadequately thought-out viewpoints. Our regular meetings in the welcoming inns of Kent, Sussex and now Hampshire, have often produced new ideas, but have invariably lasted for more hours than we had originally planned. When work, if that is what writing is, and friendship come together then the recipient is truly blessed.

This brings me to the last dedication, to my wife Edith, my best friend, which she has also been to our four boys and is now to our four grandchildren. She shows endless patience and gentle encouragement to a sometimes unsociable, and frequently unavailable, partner. I am hugely lucky to have had the support she has given with this book – the latest element in our lives – as she has given to all the things we have done in many parts of the world for half a century together.

ANDREW SETH

I echo Andrew's thanks to the many people who have made this book possible. Jose-Luis Duran, the CFO, and now CEO, of Carrefour, was generous with his time. He was articulate (in what is his third language) in giving a wide-ranging strategic view of both his company and the industry worldwide. He also provided introductions and access to his colleagues, who were similarly forthcoming and helpful – Bruno Cabasso, chief information officer, was frank as well as positive about Carrefour's information systems, Francois Bouche described its approach to global sourcing and Elisabeth Andro kindly supplied photographs.

Andrew Fowler of Merrill Lynch, for many years the leading food retailing analyst in the City, gave many hours of his time during several conversations, drawing on his wide and deep experience to give penetrating insights. Didier Rabattu, main author of the Deutsche Bank report mentioned above, provided refreshing views from a non-English standpoint. Kelly Hearn could also reflect a truly international background, and gave considered views based on deep financial analysis of the industry. An analyst of a different sort, Robert Clark, a retail market analyst, is one of the best informed and objective of observers of the retail scene, and was generous with his time and views.

Two consultants, Johanna Waterous of McKinsey and Mike Prefontaine of Deloittes, both American, were interesting in their opinions of the US market and Wal-Mart's place in it, as well as being well informed about the rest of the world.

Two elder statesmen – if they do not object to that term – gave their wise advice – David Webster, then still of Safeway, and Sir Geoffrey Owen of the London School of Economics. Dr Peter Grindrod was fascinating about the higher mathematics of data analysis in retailing.

In writing about the world market, I benefited greatly from an online course on the emerging giants (the BRICs) run by Dr Linda Yueh (2004) for AllLearn.org (the universities of Oxford, Stanford and Yale).

One should, perhaps, give a vote of thanks to technology and the Internet, which have made the task of finding information on a whole range of topics a great deal easier and quicker than it used to be.

As Andrew says, our working partnership is the fruit of a long friendship. Certainly, our working relations have been close, harmonious and fruitful; we have been able to argue, agree (mainly) and disagree (occasionally) in a way that is hard to imagine without underlying personal closeness and trust.

Finally, I must pay tribute to my wife Vicky, loving companion and support for over forty years: she has made all this possible.

GEOFFREY RANDALL

Abbreviations

BRICs	Brazil, Russia, India and China
C&C	cash and carry
CBD	Companhia Brasileira de Distribucao
CEE	Central and Eastern Europe
COO	chief operating officer
CPFR	collaborative planning, forecasting and replenishment
CSR	corporate social responsibility
EAN.UCC	a system that standardises barcodes, EDI transaction sets and so on
EBIT	earnings before interest and tax
ECR	efficient consumer response
EDI	electronic data interchange
EDLP	every day low price
EPC	electronic product code
FDI	foreign direct investment
Fmcg	fast-moving consumer goods
GCI	global commerce initiative
GDS	global data synchronisation
GMO	genetically modified organism
GTIN	global trade item number
ICT	information and communications technology
IGD	Institute of Grocery Distribution
KVIs	known-value items
MAGALI	Magasin Alimentaire
NAFTA	North American Free Trade Agreement
NGO	non-governmental organisation
OFT	Office of Fair Trading
P&G	Procter & Gamble
PCI	Produits Carrefour Internationaux
PPP	purchasing power parity
RFID	radio frequency identification

SAR	special administrative region (China)
SKUs	stock-keeping units
SOBs	state-owned banks
SOEs	state-owned enterprises
TI	Transparency International
TPF	Tesco personal finance
TWIST	Tesco Week in Store Together
WTO	World Trade Organization
XML	extended mark-up language

Introduction

Tintorn Samkamruen is piloting her four-wheel-drive through the dense Bangkok traffic. Although her maid still buys produce at local market stalls and the 'wet market', Tintorn likes going to one of the hypermarkets for their range and prices – and anyway, they are modern and efficient, like her. Usually, she goes to either Tesco Lotus or Carrefour, but a friend has told her about the new range of Leader Price products in the Big C stores. As an advertising executive, she knows that both Carrefour and Big C are French-owned and that Tesco is British, but she doesn't see much in the way of national differences between them. To her, they are just a welcome addition to the choice available, and a symptom of her country's progressive development. She hopes that the new zoning laws proposed to try to protect small local shops will not lead the foreign companies to reduce investment in Thailand.

Such a scene, unimaginable only a few years ago, could be reproduced in cities in many parts of Asia, Central and Eastern Europe (CEE), or Latin America. This book sets out to examine the phenomenon of how and why certain food retailers – mainly from France, Britain and the USA – have started to spread across the world, and what the future holds.

Two questions immediately spring to mind. First, why has it taken retailers so long to become international, when manufacturers have been doing it for a century? Second, why do they bother, when it is obviously difficult and not very profitable? It is true that one or two retailers did have branches overseas in the early twentieth century, but they were usually confined to London, Paris and New York. While manufacturers, and later service firms, planted their flags around the globe, retailers stayed mainly at home. Even by the end of the last century, the number of truly successful international retailers was tiny. Apart from luxury brands, and the fast-food giants, one can think of Ikea, Body Shop, Toys'R'Us and a few clothing stores, but one soon runs out. Among food retailers, the spread was even slower.

A list of the biggest retailers in the world by sales will show many American firms – but you will not see a Krogers or an Albertsons outside the USA. They are biggest because the US retail market is comfortably the largest in the world. In twenty years, the list will show many Chinese companies and, perhaps in fifty years, Indian. Even the mighty Wal-Mart, the most successful retailer in the world by a very large margin, started its international expansion late, and is still in only 11 countries. The ability of retailers to grow very large within the borders of the USA suggests the major reason why they stayed at home: they had plenty of scope to grow. Even now for

Wal-Mart, it is still easier to open large amounts of new space every year within the USA than elsewhere. Expanding within your home market, which you know intimately, is less risky and more profitable than entering strange new markets with an unknown culture, language, structure and competitors. The same is true, within their smaller markets, of European firms.

The establishment of what we would call a modern food retailing system – characterised by chains of multiples operating hundreds of large self-service stores, supported by an efficient supply chain – only developed in the past fifty years. Even in that time, success was not guaranteed, as familiar names struggled or disappeared, and new ones came to prominence. Success went to those who found the essence of a business model that worked for them in their particular market, and stuck to it relentlessly. The eclipse of Kmart by Wal-Mart, or of Sainsbury's by Tesco, shows how fierce the struggle was, and how unforgiving the judgement of consumers and investors. We would argue that food retailers had their work cut out first to survive, then to grow, in this jungle. Keeping up with changing tastes, investing in new technology, finding new sites, coping with regulations and legislation, quite apart from fighting competitors, all stretched most managements to the limit. Perhaps it is not so surprising, then, that in most cases, international expansion was not a priority until the 1990s.

The next question, more often asked by investment analysts than others, is, why bother? In this view, foreign markets could be divided roughly into three. The USA and most of Western Europe are large markets, with plenty of wealthy consumers willing to buy – but with entrenched and mainly very effective players already there, and often with very restrictive legislation making new store development extremely hard. At the other end are countries so poor that there are not enough potential consumers with the money to buy, and usually lacking the sort of modern infrastructure needed to run a retail multiple. In between, are those countries that are growing, often quite fast, and have at least some wealthy customers and a reasonable infrastructure. On the other hand, many are politically unstable, or have volatile economies, and anyway, they are ineluctably *foreign*. Among this group, there are some big countries that have huge potential, but also huge uncertainties, in particular those called the BRICs by economists. These are discussed in Chapter 1.

Retailers have to be very close their customers; they must understand them thoroughly, and be sensitive to their changing tastes and priorities. Sometimes they have to predict what they will want before they realise it themselves. If this is a challenge in your home market – and we know how hard it is because of some of the famous names who have failed to keep up – then how much more difficult is it in a country quite new to you. Because of the problems of adjustment, it usually takes time for new businesses in foreign markets to make money, and when the margins are as low as they customarily are in food retailing, there is very little room for error. Returns from international ventures are still lower than from those at home, and investors therefore take a sceptical view of them.

Still, some firms are now doing it. The main reason, of course, is the search for growth. Most western markets are mature, and increasingly concentrated. We discuss the effects of this on companies' policies. Expenditure on food forms a decreasing proportion of a population's total spending as general wealth increases, and food prices are currently in a deflationary stage. Consumers can be persuaded to buy more exotic foods, and more added-value, prepared dishes – but there will never be much real growth in food spending. Companies have diversified into new markets: horizontally into everything from newspapers to pharmacies, and into services from dry cleaning to banking (or, in Wal-Mart's case, from non-food into food). Food will, however, remain the product mix or a major part of it, and therefore if a company wants to go on growing, it has to look abroad. Many large food retailers are publicly owned, and stock markets demand constant growth. A company that is thought to be falling behind its rivals will see its share price slip, and that, in the end, leads to takeover and death (of the company, at least).

In this book, we will concentrate on the major players among international food retailers, focusing in particular on Wal-Mart, Carrefour and Tesco. We will also look at other firms that have started on the international road and may prove to be successful contenders – Metro, Casino, Auchan and a few others – and large companies that may in future have the resources and skills to follow them – Krogers, Albertsons and Ito-Yokado.

At one time, we would have included Royal Ahold, the Netherlands-based company that had built up easily the most successful foreign-owned food retail business in the USA. Until recently, Ahold was the fourth-biggest food retailer in America, with its Stop and Shop and BiLo chains. In 1999, *Nutrition Today* could write, 'By any definition of globalization, Royal Ahold is a successful, profitable, fast-growing, seasoned international chain, a model of today's successful global supermarketer.' Since the USA is metaphorically littered with the skeletons of failed European retailers trying to break into the market, Ahold's was a fascinating story. Unfortunately, as most readers will know, Ahold imploded after a financial scandal at its American foodservice business. The unravelling of the group is still going on, and while some pieces will survive, the international group will be broken up. Commentators will continue to be split. Some argued that it was clearly an acquisition machine, achieving more by smoke and mirrors than by real retailing skills. Others claimed that, especially in America, it had made real progress in gaining back-office efficiencies. The chief executive, Cees van der Hoeven, was a dedicated internationalist, and seemed a true forward-looking manager. Sadly, he is facing prosecution in his native country, and we shall never know if his vision would have been successful. For this book, Ahold would have been a useful counter-example, in that it kept all the fascias it acquired separate, whereas the common pattern, as we shall see, is to use one brand internationally.

We concentrate on those who have survived, starting with Wal-Mart in Chapter 2. This business phenomenon has been the subject of quantities of comment and analysis, both laudatory and critical. All American readers will be intensely familiar with it, though most elsewhere will be less so, except by reputation. From our point of view, it is essential to understand what the sources are of its unbelievable success over many decades, and to analyse its international experience. Wal-Mart is such a colossus among retailers – and indeed among all businesses – that we spend some time on the origins and philosophy that drove it to dominance in the USA. We will examine its successes and occasional failures abroad before summarising its current strategy prospects.

Chapter 3 describes Carrefour, the French group that was not only the first to enter foreign markets, but is also the most international by some way. Carrefour has dominant market shares in some countries, but seems to have struggled in others; it should be in a strong position, with its range of formats and unrivalled international experience.

Chapter 4 applies the same process to Tesco, the British operator. Our previous book (Seth and Randall 2001) described Tesco's impressive rise from also-ran to market leader in the UK. Though a late entrant to the international scene, it has made its mark in both Europe and Asia, and so far rarely puts a foot wrong.

We then describe more briefly in Chapter 5 the firms we called 'the contenders'. It seems likely that only a handful of companies will end up dominating international food retailing, and while we believe that Wal-Mart, Carrefour and Tesco will be among them, so may be one or more from this chasing group.

Next, in Chapter 6 we try to tease out some of the issues involved in going international. How do firms choose the countries they enter, and why; how do they decide on the sequence of entry, and are there emerging strategies to guide future decisions; what did the leaders do, and what lessons can we draw from their various experiences? The chapter examines the issue of standardisation against adaptation: how much can and should firms adapt without compromising a winning formula? What are the implications for pricing and range, for food and non-food? What should guide branding and fascia choice?

Then, in Chapter 7, we look at the impact of information and communications technology (ICT), and companies' use of the wealth of information (or at least data) at their disposal. The chapter analyses how firms can pursue competitive advantage through the use of ICT in supply chain management, inventory control, in-store automation and cost saving. We go on to discuss the use of information for marketing: how to analyse the vast amount of purchase data, loyalty card data and other information to understand shopping behaviour, and how this may guide decisions on segmentation and targeting. We will also look at online shopping, and speculate about possible future uses of technology.

In Chapter 8, we compare the theoretical advantages of international operations with the experience of our retailers: scale, first mover advantage, transfer of learning. How far procurement is multinational or global in practice, and what the limitations are of product field, or type of goods. How transferable is experience? What can we learn from the mistakes that retailers have made?

In Chapter 9 we move on to the social issues raised by the spread of international food retailers. Protests against globalisation have made news around the world in recent years; this chapter examines to what extent this applies to our field. How will globalisation affect local shops and shopping habits, consumer choice and eating habits: for example, will supermarkets be tarred with the same brush as fast-food outlets, and be blamed for contributing to growing obesity? We examine the impact on local suppliers and multinational manufacturers, and describe government policies as they affect retailing – planning, protection of local businesses, preservation of diversity.

In Chapter 10, we ask the question, 'What do you, as a local retailer, do when Wal-Mart (or Carrefour, or Tesco, or all three) enter your country? There are strategic options, apart from selling up: fight head on, surround and stifle, differentiate or retreat to a niche. We examine the options for selected leading local firms. Will national firms have to go international to survive, whether by alliances, mergers or acquisition?

We then move on (Chapter 11) to the strategic options for those retailers who are already international, or who will take that path. The strategy adopted by Wal-Mart is different from that of Carrefour, and Tesco is different again. Will there be convergence around a common pattern, or will players need to adopt a consciously different path?

In the last chapter, we look into the future. First, we return to the regions and countries, and try to see what the future holds. We then identify the core competences that international retailing will demand, and discuss whether any new winners will emerge. We assess each of the major competitors, and give our prognosis for their future, setting out what each will have to do to succeed.

1 The World as a Market

While we refer loosely to global players, we do not mean that our leading food retailers actually operate in all 200-odd countries in the world, or that they will in the near future. In the medium to long term, we might expect every country to offer at least some potential, but that is not the position today. In this chapter, we give an overview of the world as a market, concentrating in particular on the potential giants of tomorrow. In the final chapter, we will return to the question of how this scene is likely to play out over the next few decades.

Ambitious retailers looking outside their home base can easily make a first cut at ranking regions and countries by market potential. The normal criteria will include population size, level of economic development, geographical position, culture, sophistication of infrastructure, government policies and political/economic risk. At one extreme is the developed world: North America, Western Europe, Japan and some countries of South-East Asia, Australia and New Zealand. At the other are those very poor countries – many in Africa, some in Asia – that offer little potential for the present and can be ignored. In between are the various emerging and transitional economies.

Most countries in the developed world have a mature market for food (and the associated supermarket ranges). Many are already highly concentrated, with a handful of powerful, entrenched competitors. Some, particularly in Western Europe, are regulated by legal restrictions on store development and operations. All are attractive in that they are rich and stable economies with sophisticated infrastructures. On the other hand, the only method of entry is by merger or acquisition, a process laden with difficulty and risk. We will return to this topic in the final chapter.

The challenge is then to decide, from among the wide range of all the countries between the extremes, which to enter and in what sequence. There is no space to examine all in detail. Here, we will examine as exemplars the four large economies that show enormous promise, but also demonstrate the difficulties and risks of trying to forecast future development. Economists have called them the BRICs – Brazil, Russia, India and China. Brazil, with over 180 million people, and Russia, with almost 150 million, are big countries; India and China between them account for over one third of the entire population of the world. They are not exact equivalents of other countries but, to an extent, they can represent the range of experiences of emerging and transitional economies. In this chapter, we describe briefly how they have got to the position they are in today; in the final chapter, we return and look at their possible futures.

Brazil

The only metaphor to describe Brazil's economic path is the rollercoaster. In the 1970s, the future looked rosy. From the mid-1960s, growth had been rapid, with increases in per capita GDP averaging six per cent. Its model was far from the so-called 'Washington consensus': relying instead on import substitution and a powerful public sector; it seemed to have mastered the problem of living with inflation rates of 30 per cent, and was politically stable. Over the period 1950–80, real per capita GDP almost quadrupled (Dornbusch 1997), and there seemed every reason to see Brazil as a successful emerging economy with a very bright future. That has not happened.

Economists would argue that the old model was unsustainable. The apparent ability to live with high but stable inflation (20 to 40 per cent) was based on a highly controlled economy, with wages and prices indexed, and strict controls on financial markets and exchange rates. The system was installed during the military regime of the 1960s, and seemed to cope well. It was derailed by the double oil shocks of the 1970s. For a time, the government financed the extra costs of oil by borrowing, but when that became difficult (because other countries were also struggling to contain inflation by restricting money supply), the price rises were passed on. Within the system, this led inexorably to wage rises, which led to higher inflation, which fed the cycle even further. Inflation rose to 80 per cent, then over 100 per cent; wage increases became more frequent, and this fed the rises faster. Soon, the system was out of control, and inflation hit over 200 per cent by 1985, with wide swings from month to month.

The Cruzado Plan of 1986 tried to re-impose stability through an incomes policy and price controls. There was a short-lived boom, but soon inflation was approaching 400 per cent and rising. In the years that followed, there was a succession of plans to stop inflation: Cruzado 2, the Plan Bresser, the Summer Plan, the Collor Plan, and Collor 2. All had similar results – a short period of stability followed by raging inflation. Finally, in 1994, the Real Plan introduced a new approach, including a new currency, the real, linked to the US dollar. Economic policies took a more orthodox turn, and although the process took some time and was not without incident, it gradually worked. The old import substitution policy was abandoned, and the economy opened to the outside world. Nowadays, Brazil looks more like a 'normal' country, with inflation in 2003 at nine per cent, though also with sluggish GDP growth and high interest rates. Because of the damage done by previous policies, GDP per head is, at $2500, lower than that in Argentina ($2840) and considerably below that of Mexico ($6210) (Economist Intelligence Unit 2004).

Despite this turbulent history, Brazil has been a country in which many international businesses invested, and made money. Like many emerging economies, development is concentrated in the large cities, such as Rio de Janeiro, Sao Paulo, Recife and Curitiba. Because of the country's size – the distance from north to south is equal to the distance between London and Baghdad – companies often focus on one or two regions.

The retailing industry has modernised, led both by local companies and by entrants. The market leader is a local firm, Companhia Brasileira de Distribucao (CBD), which has around 15 per cent. Carrefour entered early, and is second. Wal-Mart started operations in 1995, but expanded slowly until it bought the Bompreco chain from the troubled Ahold in 2004. CBD is mainly in the north-east of the country, while the others are located mainly in the south.

Russia

Russia is, in Churchill's oft-quoted phrase, 'a riddle wrapped in a mystery inside an enigma'. As the source of the revolution of 1917, and the leader of the USSR, it lived in a centrally planned, command economy until after 1988. This system is hard for outsiders to understand, as it featured such things as centrally controlled prices and separate (and different) exchange rates for each major good. No market, in the accepted sense, existed. The country was powerful, and relatively well-off because of its huge oil and gas reserves. Party and state officials were privileged, but most of the population had a basic standard of living, and education and health care were free.

As we now know, the system was unsustainable: the demise of communism and the break-up of the USSR were among the most dramatic and influential events of the late twentieth century. Unfortunately for Russians, the next decade saw GDP almost halve, and life expectancy actually decline. How on earth did this happen, when the country had apparently adopted the capitalist, market model? What follows is necessarily a short and over-simplified account of an exceedingly complex process.

First, there were legacies of the old Soviet system that were to have a huge impact. In particular, a tiny elite, the *nomenklatura*, ran the system, made all the important decisions and controlled the major resources. Some of them were economically aware, and in a position to profit from the confusion and the opportunities that appeared as central authority broke down. Quite early on, in 1988, a Law on Cooperatives allowed what amounted to management theft: managers of state enterprises could set up parallel private companies (Aslund 1999). The bizarre pricing structure meant that in 1991, the state-controlled price of oil was 50 cents a ton, 0.4 per cent of the world price, while industrial goods were grossly over-priced. As an example of what resulted, well-connected managers could obtain foreign trade rights, buy oil at ludicrously low prices, and sell it abroad at a huge profit.

Secondly, Russia attempted to reform by 'shock therapy', and started to free controls in 1991 after Boris Yeltsin took charge. The economy was in disarray: as central control of the states disappeared, the government was receiving little revenue, and many shops were empty. Yeltsin's government attempted to liberalise all prices at a stroke in 1992, but the powerful managers of the oil and other commodity enterprises successfully resisted – not surprisingly, given the amount of profit they were making. Most prices were freed, but as there was little financial infrastructure, this led to runaway inflation that destroyed savings; by 1992, inflation was running at 2,500 per cent. The central bank issued large credits, which given the inflation rate were essentially free, and many bankers became very rich.

In such conditions, corruption (always present) became rife, and the powerful former state managers, the bankers and corrupt officials resisted changes that would threaten their privileges. They defeated the reformers, though there were further attempts at reform from 1993 onwards. Throughout, however, the collapse of the old system before a new one had been put in its place led to anarchy. Poverty increased: in 1989, only two per cent of Russians lived in poverty, but by 1998 that had risen to 24 per cent (and more than half of all children) (Aslund 1999).

The other major reform, and the one that has been most publicly criticised, was the privatisation of state enterprises. The general perception is that the issue of vouchers to everyone, though admirable in principle, did not work: many companies ended up being controlled by very few people, who had the contacts and access to funds that allowed them to take over large concerns cheaply. This is partly true, and especially so of the oil and gas firms, which were extremely valuable. Many other firms, the old, inefficient Soviet plants, were hardly great prizes. What is certain is that a few of the 'oligarchs' who had emerged from the previous period did gain control of huge assets. Many of the old *nomenklatura* in fact opposed privatisation, as it might deprive them of their ability to go on stealing from the concerns they managed. On this view, the privatisation was not the most important cause of the acquisition of enormous wealth by a few: that had happened already. The public perception, however, during a period when many of the population were experiencing real hardship, was very damaging.

Reform had virtually stopped by 1996. Because of the size and importance of Russia, the west continued to support it politically and financially. The IMF arranged a large loan, and foreign investment rose. Although the IMF loan was in theory tied to continuing reform, this seems not to have worked. The oligarchs and other powerful interest groups were too strong; they influenced government decisions in their favour, carried on making money, and transferred much of it out of the country. The loans may even have encouraged the government to ignore its difficulties in collecting taxes, and the fiscal situation worsened; budget deficits rose. Criminals became actively involved in politics and business. Confidence among outside investors ebbed, and the stage was set for the crisis. When oil prices fell, the government tried to maintain the exchange rate, but in the end, in 1998, Russia suspended its debt repayments, and devalued the rouble, which promptly crashed.

Since then, the situation has stabilised. Higher oil prices and stronger central government under President Putin have led to better control of finances; the budget is in surplus, inflation is lower, the economy has been growing and the exchange rate steady. The worst gangsterism has disappeared. Corruption is still widespread: in the Transparency International ratings, Russia scores a lowly 2.8 out of ten and shares 90th place with India, among others (the top country, Finland, scores 9.7, the UK is 11th with 8.6 and the USA 17th with 7.5). Much of the infrastructure needs investment, and the financial system needs further reform (Economist.com 2004a). Most worryingly, Putin shows increasing intolerance of political dissent. One of the oligarchs, Mikhail Khodorkovsky, began to take too active a role in opposing Putin's policies, and was jailed on charges of tax evasion. His company, Yukos, a huge oil firm, has been effectively nationalised. The rule of law is not universal.

Nonetheless, many western investors have returned to Russia, and locals are also active. The retail sector has seen chains take 14 per cent of the total food market from almost nothing (Euromonitor 2004). Leaders are Perekrestok (see below), Ramstor, Sedmoi Kontinent and Megamart. Metro, Spar and Auchan have opened stores, and Carrefour is planning to enter. Wal-Mart has been in talks with Koc Holdings of Turkey, whose Migros Turk chain owns Ramstor in Russia, so this may be the US giant's way in.

One feature of the market is what are known as 'quotations', and what we would call challenges. Perekrestok, for example, means crossroads in English; so does Carrefour. The Russian retailer hired a French consultant to set up the name and organisation structure; 'insiders say there is a striking resemblance between the products and pricing approach presented by Perekrestok ... and those usually associated with Carrefour' (tdctrade.com 2001).

Doing business in Russia is still different from what westerners are used to, and a great deal of change is still necessary. Many investors and commentators think that the opportunities are too great to ignore, but others are more cautious.

India

India draws on a civilisation thousands of years old: while Europe was in the dark ages, Indian mathematicians and astronomers were developing their science. The rich culture and religious life of the sub-continent has fascinated westerners, and still does. With a population of over one billion, India is already more than three times the size of the USA; with a higher birth rate, it seems certain to overtake China as the most populous country in the world. It is, as it proudly claims, the largest democracy on earth. Yet its economy has not flourished as have others in Asia, and it still not a magnet for foreign investment.

For many years after gaining independence from Britain in 1947, India followed a socialist ideology. In economic terms, this meant widespread government control, of investment and trade in particular. Everything was subject to licensing, imports were forbidden or severely restricted, foreigners could not own more than 40 per cent of the equity of a company. Like Brazil, it followed an import substitution policy, so a wide range of industries grew up; but many were technologically backward, and the goods they produced were of poor quality. Growth stayed stubbornly at the 'Hindu rate' of three to five per cent.

The British had introduced many of these controls in 1940, and some relaxation occurred in the late 1940s. However, a foreign exchange crisis in 1956–7 led the World Bank to enforce a 57.5 devaluation of the rupee. Such was the internal hostility to this that it 'led India to turn inward with a vengeance' (Panagariya 2004). This situation remained until the 1980s, when some selective relaxations were introduced. Growth improved, but was very variable. Much of the growth was fed by government spending; external and domestic borrowing financed deficits. Foreign debt rose from $21 billion in 1980–1 to $64 billion in 1989–90.

In a sadly familiar scenario, rising government spending, large fiscal deficits, increasing public debt and a growing current account deficit led to the inevitable crisis in 1991. This time, the government acted decisively, introducing reforms whose effects are still working their way through the economy. Industry was very substantially deregulated except for a few reserved areas (such as arms, alcohol and tobacco). In many industries, the 40 per cent ceiling on foreign investment was abolished; the central bank could automatically allow up to 51 per cent (and up to 100 per cent in some cases), again apart from in certain sectors. Trade was also liberalised, with import restrictions lifted for many goods. The rupee was devalued by 22 per cent.

Although all this was welcome, and did lead to an increase in the growth rate, the improvement was not dramatic. This has been particularly true in manufacturing, which has not shown anything like the Chinese dynamism. India remains a country of contrasts, with teeming cities and a huge, poor, rural hinterland. While the software and IT services industries are developing a world presence, most others are not. Michael Porter, the world-renowned guru of competitive strategy, points out that many Indians, when they leave their country, are extremely successful; many US and other corporations are headed by CEOs of Indian origin. The problem seems to lie at home.

Porter points out that 'Indians have a tremendous tendency for over-statement ... One thing I've noticed is that Indians don't take criticism very well. They get very offended.' (Raman 2004). These brusque remarks were made in a context of great affection for and interest in the country. Porter's view relates to his well-known hypothesis that what produces world-class companies is a highly competitive home environment. Indian businesses have lived in a very protected situation: to catch up, they need to learn from rivals in other countries, and they can only do that by working with them and listening to them.

According to Porter, India's business environment still has several important weaknesses. First, the capital markets are rather weak. Second, the physical infrastructure is 'abysmally ranked'. Worst of all are 'the pervasive barriers to competition'. In other words, although considerable liberalisation has occurred, there is still far too much government interference. India is, despite its many positive features, not an attractive place to do business in, compared with, say, China. This is reflected in the relatively low levels of foreign direct investment (FDI).

Retailing demonstrates how true much of this analysis is.

In the past years, a lot has been written about the so-called revolution in the Indian retail sector and the boom it has supposedly been experiencing. ... Most of the time, the euphoria has largely been based on the metro, upwardly mobile consumer. No wonder, despite all the hoopla .... the share of the 'organised' retail remains an insignificant 2 per cent or so of total consumer spending in India (Singhal 2004).

It is true that modern retailing has begun to have an impact, and that shopping malls are appearing in major cities. Most retailing, however, remains unorganised, carried on by millions of tiny shops. Most food is sold in *kiranas* (corner shops or mom-and-pop stores).

In fact, FDI in food retailing is still banned. Metro, the German group, has opened cash-and-carry outlets, but in what seems a typical fashion, local rivals are suing them. The claim is that Metro is selling to consumers, in contravention of its licence. The motive is clearly protectionist, but is surely symptomatic. Firms such as Wal-Mart and Carrefour are rumoured to be considering entry when given permission, but no early moves are expected.

World Trade Organization (WTO) rules have forced China to open its market to foreign retailers, and most commentators expect the same to happen in India. Given the state of the infrastructure, and the concentration of income in a few cities, it does not look an attractive market at present.

China

For centuries the most advanced civilisation on earth, far ahead of any other, China might have gone on to become a dominant power if it had not decided to turn its back on the rest of the world in the fifteenth century CE. Its twentieth-century history is well known: the communist party led by Mao Zedong took power in 1949, and has ruled ever since. Of greatest interest to us here is what has happened in the past few decades, as the Chinese rulers began to open the country to market forces.

The contrast with Russia's experience is striking, as China rejected the 'shock therapy' approach for a gradualist path. Russia and the other countries of Central and Eastern Europe (CEE) after 1989 were relatively industrialised, but in poor shape economically, experiencing low growth, and with considerably weakened central government. China, by contrast, had a centralised government in firm control and with great continuity. Its state sector was not yet in decline in the late 1970s when reform started, so needed fewer subsidies than those in CEE. It was also relatively under-industrialised, with a large surplus rural labour force, all conditions favourable to a gradualist approach (Yueh 2003).

China's leaders were pragmatic, starting with 'a planned economy with some market adjustment', moving to 'a combination of plan and market', finally to 'a socialist market economy'. They saw the need to modernise, as they could not keep up with more advanced nations, but did not have the pressing need of the CEE countries to rejuvenate failing industries and rejoin

Europe. They could afford, they thought, to move slowly and in a distinctly Chinese way. Their approach is still to have a dual track, with both state-owned enterprises and private companies. In such a large country, they could also experiment in different regions that were separate enough not to contaminate the rest if the experiment failed (mostly, of course, the Special Economic Zones such as Shenzhen have been a spectacular success – but it may be that they did not want too much success to cause widespread jealousy and unrest).

To see a huge country in the middle of such a dramatic transition is fascinating (both authors have visited China). The great majority of the population has no experience of a market system at all. They had lived all their lives under the implicit contract of the 'iron rice bowl'. This means that everyone has some sort of job for life, and receives a wage, free housing, education and health care, and a retirement pension. The wage is very low (a doctor received some $50 a month just five years ago), but there are, in theory, few other costs. To jump from that low-luxury but very safe cocoon to the risks and opportunities of the free market is challenging. Of course, Chinese people outside China have always shown great entrepreneurial drive and skill: they run most businesses in South-East Asia, and are notably successful in the USA. There seems no reason to doubt that they will show similar traits at home.

The transition is in progress, and after several decades shows every sign of success. Since 1978, when Deng Xao Ping initiated the economic reforms, China's growth rate has averaged a staggering 9.5 per cent (*The Economist* 2004c). This is three times that of the USA in the same period, and faster than Japan's during its miracle years. China has become one of the manufacturing powerhouses of the world, as most people can testify from personal shopping experience. With a population of 1.3 billion, and this sort of growth, it has become the magnet for companies from all the developed nations. As someone said to us some years ago, 'In ten years you won't have to ask what is the biggest market for anything – it will be China'.

Not everything in the Chinese garden is perfect, however. The gradualist path has been described as the 'easy to hard' reform sequence (Yueh 2003). The easy changes were made first, leaving until later the changes that would cause political problems and will be harder to implement. Several major problems remain. The most difficult revolve around the still-large public sector – the state-owned enterprises (SOEs) and the state-owned banks (SOBs). The central and local governments share ownership in some 150,000 SOEs, many of them of uncertain value. At present, it is not clear how and when the state could divest itself of these, nor what the effects would be – on unemployment, for example.

The SOBs have huge books of non-performing loans: 21 per cent of GDP in 2003 (Prasad 2004). Many of their other loans may also be of doubtful worth. Although there has been some progress in moving towards accepted standards of reporting and provision, most of the banks have, by western standards, low capital adequacy and profitability. It is hard to over-stress the size and difficulty of these two problems. Certainly, no quick solution is in sight.

An issue relevant to business is the lack of a recognisable and complete legal system. Laws have been passed, but their implementation is often poor and enforcement is often lacking. Added to prevalent corruption and fraud (China scores 3.4 on the Transparency International (TI) scale, and is in 71st position), this makes doing business risky. There are many anecdotes of foreign business people losing out on what they thought were perfectly proper contracts and deals (see Clissold 2004).

Other looming problems include high unemployment, rural–urban migration, lack of a social safety net and environmental damage (Yueh 2003). At some point soon, China will have to face up to the pressure on its currency, and revalue. All these are the hard decisions that have been postponed, but cannot be forgotten.

For retailers, as for other businesses, China remains hugely attractive. It had a mainly pre-modern retail industry based on markets and small shops, but this has been changing since the 1980s. In the 1990s, supermarkets started to spread, led by local chains such as Lianhua, Hualian and Nong-Gong-Shang. Several foreign retailers entered at this stage, from Japan, the Netherlands and Hong Kong, but most withdrew or reduced their presence as they could not compete with the locals. Competition is intense and margins thin; Chinese consumers have the reputation of being very price-conscious. The domestic operators not only had the local knowledge and contacts, but often received soft loans and reduced rents (Gilmour and Gale 2002).

Now, with its growing middle class and booming cities (21 of more than 3 million people) it is a tempting target. As with other sectors, it has not been easy to gain entry: negotiations have to be carried out with central and local governments and usually, a suitable partner found. This has not stopped Carrefour, Wal-Mart, Metro, Tesco and others from opening stores or buying into local companies. Since 1992, $3 billion of FDI has reached China, and the government has approved 264 foreign retailers (covering all sectors) (www.ce.cn accessed 17 March 2004). With its accession to the World Trade Organization in 2004, China has had to open up the retail sector as well as other markets completely.

Both foreign and local retailers face common problems, according to a study by AC Nielsen. Four issues are of major strategic concern: an inefficient supply chain; high staff turnover costs and other human resource issues; questions over whether to merge or acquire new businesses; and challenges in developing brand and shopper loyalty (www.Retail-merchandiser.com/retailmerchandiser/reports_analysis 2004). The very nature and size of the country make logistics a problem – but no more, in principle, than the USA (the two have a similar-sized land mass). What is lacking in China is the century or more of development that has gone on in America to produce its modern supply chains.

There is no doubt, from the success of the foreign entrants so far, that their formula is attractive to many Chinese consumers, so it is a market that anyone aiming to be an international retailer will have to succeed in.

What these four examples show is that transitional economies share many of the same challenges. They have chosen different routes, but their positions are converging. Parallels exist in the other countries in similar situations.

We now move on to see how the major international retailers have exploited the opportunities, starting with Wal-Mart.

2 Wal-Mart: The Colossus

The Wal-Mart story is unique in retailing. It is unique because for thirty years it was the vision and actions of one man which created a retail colossus that covered the length and breadth of America in a way nobody else had done before. Few individuals have exercised the influence that Sam Walton did in his business lifetime. His personal achievement was simply staggering, a stunning example of the classic 'rags to riches' American dream. From the smallest of small-town beginnings in Rogers, Arkansas, in the rural American mid-west, Walton rose to command the greatest personal fortune ever amassed in US history before Bill Gates. From an unprepossessing start as a store assistant in the J.C. Penney department stores, Walton drove his own business ahead with such persistence that today it is not just the biggest in America, but is ranked first in sales in worldwide business, ahead of such commercial giants as Exxon, IBM, General Motors, and General Electric. Walton was a true retailing phenomenon, an entrepreneur to delight the most demanding of critics, who took enormous pleasure in doing things his way, in swimming, as he liked to tell anyone who would listen, 'against the current'. Once he had proved a principle to his satisfaction, he was consistent to the point of utter ruthlessness in sticking to the truth he had learned, and making sure that colleagues were equally aware and disciplined. He was in many ways a simple man, whose business approach, as we shall see, depended on the application of basic tenets which created success across an enormous swathe of retailing activity, and which have stood the test of time not just for thirty years in Sam's own lifetime but since then for more than a decade after his death in 1992. There is no story quite like it.

Sam was always astonishingly determined and ambitious, with phenomenal powers of self-motivation and an ability to persuade others. His brother, Bud Walton talks about him (Walton 1993) in this way:

> From the time we were kids, Sam would excel at anything he set his mind to. I guess it's just the way he was born. Back when he carried newspapers, there was a contest. I've forgotten what the prizes were – maybe $10, who knows? He won that contest, selling new subscriptions door to door, and he knew he was going to win. It's just the make-up of the man.

The make-up of the man was something the Wal-Mart organisation was to learn a great deal about over the ensuing thirty years. Over those hugely successful years, Sam made himself more and more of an iconic figure, the stuff of American business legend. There were to be a lot of contests, at all kinds of levels, and in all kinds of places, and not just with Wal-Mart's constantly growing range of business competitors. As the years passed, Sam's adversaries became more and more significant. When he began trading, Cincinnati's doyen company, Procter & Gamble (P&G) did not consider him worth selling to. Today Wal-Mart is streets ahead of anyone else in turnover, as a P&G customer. Whoever and wherever it was, Sam had no doubt at all, as Bud had suggested, he was going to go on winning. He created a retail juggernaut that like Attila the Hun, swept all before it, taking great pleasure in burying competitors who tried to imitate its approach, or worse still, stand in its way. It tried, and often succeeded in, setting its own rules or modus vivendi, and local communities in the US have found themselves radically affected by the presence, or impending entry, of Wal-Mart in their midst. Wal-Mart has its own, unequivocal way of thinking which has made it a different kind of competitive business from anything American retailing had seen before. It polarises responses wherever it goes.

The principles that Sam Walton made his own were blindingly simple. Offer the lowest possible prices, all the time, everywhere, on everything. Be sure everyone knows this is what you are doing. Keep your costs lower than they were last week, or last year, lower than any of your competitors', and keep the process of cost reduction continuous across all aspects of your business. Singlemindedly pursue volume growth – make your company the biggest in its sector, in its industry, in the country, and, one day, in the world. Ensure that your own teams know absolutely, all the time, what your strategy is, and that it is not about to change. Ensure that they implement it faithfully – using everything from cheerleading encouragement publicly delivered, to the most autocratic instruction, to make sure this happens. Apply these same tactics to your suppliers, be they big or small – negotiate ruthlessly for lower costs by offering them the prospect of ever-increasing sales and market share, providing they bring their own costs down. Finally, use the inherent and over-riding appeal of the message – 'Lowest Prices, Always' – for customers, to cajole and browbeat local, national and even international communities to give you the headroom and licence needed to make the ongoing process of explosive Wal-Mart growth accelerating and continuous. It is in essence the simplest of capitalist visions – lowest costs plus lowest prices means fastest growth for everyone playing in the game. Among the participants, there are no losers, only winners. Applied with the consistency and firmness which Wal-Mart provides, it becomes the most powerful and relentless of business bandwagons. How 'good' it is for society as a whole, is, in some quarters, a subject of some argument. That it has succeeded, continues to prosper, and has many more good years ahead, is however not in question.

Wal-Mart's progress can be traced through three distinct but equally striking and successful phases. The first was the early manifestation of Sam's vision in small-town rural America; the second, more than a decade after he started, but still driven forward with Sam at the helm, was the more comprehensive, frontal assault on US non-food as well as food retailing. This was still located in the US and it took Wal-Mart forward to become the powerhouse it is today, a force to be reckoned with across the entire US and in most sectors of customer retailing. The third, and perhaps the most surprisingly successful of all, is the past ten to fifteen years (1990–2005) when new chiefs arrived to run the Wal-Mart machine ; first David Glass, anointed by Sam as his successor, and latterly, Lee Scott. They have maintained the highest levels of business performance, and driven Sam's original vision and ideas forward with clarity and persistence. It sometimes seems as if Sam is still there, at their side, encouraging and blessing their every move. Managers said the same thing about Disney long after Walt was no more around to lead and inspire. Wal-Mart today may be a great deal bigger than it was when Sam left, but it seems no different in nature. It has grown even more quickly in the US, taking on new markets and a host of new store formats. It has pioneered and exploited with great verve the largest one-stop supercenters that are already such a feature of the US landscape, and are currently being built at the staggering rate of more than 200 each year.

Finally Glass, Scott and their successors have taken Wal-Mart into a dozen international markets, and from the outset they have not been daunted by the novelty or size of the countries they have selected. From neighbouring Mexico and Canada, they moved to the biggest European markets, UK and Germany. Today Wal-Mart is well represented in Japan and China, so uniquely among world retailers, it has a strong presence across the major and developed markets of the global triad. Sam would feel, perhaps, that his chosen successors have done him and his philosophy proud, not only in style and substance – much of which they inherited – but also in global reach, which has been their achievement. It has been formidably consistent, one the market recognises in Wal-Mart's ever-ascending share price. Its principles have been straightforward and uniformly applied wherever they have gone.

It is worth enumerating what these principles are. Formulated by Sam in the earliest days, they have not altered significantly under his successors, and throughout they have been rigorously applied in whatever store format Wal-Mart has been present. Cheapest possible pricing is at the root of the policy. Sam talked about his first store in Newport Arkansas:

> *Here's the simple lesson ... which eventually changed the way retailers sell and customers buy right across America. Say I bought an item for 80 cents I found that by pricing it at $1 ... I could sell three times more than by selling it at $1.20. I might make only half the profit per item but because I was selling three times as much the overall profit was much greater. Simple enough. But this is really the essence of discounting ... you earn far more at the cheaper retail price. In retailer language, you can lower your mark up but earn more because of the increased volume. Things began to clip along pretty good in Newport in a very short time ... (Walton 1993).*

and to clip along even better elsewhere in the years ahead. The pricing recipe has not changed since Newport days. In 2004, Lee Scott put the argument in moral terms – twenty per cent of Wal-Mart customers had no bank account and lived from pay cheque to pay cheque. They deserved the opportunity to buy goods at Wal-Mart price levels. Banning superstores in favour of a utopian vision of small-store retailing hit those who could afford it least.

'It simply means that they can't have as good a life, because you have chosen *your* image of the world versus what is the most efficient manner of serving the consumer', he said. Expressed in this way, as an issue of society governance, it is hard to argue with Scott's statement or the Wal-Mart approach. As Sam admitted, there is nothing earth-shaking or even novel about the Walton pricing 'lesson' – business has worked this way from time immemorial all over the world. Discounters with similar philosophies of pricing exist in most retail markets and sectors. The striking thing has been the way in which Wal-Mart for four decades has translated the simple discounting truth through its entire company, and corralled everyone into driving home the message of 'lower prices, always', to create lasting competitive advantage for Wal-Mart in its many marketplaces.

The day Newport saw it all start was 2 July 1962:

> The day which would alter for ever the suburban landscape in which so many Americans live. There was not much retail presentation in the operation – it was strictly bargain basement in style. Racks of clothes hung from metal pipes and … the goods, from automotive supplies to toys and sporting goods, were stacked on tables. There were three checkout stands … twenty five staff, mostly women, paid 50–60 cents an hour, well below the minimum wage of $1.15. Many of the goods were junky … [they were all that Walton at that stage could obtain]. But the prices … they drew in the shoppers. At that time, the manufacturer's suggested price was what most retailers charged. Wal-Mart offered a stark contrast … savings of 20–30 per cent across the board with most items backed by a manufacturer's guarantee (Ortega 1999).

Except for the scale of operation, from one small mid-western store in 1962 to thousands of discount stores and supercenters today, nothing has changed. The consistency is remarkable.

Wal-Mart's steadfastness has been an admirable characteristic. As Sam put it:

> We started out swimming upstream and it's made us strong, lean and alert. We … have our own way of doing things. It may be different and it takes some folks a while to adjust to it, at first … and whether or not other folks want to accommodate us we … stick to what we believe in because it's proven to be very, very successful.

The next key element in Wal-Mart's permanent dedication to keeping costs low for its customers has been a ritualistic and well articulated belief that 'a dollar saved is a dollar passed on to the customer'. Always the emphasis is on securing the best possible pricing from suppliers so that the company could turn around and pass the savings along to its customers. Wal-Mart aimed, and still aims, to be the prototype 'lean, mean merchandising machine' (Turner 2003a). In return for recognition and support for this policy, Wal-Mart offers its suppliers volume, volume and then more volume, and on the record it has delivered handsomely with its side of the bargain. Not everyone has enjoyed the experience; and it took time for the company to fully engineer their approach with the biggest supplier companies but, eventually, they did. Once it had happened, there was simply no stopping the process.

'Sometimes it was difficult to get the biggest companies to call on us at all' Sam noted in 'Swimming upstream' (Chapter 4 of his autobiography) and 'when they did, it was to dictate to us how much they would sell to us and at what price. P&G allowed me a 2 per cent discount if we paid within 10 days and if we didn't they took the discount right off ... we were the victims of a great deal of (vendor) arrogance in those days.' How life was to change for these two formidable companies over the next forty years. Twenty years later, P&G finally and abruptly came to heel. It started to understand who was by then calling the shots, even with the biggest consumer goods company in the world. 'We are in your shoes now' proclaimed the P&G ads in the big retail magazines of 1983–84, announcing the appointment of Brad Butler as their new trade relations supremo, and recognising publicly once and for all that Wal-Mart needed to be dealt with specifically and cooperatively to ensure P&G got its share of its burgeoning business volume. Shortly afterwards, Wal-Mart welcomed into its Bentonville HQ large numbers of P&G negotiating 'partners' charged with getting P&G market shares in Wal-Mart moving upwards. They succeeded in their mission, albeit at a price in both economic and psychological terms.

It was a watershed for US manufacturers as a whole, and for retailers, a clear sign that 'the times they were a changin'. Sam Walton says:

> In those days we desperately needed P&G's product whereas they could have gotten along just fine without us. Today we are their largest customer. But it wasn't until 1987 that we turned a basically adversarial relationship into one we like to think is the wave of the future – a win/win partnership between two big companies both trying to serve the same customer.

For P&G it may have been perceived as a relatively painless transition which certainly paid off for Cincinatti as well as Bentonville. Today P&G is selling more than one third of its volume in the US to Wal-Mart, an enormous percentage for this highly successful business, but the dependency relationship has changed utterly in the period. P&G are now less likely to pull out of a deal, or raise its voice, since the penalties would be prohibitive if they did so. The Beast of Bentonville has turned on and tamed the smartest of its mid-western hunters.

In a different part of the forest, the case of the Rubbermaid company is instructive. Like P&G, Rubbermaid, a winner of US national business awards and a $2 billion company, with brands like Rubbermaid containers, Grace baby products and Waterman and Parker pens, has its satellite office in Bentonville on the Wal-Mart site – this has become a virtual sine qua non of supplier success today and nearly 500 companies have chosen to run up their flags on the Wal-Mart premises. The Rubbermaid office is practically 'a shrine to Wal-Mart'. 'We wanted our office to be consistent with Wal-Mart's culture of simplicity and frugality' says Steven Scheyer, Rubbermaid's President insouciantly. If the language speaks of kow-towing to the retailer, it is unsurprising as Rubbermaid had been through the fire in their dealings with

Bentonville. Some years earlier in response to their own increases in cost, Rubbermaid endeavoured to push price increases through its distributors. Wal-Mart in a not atypical manifestation of its corporate power simply de-listed the entire company range and replaced it from other sources. This resulted in Rubbermaid weakening so significantly in the market, that four years later Rubbermaid itself became a victim and was taken over by Newell. Is it surprising that its new owners have decided to pay the price, almost any price, to restore a critical relationship, one that can mean the restoration of volumes that might be a quarter or even a third of potential total company business? (*Financial Times* July 2004)

Newell's policy reversal, and its willingness to identify itself with its destroyer and eat humble pie, is clear confirmation that in the US (as already seen in parts of Europe, notably the UK) the balance of power has shifted irretrievably from manufacturer to retailer. When it can drive suppliers out of business, has the trend gone too far? Not according to today's Wal-Mart hierarchy. Tom Coughlin, Wal-Mart's former Vice-Chairman and a frequent spokesman on this issue says, 'If I were a supplier, here is a company that gives me a new chain of stores every year.' Rubbermaid are certainly happy with the state of things now they are back in distribution. Steven Scheyer went on record as calling the Wal-Mart negotiation approach 'simply straightforward'.

> Other retailers [he said] ask for rebates, cooperative advertising payments and listing fees. But Wal-Mart just wants the best possible quality at the lowest price – it's a net–net proposition and so, easy to read.

An outside observer might conclude that 'Rubbermaid had been brought to their senses', but Wal-Mart would never be caught using such brutal language.

Yet Wal-Mart does lay itself open to the accusation that it uses its power to demand exclusive product and demand lower prices. Recently Levi Strauss, the embattled jeans maker, has produced a special line of merchandise for Wal-Mart, called 'Signature' priced at $10, and there are many cases of similar 'exclusive contracts'. 'On most products as you sell more you earn an opportunity to reduce your costs' said Tom Coughlin. Lee Scott admits he is 'not terribly sympathetic' to companies who protest about Wal-Mart squeezing their margins. 'We make about 3 cents on the dollar. Most people we buy from have a higher return than we do.' Scott would probably say this is the *raison d'etre* for the process of price and margin reductions continuing ad infinitum, and he would point out that Wal-Mart does not pocket the gains, it passes them on. The process has become an organic one and there is no doubt that Wal-Mart is ferocious in its search for purchasing cost gain. The *Financial Times* (12 August 2004) reviewing Wal-Mart's latest results, noted that there had been gross margin gains in eleven of the previous 12 quarters. Increasing drive for global procurement was becoming a key element of Wal-Mart advantage, especially in clothing. Wal-Mart's own direct purchasing involvement seemed certain to provide potentially big percentage gains – estimated by Deutsche Bank at 4–6 percentage points.

Asda UK has been able to introduce 8000 of its 12,000 new lines, noted in former CEO Tony de Nunzio's latest report, as a direct benefit from Wal-Mart global sourcing. It's not all good news – at least in an American election year. There was a strident reaction in 2004, from John Kerry among others, to Wal-Mart's deliberate opening up of sourcing from China – estimates of up to $15 billion have been admitted including gains from suppliers from the same source. Of course Wal-Mart is by no means alone in this. Tesco and Carrefour are doing the same thing. Nor has Wal-Mart pre-empted the market. But its scale makes it visible and has generated comment in high places. However, the simple overall message seems to have struck home with the customer – Wal-Mart's core appeal in the US, but now also in its successful markets outside the US, has always been and continues to be to the less affluent. This is the group that welcomes lowest cost from wherever it comes, and needs the lowest prices, preferably from a one-stop location. A large group of customers are clear they trust the uncomplicated message and in the US they have seen it in action for long enough to know how it is achieved. The same applies in Wal-Mart's most successful foreign market, the UK, where a strong Asda price brand has been strengthened by the additional clout that Wal-Mart has provided in a consistent way to the Asda position. Lowest prices, based on lowest possible costs, is a simple message. Marry this to unparalleled shopping convenience – everything under one roof – and you have a true winning formula.

There are three key elements where Wal-Mart extracts significant and worldwide cost advantage. They are first, as we noted above, sourcing and logistic costs; second, keeping corporate overhead costs to a minimum; and third, low, fixed wages and salaries. Taken together, and spread across the massive, growing volume they represent huge competitive advantage, wherever they compete.

Keeping down the costs of running the business has necessarily applied to the biggest cost of retailing – the company's own wage bill costs. We have seen how Sam started off with a wage bill set at very low levels, way below the minimum wage in the 1960s. Not much has changed. Wages and salaries are kept to a minimum and Wal-Mart has fought a tooth and nail battle to keep labour non-unionised across the company – it is a battle that they may now be beginning to lose, and indeed Wal-Mart have ceded the issue in China. Today a new hire can still earn as little as $8 an hour, perhaps 25 per cent lower than a unionised equivalent in the next-door supermarket might take home.

Here again the Wal-Mart advantage may now be eroding. In February 2004, after a five month strike, California supermarket workers agreed to cede some wage and benefit advantages to the employers. The workers had taken the strike primarily to stiffen their position ahead of Wal-Mart's major superstore expansion plan, scheduled for Inglewood, California in 2005 (discussed below). Wal-Mart will of course point out that in considering its wage and salary costs, the benefits accruing from its share save and bonus programmes need to be taken into account, and there is no question that many employees, at a range of different levels, have earned large sums from Wal-Mart's explosive growth over the years. Wal-Mart has offered employment to groups of workers in society who have found jobs difficult to get. The 'Goldies'– groups of over-50 workers – are a significant feature in their US workforce. Asda UK have successfully recruited in the same way, and this policy has community appeal and may be a part of the perceived customer service advantage that Asda enjoys. Wal-Mart has recruited graduates deliberately from cheaper – southern and mid-western – campuses and has achieved high performance from them at lower costs through recruiting this way. Finally, it can point out that, despite Sam and his family joining the group of richest people in America, the policy of minimising fixed wage costs applied across the board – there's no difference even at top management levels. In the late 1990s, of the fifty highest paid individuals in discount retailing in the US, not a huge catchment group, Wal-Mart possessed only two – the CEO and his number two, and they were placed at 19th and 35th positions respectively. Accusations of 'penny pinching myopia' and being 'in thrall to the almighty dollar' are fashionable among US critics, but the universal approach to wage and salary costs is impressive.

But storm clouds now threaten many of Sam's venerated people policies. They are being challenged externally and in some cases within the enterprise itself, and perhaps seriously, for the first time. Wal-Mart is venturing into a new and demanding world in which its capacity to pilot a consistent course will show if it is capable of continuing to grow at a historic rate. Meanwhile the hallowed routines of iconic corporate behaviour at Bentonville persist. The most theatrical of these is the famous Saturday meeting, well described in Graham Turner's *American Odyssey* (2003a). For many outsiders this personifies the folksy, simple-talking outlook on life that surrounded Wal-Mart's beginnings. Wal-Mart does have a humorous streak which Sam described as 'whistling while you work'. He was persuaded once to dance the Hawaian hula down Fifth Avenue, New York, after losing a bet on business results. But this behaviour is something of a veneer, and the real Wal-Mart has an intrinsically harder edge. Internally, Turner was told, company meetings are characterised 'by a great deal of hardball'. It is hard to imagine otherwise. We have seen how brutal supplier negotiation can be. Perhaps the folksy side of things is an apology for having to be tough the rest of the time.

Stalk and Lachenauer (2004) say that 'winners in business play rough and don't apologise', instancing Wal-Mart in their introduction to the theme, as classic hardball players.

> They pursue with a single minded focus competitive advantage and the benefits it offers – leading market shares, great margins, rapid growth and all the intangibles of being in command.

Wal-Mart's unique success has been to build this uncompromising business culture, but also to preserve a corporate ethic that has tried to emulate the spirited entrepreneurial ideas and style of its founder. It is not afraid of risk or of moving quickly to respond to market opportunity ahead of competition. Given the results, it is hard to quarrel with the combination of toughness and risk-taking that has emerged.

But it may now be getting tougher to keep up the breakneck pace. There's far too much external interference for Wal-Mart's comfort. In an unguarded moment, Lee Scott described his typical working day – 'my mornings start with reading sales, followed by a visit from our general counsel'. Legal and labour compliance problems have mushroomed, and through a twelvemonth period Wal-Mart has been assailed by a horrific series of major governance challenges. All the ensuing occurred in 2004 to date. Lawyers representing 200 illegal immigrants are suing the company, alleging that Wal-Mart staff knew they were illegal entrants and conspired with contractors to pay them low wages. Simultaneously, a Wal-Mart superstore in Quebec looks likely to become the retailer's first unionised store in North America after the provincial labour board said that workers were entitled to union recognition. Naturally, this case could set important precedents, thus eroding much of the company's long-standing wage cost advantage through time. In April 2004 the Inglewood, California, voter rejection of Wal-Mart's planned major supercenter incursion into the state constituted a body blow to its expansion strategy (discussed below). But none of these reversals compares with the news which broke in June 2004 that Wal-Mart was being forced to defend a class action, brought by 1.6 million women employees, involving the company in dozens of law suits over its employment practices.

In what the *Financial Times* described as 'the grand-daddy of employment class actions', Wal-Mart is accused of systematically denying equal opportunities for pay and promotion to its female workforce. Mona Williams, the Wal-Mart spokesperson, claimed that the clearance for the class action which was granted in a San Francisco court in June 2004 'had nothing to do with the merits of the case'. Nevertheless the case is regarded by the company as material financial risk. Were they to elect to settle, the damages could possibly run to billions of dollars. Wal-Mart has certainly responded to the problem, setting new diversity targets, and warning its own management that non-compliance with the law's requirements in terms of minorities' pay and promotion will bring salary reductions for those responsible – recognition that the seriousness of the position is appreciated from the top. 'Until now' said Brad Seligman, counsel for the plaintiffs, 'they've never faced a trial like this. Lawsuits by individual women were nothing more than a pinprick. Now however the playing field has been levelled.' Even today the Wal-Mart net pay level is a huge advantage to the business – the average hourly wage is just $9.64 an hour. The challenge has been called 'the Microsoft phenomenon' of size and scope, driving intense scrutiny and potentially large-scale, time-consuming litigation. It has been called not only a case for big money but one that is almost impossible to defend. The case, and the overall background of increasing litigation, points to more serious strategic worry for the company. Not only will Wal-Mart have to concede the need for additional legal, PR and

Human Resources staff, but also, perhaps more significantly, the diversion of business leadership from the task of driving growth and margins could be significant. What Wal-Mart must fear most is becoming a visible magnet for social enquiry, thus watering down its culture of strength and entre-preneurship which, as noted above, has represented its twin performance hallmarks. Rallying the troops to provide a persuasive and determined response has begun – 'We're under scrutiny like we've never been before and we've got to tell our story like we never have before', said Betsy Reithemeyer, VP of Corporate Affairs. Worryingly for the business, Wal-Mart's explosive growth means it is never short of influential enemies, and this is a new chapter for Bentonville, one that Sam never had to write – defending the citadel against a range of new attacks.

Sadly for US corporate business, there will be many who want it to fail. In recent months Wal-Mart has become increasingly aware of this unpalat-able truth, and is changing its corporate approach, apparently permanently, taking a much higher federal and national profile in the US in order to represent its position better. Wal-Mart is strengthening its lobbying position in Washington, and has become (2004, a Presidential year,) the largest corporate donor in the US, a huge change over four short years; in 2000 the company ranked 771st of US companies on this same measure. Jay Allen, senior VP of corporate affairs for the company noted 'frankly there is a need that exists today … with everything that's going on, for people to under-stand us better'. Wal-Mart has made big funding contributions to congres-sional and senate candidates (220 of them at the last count), unsurprisingly 85 per cent going to Republicans. Ray Bracy, international corporate affairs VP, said 'until recent[ly] the biggest issues had been local … but more and more as we have become big, and the target of criticism for many … we recognised that there were looming and large national issues'. Wal-Mart may be trying to have its cake and eat it; there are comments that it is staffing its lobbying offices sparsely, and on the cheap, but the fact remains that this kind of approach and investment betokens a big change of heart from tradi-tional Wal-Mart mores. Sam would not have liked it.

The public image of the company has been taking a battering and nowhere more visibly than in the protracted battles in which the company has been engaged, over many years, and in many places, in fulfilling its goal of increasing the penetration and number of Wal-Mart outlets across the US. The process has developed into a virtual civil war, not just setting the company against town and city governments, but dividing communities against themselves, as individuals take sides in what have regularly become bitter, impassioned encounters. Even the highly paid consultants and learned academics who have reviewed the increasingly bruising arguments are unable to agree where right lies. Few issues fire up US local communities more violently than news of the impending arrival of a Wal-Mart. Ortega (1999) devotes several entire chapters in his *In Sam We Trust* work to the confronta-tions that began to break out as the company accelerated its supercenter expansion in the 1990s. Wal-Mart did not win them all either. In Lancaster County, Pennsylvania ('God's country'), a highly organised protest movement stopped the building of six such stores. The final comment was a back-handed compliment to the company's hardball negotiating approach by John Jarvis, the movement's leader:

The good thing about Wal-Mart was that it was big enough, nasty enough and aggressive enough to make the problems of uncontrolled growth clear.

The issue is a persistent one, all over the US, and if anything the arguments are getting bigger and more bruising for all concerned particularly as the latest Wal-Mart strategies are to put more store locations in and around the big cities of the US, not, as hitherto, to concentrate more on out-of-town sites.

Inglewood, California, was the scene for the latest highly public round of the battle. Wal-Mart had planned to build 40 supercenters in Los Angeles county and chose the poor and mixed-race community of Inglewood to make its first sortie, envisaging a store the size of seventeen football fields, and devoting major energy and PR drive to their case. They sought to bypass the local officials by taking the issue of the store's rationale direct to Inglewood voters, who they were convinced they could persuade of the merits of the case – based on new jobs, tax revenues support and of course, lowest prices. As the day for the vote grew closer, hostilities became a daily occurrence and both sides increased their levels of support; the anti movement brought in the local congresswoman, Maxine Waters, and flew in Rev. Jesse Jackson to bolster their case. Jackson is known for a fine and vivid line of Wal-Mart rhetoric, calling their store staff 'twenty-first century plantation workers', and likening the company to a mammoth-sized gorilla. At the end of the day Wal-Mart lost the battle, a significant majority coming out against the proposal, and the reversal is bad news for the company's approach to California as a whole. Consumer militancy had again inflicted a defeat on Wal-Mart, crowing, at the post-vote celebration party, (*Los Angeles Times*, 7 April 2004) 'dollars can't buy the people. They wanted a good fight and they came to the right place.'

There are many more such battles to come as Wal-Mart seeks to extend its discount superstore operations into the big cities of the US. Already communities have begun to pass new sets of ordinances, designed plainly to fetter the Wal-Mart approach, limiting the size of outlets to 100,000 sq. ft. The company response has been to design stores to fit just inside such constraints. But the real problem for Wal-Mart is to make the case stick at a conceptual level, where more and more people believe Wal-Mart forces small retailers out of business, replaces well-paid jobs with poorly paid ones, creates traffic problems, and worsens the character of the community itself – something that Americans have always valued highly. Neil Buckley (*Financial Times* 7 July 2004) points out that measuring Wal-Mart's impact on jobs and communities is inherently tricky. Ken Stone, a retired Iowa State academic, concluded in 1997 that:

Rural communities have been more adversely affected by discount stores than by any other recent factors ... What Wal-Mart has done is really decimate our small towns to the point where it becomes very inconvenient to live there.

Conversely, another study of 1750 Wal-Mart openings, by Emek Basker of the University of Missouri, stated that a Wal-Mart entry into a county might increase employment after five years (Basker 2005).

Prior to the Inglewood vote, noted above, two simultaneous studies, one paid for by the town council and the other by Wal-Mart itself, reached diametrically opposite conclusions regarding the consumer choice and economic effects of the planned Wal-Mart California strategy. The issue is complex and is unlikely to be resolved by more academic treatises. More compelling is the chilling remark by Professor Stone on what happens when Wal-Mart is forced on to the retreat by a community – the unintended consequences often are that when Wal-Mart is driven to stay out, it 'goes on to the next community and draws the trade right out of the original town.' This is what happened in Vermont state, which marshalled its anti-Wal-Mart resources so successfully, it claimed a unique state wide victory. Wal-Mart then built stores on the state perimeters in New Hampshire and New York, took trade away, and forced the state legislators to come to heel, and allow them to enter after all. God appears in these head to head encounters, to end up on the side of the big battalions. The game goes on at a frenetic pace.

Wal-Mart's ability to pressure, debilitate and force mainstream business competitors to throw in the towel is universally recognised. It started of course with Sam, planning how to tackle Kmart and Target stores:

> *We decided instead of avoiding our competition, or waiting for them to come to us, we would meet them head on. It was the smartest decision we ever made. (Walton 1993 p. 242)*

Bud Walton confirmed this: 'Competition is very definitely what made Wal-Mart'. He describes Sam's well-honed approach to competitive intelligence, essentially snooping on everyone who might help his growth – 'there may be nothing he enjoys more than going into a competitor's store and trying to learn something from it'. It is a primary part of the company's strategy, and its competitors know it well and, if they are any good, take their own steps to meet it and stay ahead. There have been successes, some of them remarkable and even durable. Tesco in Britain have gained in share and momentum following the take-over of a successful Asda competitor by Wal-Mart in 1999, even though Wal-Mart itself has made handsome gains. Perhaps the denouement here, if there is to be one, is still years ahead. Wal-Mart could afford to pressure Tesco margins, and it might be in its worldwide interest to do this. A lot may depend on how spirited Tesco, a dominant market leader, chooses to be vis-à-vis Wal-Mart's UK aspirations. It may care to read the story of Kmart (Text Boxes 2.1 and 2.2) when it reflects on how hard it wants to try.

Wal-Mart is a force for creating focused business pressures on thinking competition – it is its imminent arrival in California which made the collective retail chains there take steps, even including a lengthy workers' strike, to ensure their wage and benefit costs were at a level where they could compete with Bentonville's planned arrival. As Wal-Mart would say there's one big winner here – the customer.

BOX 2.1

WHAT KILLED KMART?

1962 was a banner year in American retailing. Sam Walton opened his first Wal-Mart store in Rogers, Arkansas. Nobody paid any attention. The sixty-year veteran retailer, S.S. Kresge opened its first Kmart discount store in Detroit, following it with seventeen more that same year. Everybody noticed – Kresge were a big and long-established US retailer. Ten years later Kmart had 1200 stores, ten times as many as Sam Walton, and the company changed its name to Kmart, reflecting the significance of the new discount operation. However 1990 saw Wal-Mart sales sneak ahead of its rival despite a huge Kmart equity offering, several acquisitions (Walden Books, Builders' Square, The Sports Authority, Office Max, Borders) and a move to Europe, Mexico and Singapore.

As Wal-Mart growth exploded, Kmart fortunes went in the opposite direction. Acquisitions were sold off, the company experimented with the Big Kmart format – imitating guess who – the Martha Stewart brand was introduced and expanded into several categories. In the year 2000, both companies acquired new CEOs. Lee Scott took over at Wal-Mart, Charles (Chuck) Conaway became Chairman and CEO at Kmart. Within eighteen months – by January 2002 – Conaway's company filed for Chapter 11 Bankruptcy Protection and that year he left the company. What had gone wrong? Why did Kmart fail? More significantly, how could two companies with identical retail profiles perform so differently in such a short space of time?

Ironically, Kmart was a model for Sam Walton all his business life. Harry Cunningham, an early, successful Kmart CEO, notes wistfully in Sam's life story, 'Sam adopted almost all the great Kmart ideas'. Sam, diehard competitive intelligence gatherer that he was, was forever dropping in on Kmart, to find out what they were doing – it was a hallmark of his fiercely competitive behaviour. Once he was winning, anyone with a notebook or a camera had better not be found in a Wal-Mart store. This one difference is symptomatic of the cultural divide between these two companies. Kmart lacked competitive culture, believing their customers were happy with what they were getting. Right to the end they ignored competitors nipping at their heels, feeling that there was no need to change a well-tried traditional formula. Obstinacy and a lack of competitive spirit pervaded Kmart management.

Kmart's strategy was to aim to be biggest, and to 'score home runs' rather than patiently make incremental changes. Wal-Mart wanted to be best and developed the formulas that made them biggest. This was a crucial difference between the two. The Kmart strategy was high risk – they fought directly on Wal-Mart's battle ground, even when it was abundantly clear that Wal-Mart had many more answers. As we shall see, this insouciance led to their final undoing. Target, sensibly, took a peripheral route based on differentiation, which paid off handsomely, despite sharing Wal-Mart's store formats. There was a further gap between Wal-Mart and Kmart in their ability to execute successfully. Wal-Mart worked assiduously at its supply systems and information. Kmart constantly changed tack from area to area, and across its diverse store range, never capitalising on potential scale strengths. Even at the end, IT systems were not integrated – a huge problem for a company trying to keep pace with the Wal-Mart ever-reducing cost base.

Food was symptomatic of Kmart's failure to establish a customer-driven culture. As Wal-Mart was growing its every-day-low-price (EDLP) offering to become the biggest food retailer in the country, and Target building a niche reputation for quality and differentiation, Kmart did neither and went nowhere. Their attitude to suppliers was lackadaisical and relied on tactics. Policies were developed 'on the hoof', and there was no consistent communication or shared purpose in supplier dealings. Kmart had a mentality problem, process disadvantage, and a weak and ever-changing leadership structure. Roles and responsibilities were simply not clear. Leadership changed so frequently that most managers barely knew a new leader's name, far less his aspirations. By 2000, when Conaway took over, it was clear the company was in poor shape – but it was at least still making profits. But even this was not to last much longer.

Conaway's strategy – another Kmart home run sally – was long on bravura but short on analysis. He elected to take on Wal-Mart at its own game. In 2001, he announced price cuts on 10,000 items that brought Kmart's prices below Wal-Mart's. He then doubled the reductions, in a second phase, to 20,000, and with his Kmart revived 'Blue Light Always' programme, ordered heavy increases in inventory to meet expected increases in demand. Wal-Mart, recognising frontal threat to its EDLP promise, responded characteristically. Invoking 'help and support' from its 'partner' suppliers, Wal-Mart used their cost reductions to fund its own across-the-range price cuts. Kmart had fundamentally misread its market and the strength of a competitor. Wal-Mart reacted with speed and resolve to the challenge, cleverly minimising its outlay by generating a fighting fund from supplier budgets. Conaway's initiative rebounded swiftly on his weakened company, now threatened with increasing liquidity problems, caused by huge unwanted inventories. Disaster was quick to follow.

Kmart has emerged from Chapter 11 and trades profitably again. For a company which made so many mistakes, and which simply had no strategy to deliver competitive advantage, it might consider itself lucky still to be around. Can it be restored to its former glory? (See Text Box 2.2).

BOX 2.2

CAN KMART RECOVER?

When a slimmed down Kmart emerged from bankruptcy protection in May 2003, few believed that eighteen months on, it would itself acquire an erstwhile US retailing powerhouse – Sears, once the world's leading retailer, with a pedigree stretching back to 1886. Kmart had itself undergone significant restructuring, including selling many stores and ruthlessly cutting costs. Profitability had returned to the company for the fourth successive quarter in the third quarter of 2004, this after thirteen successive loss-making quarters through the disaster years of 2001–2003, when Chuck Conaway's adventurous price cutting strategy had bankrupted the business, in a vain attempt to compete in price cutting terms with the Wal-Mart US colossus.

However, new Kmart with its reduced store count is a pale shadow of its former self. Now ranked eighth among US retailers, sales fell again by 13.7 per cent in the latest quarter to a shade over $4 billion, a tiny (seven per cent) proportion of Wal-Mart's quarterly revenues. What is new to Kmart is that for the first time it has acquired a leader with genuine commitment and focus – a chairman who is clear about competitive advantage, the need for results and how he is going to deliver. Eddie Lampert, 42, the 'Sage of Connecticut', (so called because he models himself as a hedge fund manager on Warren Buffett, the legendary Sage of Omaha), has a powerful reputation and a fifteen-year track record. He has invested in old-line companies that can be managed to throw off lots of cash, and he has indicated that he intends to fashion Kmart to become a powerful investment vehicle. Lampert through his fund, ESL Investments in Greenwich, owns 50 per cent of new Kmart. The potential for change at Kmart is suddenly striking.

Lampert is already successful where his predecessors in old Kmart failed conspicuously – in driving cost effectiveness management through the business and generating a multi-billion dollar cash hoard in quick time. On 17 November 2004, Lampert revealed an agreed bid for Sears, valuing the merged business at $11 billion. The stock market reacted positively to the news and shares in both elements of the new merged company rose immediately and by double figure percentages. Lampert, chairman-elect of the new company, claimed that the combination was 'extremely compelling' for customers, associates and shareholders. He went on, 'it will create a powerful leader in the retail industry, with greatly expanded ... distribution ... brands ... and improved scale and operating efficiencies'.

Will it? Who does Lampert see as his target audience – retail customers, or his hedge fund shareholders? Their requirements could be very different. Answering this question may reveal how likely it is that Lampert will be able to develop a powerful competitive retail vehicle and brand.

Sears itself has experienced the endemic growth failure affecting Kmart, partly because it too has problems with those same competitors – Wal-Mart and Target – and partly through problems of its own, where Home Depot have been gaining share at Sears' expense, and the company has resorted to a new 'off-mall' strategy in an attempt to create an area of retail space it can occupy more profitably. The new 'Sears Grand' strategy has been touted by Sears – through Alan Lacy, their CEO – as 'the way to jump start our strategy to grow the brand off-mall'. So far results are unclear and if anything Sears' revenues trends look as weak as Kmart's. Off-mall could finally mean little more than running for cover.

What is evident is that it is Wal-Mart's presence, its scale and focus, which have created the impetus for these latest moves. Only by driving costs down can companies like Sears and Kmart hope to survive – separately or together. So there is an elemental logic to the merger, and the synergies resulting will be a worthwhile platform from which to drive a more profitable business forward. Alan Lacy states ambitiously that 'this is a fabulous merger – a great combination of two very fine companies and brands'. Aylwin Lewis, hired from Pepsico (Yum brands) and appointed by Lampert as CEO of the new Kmart wing of the company, says 'the move will turbo-charge Kmart. I am here to build a super-retailing brand in the US.' Lewis's focus would be on customers and he appears unconcerned about Wal-Mart breathing down his neck: 'our goal is to win, relative to our strengths and serving our customers' unmet needs.' There is clear evidence that Lampert and his lieutenants realise they are now playing in a big game, against the biggest of competitors, and that they need high-calibre management and a competitive strategy, as well as cost savings, to win through. Will they be good enough? If he can't breathe life into his merged company, will Lampert simply move his pile of cash to new, more rewarding territory?

The weakness in the argument seems to be that combining two weak players rarely produces one strong one. While revenues move merged Kmart to third place in the market, it is not yet by any means a secure position. Sales growth is absent, and no amount of cost cutting will of itself reverse this decline. More significantly the two parent brands, while long-established and even iconic in their heyday, have lost virtually all their one-time lustre. Neither stands for anything much more than 'yesterday's hero' in today's competitive US market. Wal-Mart is the price and cost marker, the leviathan Kmart cannot ignore, but alongside Wal-Mart there are now a range of relatively well differentiated companies, some local, some national (Home Depot in home products, Best Buy in appliances, Target, like Wal-Mart, everywhere) and these players have a perceived brand quality that both Kmart and Sears now lack.

There are problems with both business models. Adding Sears brands to the Kmart range will not make the latter a better competitor to Wal-Mart. Sending Sears stores off-mall will not of itself do so either. This will take time, money and professional skill – whether Lampert's team have this in sufficient depth and whether Lampert himself has the customer dedication and the patience to stay with the brand-building task, only time will tell. What is clear is that, for the Sage of Connecticut this is new territory.

Michael Silverstein (Silverstein and Fiske 2003) seems to have made the key point. 'Wal-Mart just does trading down' he notes, whereas Costco – but also H-E-B, Target, and British Tesco – 'do trading up as well as trading down'. It gives them flexibility, a more inclusive consumer offer, and best of all, the capacity to stand up to the colossal purchasing power of Wal-Mart. Where this idea will go in future is less clear. Silverstein says that, 'At some point … trading down will have played out', and feels that the ultimate winners may be the players who can take their market in either direction. However, it is hard to see the appeal of low prices on the majority of goods being anything other than a primary long-term consumer appeal, especially in the less-rich countries into which Wal-Mart will increasingly venture. Today's lesson is that in a segmented market, which all developed economies would expect to have, both strategies can prosper, *if efficiently operated*. These three words matter most.

Wal-Mart's international progress has in overall terms been less smooth than its domestic development. Today they are present in ten markets outside the USA, with around 1500 stores, the largest number in Mexico, but with significant numbers in the UK – probably the most happy single Wal-Mart acquisition – Brazil, Canada and Germany. With sales of $47.5 billion, international is a significant and already fast-growing element in the portfolio, and its growth momentum at least matches domestic growth – sales up nearly 17 per cent in 2004 and profits up slightly more – at $2.3 billion, and growing quickly. The picture looks strong from an investment viewpoint, especially as Wal-Mart still has small market shares in most of the markets it has entered, and has chosen to position itself across the triad, and in the most significant world markets. Prospects for future growth are therefore excellent.

However, Wal-Mart has made mistakes, some visible and damaging. 'Traditionally', notes *The Economist* (*The Economist* 17 April 2004) 'retailers have not been good at going abroad' – Tesco and Carrefour might argue with this – 'and Wal-Mart is no exception'. As recently as 16 December 2004 Constance Hays, writing in the *New York Times* (*New York Times* 16 December 2004), observed that overseas ventures have yielded mixed gains for Wal-Mart, describing the position as 'an American formula, lost in translation.' Wal-Mart's formula has been good in America's border countries, successful in Canada for instance, and in Mexico where Wal-Mart is the biggest private employer. The Asda purchase in the UK in 1999, for $10.7 billion, has been a success, taking Asda temporarily past Sainsbury's into second position in the UK market. Today Asda apparently makes 50 per cent of Wal-Mart's international profits, a significant proportion from a still quite modest market share, and in a medium-sized market, fully justifying the investment. Five years on, Asda is a highly rated UK company in its own right, and has held its character and reputation post the acquisition. It prides itself on being a first-rate employer, a fast growing innovator, on being a clear price leader – an Asda heritage as well as a Wal-Mart imperative. Importantly, on employment and community support practices, where it has worked to avoid some of the US community-driven and litigation problems noted earlier, the Asda leadership – with Tony de Nunzio as its CEO until 2005 – has played its cards with sensitivity.

If the UK is a relative success however, Japan is at best in the 'not proven' category. Here Wal-Mart has been more cautious, starting with a nominal six per cent stake in the Seiyu company, fifth biggest in Japan's important market, and then raising its share to a controlling 38 per cent with an option to take two thirds of the company in 2007. Wal-Mart stated that in Japan, 'they have had the ability to look at what worked and what didn't work as we expanded elsewhere in the world' (Craig Herbert, COO International, *Financial Times* 13 December 2002) The way ahead is unlikely to be smooth, as both Ito-Yokado and Aeon are Japanese retailers with leading market shares to defend, and alongside Wal-Mart/Seiyu, Tesco will be present and ambitious to grow. Herbert claims that the step-by-step approach is 'a very good one for this market.' It is certainly conservative – Wal-Mart had made one earlier and abortive attempt to enter Japan and failed. There seems no doubt that Wal-Mart understands now that Japan is highly distinctive and will require an appropriate local approach, and business learning. It sees key advantages as global sourcing power and the information systems it can apply to the task.

Meanwhile in the small fishing town of Numazu, Wal-Mart is pioneering the US supercenter approach, hoping they have set the cost and price components at a sufficiently competitive level to succeed. The company have been disappointed by the pace at which Seiyu as a whole, is working for them and in August 2004 Wal-Mart expressed an interest in investing in Daiei, Japan's third biggest retailer, a struggling company, 'the archetypal zombie company, on permanent life-support from indulgent lenders' (*Financial Times* 17 August 2004). Wal-Mart confirmed an interest in finding additional opportunities in Japan. Commentators were uniformly critical of the projected deal, 'the poster child for Japan's walking dead' was the way Lex of the *Financial Times* described Daiei, noting that their projected margins at three per cent were half those being earned by Wal-Mart elsewhere. Its strategy in Japan looks to be in some disorder, with a sensation that Wal-Mart is casting about indiscriminately for a way of boosting growth in this difficult but major market.

If Britain has worked, and Japan is at best unproven, Germany, entered in Wal-Mart's first European foray, has been a disaster, severely damaging the Wal-Mart brand and international reputation. Anything it could get wrong when it bought both Wertkauf and Interspar, two divergent German store chains, in 1997, it did. German legislation acutely hampers the traditional 'Lowest Prices, Always' strategy. Labour laws are restrictive and the locations available to build big stores has been even trickier to find than in the US. Expansion has not happened – it still has less than 100 store sites – and the long-established and trusted German discounter cohort have risen to the challenge and been happy to see off the intruder. So far Wal-Mart has lost what, in Germany, has been a small fortune, and apart from the issues noted above, it has been its lack of success in developing a trusted German customer culture that has been the most glaring failure. Shipping in serried ranks of US expatriates who have not understood the admittedly unusual German trading practices, such as the stores closing for the day at the end of afternoon business, has been gauche. Not insisting that these same expatriates could speak some German was unforgivable. The result has been the collapse of a vaunted business ethic and a reputation that has made no appeal and had no competitive edge in the world's third biggest trading market. Wal-Mart is not out of the woods here and seems uncertain of the next move.

By comparison, China is still a market where Wal-Mart is embryonic – it has about forty sites as we speak. Once again, however, we see a company recognising the market's ultimate significance and playing its cards with great care. Wal-Mart have started by building a formidable listening post in China, which enables it to understand the market, get to know the political regimes and constraints, and build sourcing capabilities. There are signs that Wal-Mart's purposefully constructive approach is paying off in China. The company appears to have a good working relationship with central government who see the chance of using Wal-Mart's array of knowledge and techniques rapidly to equip their own retailing industry. This may have catapulted the company for the time being into a position of real advantage vis-à-vis international competition, notably Carrefour – who have had problems with government – and Tesco, who are barely out of the starting blocks. If Wal-Mart can parlay this lead into a long-term supportive relationship, its super-center approach in China may be able to move rapidly ahead. It has also had time to decide how much variation to the standard US approach may be needed in China, and there are signs of flexibility in what it is doing – with product range and even with union membership for example. This could be invaluable for the international business in the years ahead.

So summarising international experience, we can say that there have been successes, some that are now trading maturely and making good returns, but in some of the big single markets, Wal-Mart has not moved with the sure touch it showed back home. The absence of a set of local/global trading approaches which give the company confidence that it knows what it is doing when it appraises and then takes a stake overseas must, so far, be accounted a significant process weakness, and the need to develop a confident international trading mentality may be the overriding business priority for Wal-Mart. After all, it is from international markets that, long term, most of the company's growth must come. These concerns are, it must be said, currently well compensated for by the quality of company results, which show overall a growing company division, making highly attractive year-on-year trading margins from fast developing volumes. This will buy some valuable flexibility – and what this means is that Wal-Mart's international managers have room and time to learn. The conservatism of Asian moves suggests they are well aware of this priority.

We can now start reviewing the Wal-Mart achievement over the 42 plus years of its life, evaluating what it has done, and seek to determine what kind of future the world might be contemplating from this amazing enterprise. Sam Walton, entrepreneur American folk-hero and business-leader extraordinary, would no doubt be happy, twelve years on, to see how his successors have performed with the legacy he gave them and the business he founded which still carries his name. Sam might reflect that Glass, Scott and their colleagues have had to contend with pressures that Sam barely identified, and that the explosive growth which he began and which they have carried on have made Wal-Mart 'the cynosure of neighbouring eyes', a target for the world to aim at, and subject, therefore, to what Americans have come to know as the 'Microsoft phenomenon', a deep and searching level of scrutiny, reserved for the biggest and most impregnable of their commercial institutions.

The facts speak for themselves. It took Sam's successors just ten years from his death in 1992 to make his company the biggest, not just in the USA, but in the world, a position it has now held for three consecutive years (*Fortune* 26 July 2004). At $263 billion, it showed a top-line revenue increase of seven per cent over the previous year, and posted an increase in profits of 13 per cent. It hired a further 100,000 workers, taking its worldwide total to a world-leading 1.5 million people. Interestingly, however, Wal-Mart ranks merely twelfth in the world list for absolute profits earned, behind the oil majors, General Electric and Citigroup for example, some confirmation of the low-cost/low-prices strategy it follows and of a continuing intention of Walton's mandate to return cost reductions to the customer. An important and growing element in Wal-Mart's successful drive to raise revenues and profits has been the international business. Revenues in 2004 were up by 16.6 per cent in the year at $47.5 billion, and profitability at $2.3 billion, up 18.6 per cent on a year ago, also outstripped Wal-Mart's increase in US profits. By first quarter 2005 sales were rapidly approaching $300 billion.

A staggering feature of the 2004 picture is the rate at which Wal-Mart is adding supercenters across the US. This is a store format that is relatively recent, yet already it represents Wal-Mart at nearly 1500 store locations, almost half the US total. As a clear sign of recent strategy change, it had seemed some years ago that Wal-Mart might be reaching superstore saturation, and would have to turn to the smaller neighbourhood stores for growth. Not a bit of it – to date there are a mere 64 of the latter while superstore development steams ahead. The opportunity has apparently surprised even Wal-Mart's own top team – in *The Economist*'s 17 April 2004 report, Tom Schoewe, Wal-Mart's CFO, accepted that there had been a recent and definite change of tack, following the realisation that 'America's suburbs can absorb many more supercenters than the company had previously supposed'. The article continues, instancing the suburb of Scottsdale, a newish, upper-crust and highly desirable community in Phoenix Arizona, where six huge Wal-Mart supercenters can be seen to be doing good business on one single 20 mile stretch of road. 'This shows you what can happen' said Schoewe. One wonders how many US cities will be as compliant as Scottsdale in welcoming Wal-Mart with this degree of largesse. What *The Economist* calls 'prickly' California has shown its hand in unmistakeable fashion through the Inglewood voters' rejection. As Wal-Mart moves to tackle big city suburbs, full of voters who can be mobilised to take a stand, and who have some sense of the wider social issues at stake, one's sense is that Wal-Mart will have its work cut out to keep up the pace of expansion. It will learn as it wins some key battles, but so will its adversaries.

What is clear however is that the Bentonville machine today is motoring at full throttle – there is no reining back at Wal-Mart's HQ. The company continues to buy land in the US 'at an astonishing rate' (*The Economist* 17 April 2004) 'taking decisions on a monthly basis to buy land worth $1 billion'. Even now, Wal-Mart accounts for a mere eight per cent of US retail sales, which big though they are, is as a figure a long way from market dominance. Silverstein (Silverstein and Fiske 2003), given his belief that business development followed a one-track and down-trading approach at Wal-Mart, grudgingly gives it 'three years of decent growth left'. Darrell Rigby at Bain disagrees – 'there is plenty of room to go on growing to 2010' he says. This could create a company with sales of around $400 billion in just five more years. In May 2005, Wal-Mart confessed to a 'disappointing quarter' with sales up only 3%. Lee Scott observed 'We've changed the company' in response to widespread US criticisms. The share price has dropped more than ten per cent in 2005 to date. Could the big Bentonville machine be slowing down for the first time?

The catalyst ahead will be Wal-Mart's ability to create an American-size business from its international division. If it can do this – and there seems no reason why the brand proposition should not work in the rest of the world – it can afford a distinct slowing up in US growth and still drive forward rapidly. This raises questions addressed earlier. Can Asda Britain create the kind of overseas model to which Wal-Mart aspires in more places? Can the company sort out its big German problem, and move ahead with purpose in Japan? Is Wal-Mart clever enough and now well equipped enough to make money quickly in China where competition is in place, and many have failed? Suggestions have even been made that Wal-Mart might bid for its seemingly vulnerable worldwide rival, Carrefour, now trading weakly at home in France, and perhaps offering investors a holding structure that would facilitate a Wal-Mart bid. This would be a double win for Wal-Mart, giving it a hugely strong European position and a massive and immediate step change in international revenues. While Paris will naturally dismiss this manifestation of *'le défi Americain'*, worldwide investors might applaud eagerly. It would be an exciting contest.

Whether growth slows, holds or even, with international savvy and a renewal of ability to generate growth from Europe and Asia, increases in pace, Wal-Mart is very big, will remain very big, and will be around, for many more years – this writer suggests at least a decade. If Unilever can last for 100 years and P&G for nearly 200, why cannot Wal-Mart do the same? Maybe they can but the 'Wal-Martisation of everything' does not make the intelligent world universally happy. John Plender had this to say (*Financial Times* 22 December 2003): 'The elephantine march of ... Wal-Mart across the economic landscape becomes more awesome very day.' Plender goes on to reference P&G's worldwide accounts showing one third of its US sales go to Wal-Mart; and that its total worldwide sales now compare unfavourably with Wal-Mart's total outside America. 'As Wal-Mart expands everywhere from UK to Japan ... where I wonder will it all end?' laments Plender. It's a fair cop. P&G are a great company, with a justified reputation for highly tuned strategic management, and a roster of the finest world brands. If Wal-Mart can tuck P&G away in its back pocket, can any company stay out of their clutches? Whether they do or not, should this worry us?

Is a continuously growing Wal-Mart good for America and good for the world? Have Wal-Mart's leaders the skill and sensitivity to dominate world retailing into the indefinite future? Taking the second question first, I suggest the verdict must still be cautious – it is not yet certain that they have. There are two formidable challenges facing them in pushing operations ahead in their key markets. The first is the issue of governance in the US. Will defending its policies and practices both divert leadership and management from achieving their business goals, and in turn erode some of the advantage which low-cost operating and specifically low salaries and wages have brought to the company from its earliest beginnings? There must be some degree of risk of this happening. Probably the company has enough momentum to maintain growth and margins for more years in the US, but it would be a brave man who said that the issues of the female employee class action and California voters' rejection do not put two worthwhile spokes in the Wal-Mart growth wheel.

Secondly and more importantly, does Wal-Mart have leaders with sufficient analytical skill, flexibility, and perhaps most significant of all, humility, to develop confident business expansion models for the rest of the world? By any standards this is 'a big ask' for the company, and so far the response has been indifferent. They have the undoubted advantage of a core customer proposition both powerful and uniquely focused – 'Lowest Prices, Always' – has intrinsic, perhaps infinitely durable, appeal. Can this be married to an operating culture in markets as far apart and as different as, say, Berlin and Tokyo, which will enable the Wal-Mart machine to power ahead in key growth markets? Once again, the verdict today must be at best, very cautiously optimistic. There are signs (Japan and China) that Wal-Mart are treading the international ice more gingerly, learning carefully as they go along and before they commit the company fully to a country strategy. The contiguous markets of Mexico and Canada appear in good shape, and Asda Britain is being sensitively pushed forward.

So to answer this question of international capability, surely Wal-Mart from the world's richest and best educated country, with an infinite capacity to generate high-ability managers, can equip itself to build confident operating models across the world? It will require the marriage of worldwide strategy, a strong core-brand proposition and top-level local management skill – but surely again, Wal-Mart leadership must now be well seized of this requirement? The next few years will show how far they have travelled.

The final question – is a continuously growing Wal-Mart good for America and the world? Lee Scott, reported in the *New York Times* on 6 April 2005, was unequivocal – 'Wal-Mart is good for American consumers and good for our 1.3 million American workers' he said. However, there will be many different answers. Lots of people, paid up members of the 'Beast of Bentonville' supporters group, will respond with an emphatic negative. In a national on-line poll, held by Jobs with Justice, a coalition of local community groups across the US, Wal-Mart was named 'Grinch of the Year 2004' (Grinch is the equivalent of Scrooge – a mean, low payer). This 'reflects growing concern that working families have with this mega corporation' said their director, citing wages so low that its employees were often eligible for food stamps, its habit of locking overnight employees into its stores, and the massive sex discrimination case noted earlier. There is no question that Wal-Mart is deeply unpopular with a significant section of the community, and that this group are often both intelligent and articulate about the company's many perceived shortcomings. For them big is anything but beautiful.

Yet who can argue with Wal-Mart's business achievement, created initially in the world's most free market, by ordinary but determined people, and from humblest rural beginnings? Is not this a story exemplifying exactly the American dream? Is Wal-Mart's highly charged competitive approach to business, its determination to play hardball with suppliers, even with its own people, in order to push through a 'Lowest Prices, Always' proposition inadequate, immoral or in some way wrong? We do not think so. Neutral commentators point to the inherently good effects Wal-Mart has on markets as a whole, describing its influence as liberating and even cleansing. The Chinese appear to be signing on for this at a national level. Once we start aiming off because it is too large, too powerful, or too determinedly aggressive, surely we question the ethic on which innovation and growth in free societies is built. Wal-Mart has aimed its brand unequivocally at the world's largest and most developed countries – just those markets that are best equipped, where checks and balances are needed, to ensure appropriate consumer and business ethics are protected. There is no attempt to stay on the periphery, or hide in safe places, although that, by some considerable irony, was how founder Sam began things, in forgotten parts of America where for some years nobody noticed. Given the transparency of the Wal-Mart strategy, and despite popular misgivings, Wal-Mart has on balance been a powerful force for the good in US and now world retailing.

3 Carrefour: The Pioneer

Carrefour is the second-largest retailer in the world, though second to Wal-Mart by some way, with sales of €70 billion ($86 billion) in 2003 to Wal-Mart's $250 billion. It is easily the most international, with operations in some thirty countries in Europe, South America and Asia. It was a pioneer in developing hypermarkets, and in venturing abroad. After its merger with Promodès, it has a full range of formats – hypermarkets, supermarkets, convenience stores and hard discounters. With leadership positions in many of the countries it operates in, and its depth and breadth of international experience, it is a formidable competitor. In 2004, however, it was facing fierce price competition in its home market of France, potentially a serious weakness.

Carrefour's origins, like Wal-Mart's and Asda's, lie in the early 1960s. Its founders, Marcel Fournier and Louis Defforey, opened a 650 sq. m. (7000 sq. ft.) store in a basement in Annecy, in the Haute Savoie department of France. (Much of the history that follows is based on AGSM 2000.) Their real leap into the future came soon afterwards, when they opened the first Carrefour hypermarket in Sainte-Geneviève-des-Bois, near Paris, in 1963. The name Carrefour – which means crossroads – was based on the store's position near the intersection of five roads. The store covered 2500 sq. m. (27,000 sq. ft.) and had parking for 450 cars; products offered included groceries, clothing, sporting goods and other non-foods; prices were low. Although similar stores existed in the USA, and would soon appear in Britain, they were a novelty in Europe, and French consumers flocked to buy.

Recognising that they had a winning formula, the directors led a rapid expansion. Between 1965 and 1971, sales growth rocketed ahead at more than 50 per cent a year. Building on the idea of size, Carrefour moved up a gear in 1970 with a commercial centre of 25,000 sq. m. (270,000 sq. ft.). Nothing on this gigantic scale existed anywhere else, and Carrefour continued to develop its hypermarkets wherever it went – though usually at the 10,000 sq. m. (100,000 sq. ft.) level.

The essence of the hypermarket model is similar to that of Wal-Mart: low costs, convenience, price. Carrefour bought sites outside towns, where land was relatively cheap and access good. Its construction methods favoured simplicity, and it reckoned to build a hypermarket at a cost per square metre of about a third of traditional competitors. This allowed it to set prices at a discount level around five to ten per cent below its rivals. Low prices, combined with the convenience of free parking and one-stop shopping, formed a winning offer.

As competitors began to copy the successful formula, Carrefour saw the need to differentiate itself. While Wal-Mart stayed focused on its price-driven strategy, Carrefour started to position itself slightly differently. It had always aimed to be more than a warehouse selling cheap goods, rather it tried to offer a rewarding shopping experience for the consumer. Aiming to be seen as the leader in every fresh product category – reflecting perhaps its French heritage – it developed local buying and own label products. Buying locally, in a country such as France, allowed it to respond closely to customers' preferences – and would prove attractive internationally. Own label (private label) started in 1976 – again a pioneering move in its time – and enabled the company to offer reasonable quality at prices 15 to 35 per cent below that of national brands.

The first move abroad also came early, with a store opened in neighbouring Belgium in 1969. In 1973 it opened in Spain, and in 1975 in Brazil. Why did it venture so far from home when its domestic market still appeared to offer room for growth?

One story is that the owners were reacting to an increasingly socialist government climate in France: they thought that their business might be nationalised, so decided to start to move it somewhere safer. Carrefour itself does not confirm this version, but does say that the choice of countries was influenced by economic, political and personal factors. One director was interested in Spain, and the other in Brazil; the opportunity to develop vineyards in Brazil may also have played a part. It is also true that the French government, prompted by protests from the many small shopkeepers threatened or put out of business by the large multiples, passed laws limiting large-store growth, and imposed a tax on sales to provide pensions for small shopkeepers forced to close down.

Whatever the combination of motives, the company moved into Argentina in 1982, but then paused for a while. The early initiatives did not meet instant success, indeed they ran into some difficulties. The hypermarket in Spain, opened under a French name, struggled. The first few years in South America were very tough, and Carrefour thought about withdrawing. It learnt its first, vital lesson early: 'adaptation is *always* the key', in the words of CFO Jose-Luis Duran (now CEO).

Luckily for Carrefour, it persevered. South America in particular was to prove a gold mine. Conditions were ideal: growing economies, a burgeoning middle class, and little or no competition. Modern, attractive stores offering huge ranges at keen prices quickly became favourite destinations, and Carrefour made outstanding profits for several years, before increasing political and economic instability, together with growing competition, made the markets much more difficult.

The experience of the good years must have given the company confidence, for in 1991 it embarked on a new phase. At home, its position had been reinforced by the takeover of Euromarché: it had recognised the importance of having a strong domestic base on which to build. Daniel Bernard joined as CEO, with the brief to make internationalisation the main target. At this point Carrefour was only fifth or sixth in Europe, and only in five countries in all. It set out to change that.

Between 1991 and 1999 it opened hypermarkets in Europe, Latin

America and Asia: Greece, Portugal (1991), Italy, Turkey (1993), Poland (1997), Czech Republic (1998), Mexico (1994), Chile, Colombia (1998), Taiwan (already opened in 1989), Thailand, Malaysia (1994), China (1995), South Korea (1996) and Indonesia (1998). Although the hectic pace slackened, further stores were built in the next few years in Switzerland, Slovakia, Romania and Japan.

Not all countries proved equally welcoming. Carrefour hypermarkets in both the UK and USA were unable to make much headway against entrenched competition. In the USA, Carrefour opened a 31,000 sq. m. (330,000 sq. ft.) hypermarket in suburban Philadelphia in 1988, and a second in New Jersey in 1992. They spent little on advertising to educate consumers, who found the range and selection unappealing. Local competitors cut prices, and labour unions picketed over conditions. In 1993, Carrefour admitted defeat and withdrew from the market. They also withdrew from Hungary in 2003 after a few months, accepting that they had arrived too late to cope with existing competition.

The final phase of development that produced the current Carrefour came in 2000 with the merger of Carrefour and Promodès. This brilliant strategic move took rivals and commentators by surprise, and vaulted the new group into first place in Europe. Until now, the two firms had been fierce competitors in France (Promodès had few international activities). Promodès brought a range of formats: hypermarkets, supermarkets, hard discounters, some convenience stores, cash and carry, and foodservice. The business was lean and well run, and brought experience of operating franchise stores. It was a good fit for Carrefour, giving them a much stronger and broader local base, and the opportunity for cross-border synergies. It also brought a second set of family shareholders, which may bring problems in the future: we will return to this issue.

What sort of retail animal is Carrefour now? It is very international, with 76 per cent of its 6067 stores outside France (17 per cent outside Europe). On the other hand, just over 50 per cent of sales and 66 per cent of profit (earnings before interest and tax (EBIT)) are from France. Latin America and Asia provided only five per cent of profit in 2003 (Carrefour Annual Report), reflecting low margins in Asia (three per cent), and almost non-existent ones in Latin America. As with all retailers, international expansion is a long-term strategy; the firm recognises that the golden years in South America will not return, but they still see worthwhile returns in time.

Carrefour aims to be in the top three in every market in which it operates. Within Europe, which it now defines as its 'home market', it is leader in France, Spain, Belgium, Greece and Italy. It is number one in Taiwan, and still has leading shares in Latin America. Elsewhere, its record is mixed. In South Korea, it has struggled against strong local competition and Tesco, and in Thailand it has lost its leading position, now trailing at fourth. Tesco, more used to high capital intensity from its home market and therefore more used to paying high prices for land, has bought better sites, and operated them better too, with more sensitive local adaptation.

In both South Korea, and especially in Japan, Carrefour has been criticised for going in with the wrong format and position. It entered these markets with its standard hypermarket, with pricing at the discount level. Both, but particularly Japan, are markets very concerned with quality (see Text Box 3.1). Moreover, Japanese housewives do not have large storage areas in their small homes, and they shop frequently. Carrefour has learnt these lessons and adapted, but it is strange that the most experienced international retailer should make such mistakes. Japan is known to be a difficult market, and in late 2004 Carrefour announced that it would withdraw from the country.

BOX 3.1

CARREFOUR IN JAPAN

Carrefour got off to a tumultuous start in Japan when it entered the market in December 2000, where it misread consumers and alienated wholesalers on arrival. Though it was initially attracted to Japan by consumers' high disposable incomes and a decade of decline in land prices, sales slumped as consumers, expecting more French delicacies and products, were put off by the ordinary, low-priced Japanese goods.

The French retailer also faced hostility from wholesalers, after it tried to procure products directly from suppliers and refused to accept the traditional Japanese multi-layered supply system.

Carrefour, which currently has eight stores in Japan, hoped to get off to a fresh start late last year when it opened three stores in the Kansai area, located in western Japan encompassing Osaka and Hyogo prefectures. The company focused on western Japan where lower prices are more likely to lure shoppers than in Tokyo.

It revamped its outlets and gave them more of a French feel, adding an area where consumers could buy fresh baguettes and croissants. Carrefour also added cut portions of fruit and a wider range of ready-to-eat-meals, which carry a higher profit margin than other food.

But observers say the retailer has had an immensely difficult time competing with Ito-Yokado and Aeon, Japan's top two retailers, both of which boast huge economies of scale. The two retailers are able to source some items directly from their suppliers, enabling them to offer the same goods as Carrefour at lower prices.

'Carrefour needs to get scale in this country, and they can't get the business model they want and truly compete until they have scale,' said David Marra, a retail specialist at AT Kearney, the consultancy. 'They haven't settled on a store format that works.'

Source: 'Carrefour denies exiting Japan despite problems' by Mariko Sanchanta, *Financial Times* 12 October 2004. Note that they subsequently reversed this decision.

In China, on the other hand, they have been strikingly successful. Recognising the huge potential early, they entered the market in 1995. Many, if not most, large American and European companies have been eyeing China greedily: with 1.3 billion population and very rapid economic growth, it is the future market of all future markets. It is also, as many have found to their cost, a complicated and difficult market to operate in (see the discussion in Chapters 1 and 12). Companies have to have connections (guanxi) at central, regional and local government level; they have to understand the very different local culture; often they need to find and work with local partners; and they have to adapt their operations to a vast country that often does not have the infrastructure that they are used to. Carrefour started well and expanded rapidly, but in 2001 ran into difficulties. True to its pioneering culture, it had built hypermarkets in 30 cities, while Wal-Mart had entered only four or five major centres, as the central government had wanted. The central government objected to Carrefour's somewhat free-wheeling ways, and stopped it in its tracks. To its credit, the company again learnt quickly. Having re-established good relations with the government, it was very helpful during the SARS crisis, and supported Shanghai in the city's bid for an international exhibition. It is now once again a good corporate citizen, and allowed to continue expanding.

Apparently, the name Carrefour transliterates into Mandarin as 'happiness and prosperity', and many Chinese refer to any hypermarket as a 'Carrefour'. This is a lucky edge, but the key to success is still the stores themselves. Some are spectacular (see plate section) and the choice of local partners has worked well to deliver an offering that local people find irresistible. It may be that the rapid expansion helps in supply chain management, as Wal-Mart has found it a logistical nightmare to deliver to a small number of very widely scattered outlets. Carrefour is also launching Dia hard discount shops in China, and seems to have a bright future there.

Given this somewhat mixed bag of results, is it possible to discern a strategy behind Carrefour's international expansion? From its early days, it identified the fact that if it could enter a market that was beginning to develop reasonably quickly, with a growing middle class, they could grow together. It achieved this in Spain in 1973, in Brazil in 1975 and in South Korea in 1996.

In principle, Carrefour selects foreign markets using three models: commercial, economic and financial. With the commercial model, it examines how the hypermarket format would fit in (it always tries to enter using hypermarkets): how is the retail industry structured, can the hypermarket work, can it be adopted, is our range suitably adapted, what can we offer consumers? The economic model looks at pricing strategies, cross-border synergies, links with suppliers, competition, social/legal/fiscal issues, personnel and real estate factors. The financial model analyses possible financing packages, whether to own or leaseback, debt and capital structure and possible partnerships.

When it enters a new market, Carrefour's senior managers stress how hard they try to be local: to them, being local means knowing local, regional and central governments, local suppliers and so on. As we have seen, Carrefour does not always live up to this, or perhaps does not lay enough stress on knowing local consumers. Critics say, for example, that it uses too many French managers rather than locals. Its answer is that in some countries, such as China in 1995, no locals know anything about modern retailing, so it has to employ French managers to begin with. This is a fair point, and it is true that, where Tesco has bought local companies and their managers, Carrefour has spent considerable sums on training its next generation of local staff.

Seeing itself as a pioneer, Carrefour generally prefers to create a new company rather than acquire an existing firm, though it does operate partnerships and joint ventures where it sees real benefits. It sees its positioning as a differentiated, innovative retailer. Although it points out that, in most countries, its main competitor is not Wal-Mart or Tesco, but a local firm, it is aware of the multinational rivals. It respects Wal-Mart, for example, but is not frightened of it. 'Wal-Mart has an extraordinary back office, we have an extraordinary front office' is their view (Duran 2004). Where it competes directly with Wal-Mart, Carrefour feels it has a better commercial model, better local adaptation, and a stronger local pioneer spirit. As a result, it claims, it achieves higher sales per square metre than its giant rival.

This is partly due to its relatively decentralised management structure. Where Wal-Mart will buy one-and-a-half million toy dogs centrally, then decide where they will be sold, it is the local Carrefour manager who leads in product selection. This decentralisation is the Carrefour tradition, and enables the local buying referred to earlier.

> *One Carrefour store manager (who incidentally was paid FF12,500 per month versus FF2,500 two years earlier … in a smaller competing … chain) made the following comment. 'My previous job was demoralising. It took a month to get authorisation to buy something for the store that cost FF14. Now I am free to make all of my own decisions. I can hire ten people, buy a new refrigerator unit, or hire a band for a parking lot festival.' (AGSM 2000)*

Operating in very different markets, with sometimes extreme conditions such as hyperinflation in South America, makes a degree of local independence essential, and Carrefour itself sees this as one of the key success factors behind its expansion (there is, of course, some regional and international structure – see Text Box 3.2).

BOX 3.2

CARREFOUR'S INTERNATIONAL MANAGEMENT STRUCTURE

Originally, there were just two levels, headquarters and stores. The head office dealt with strategy, finance, technical matters, and new store location. It also acted as a source of shared information and experience.

As the organisation became larger and more complex, more levels were added: regional offices within a country – say Spain or France – would report to a national head office, which reported to a European officer, and similarly for other regions. After 1998, the regional managers were posted in their regions rather than in Paris.

Each department was responsible for producing forecasts of both sales and margins; the store manager would negotiate and agree these, and pass them to head office. Although the head office controller would vet forecasts against past performance, company strategy and similar stores, the final say rested with the store manager. These managers were then judged on performance against the forecasts, and rewarded for 'good' performance, that is, some subjective judgement was involved.

It is department heads who do the buying, and they can buy either from Carrefour central purchasing, or locally. As local specialities and fresh produce are seen as an important element in differentiation, local buying could account for up to thirty per cent of a store's sales.

Pricing is also a local responsibility, within the overall low-price policy. Each store would check the prices in rival shops, and price against these. Sometimes, this resulted in Carrefour stores in the same city offering a product at different prices. Centrally purchased products are sold to each local store at a fixed transfer price.

Such a degree of independence is very attractive to managers, and in principle, anyone could start from the bottom and work all the way to the top of the company. Most store managers were internal appointments, and extensive training is a feature at every level.

A possible downside of this decentralisation was that for some years, store managers placed little emphasis on IT and sophisticated communications; all they needed was basic till data and sales, and the fax remained the usual means of communication with head office. As a result, Carrefour probably under-invested in information and communication technology (ICT) compared with some of its competitors, and now has to catch up (see further discussion in Chapter 7).

Local freedom is not unconstrained. The basic business model of any multiple retailer is based around economies of scale and central purchasing, and Carrefour is no different. In own label and non-food, these are fundamental.

In non-food own label in particular, the central global purchasing department based in France buys between 60 and 80 per cent of ranges. It can make 10 to 15 per cent savings in this way. Carrefour also participates in the GNX online auction for some items, especially raw materials, and reckons to save on average 12 per cent over traditional methods.

Major brands, however, are not bought centrally, even where, as in consumer electronics products, there would seem to be a good case for doing so. There is a mechanism through a central office in Geneva to negotiate global agreements with brand owners such as Procter & Gamble or L'Oréal, but the agreement only covers ways of cooperating to mutual benefit over the coming year. Price negotiation is still carried out locally. Carrefour recognises that it needs major brands to attract customers and add quality and excitement to categories.

There is also now some centralisation in information technology (IT). As mentioned, one result of management decentralisation was a lack of interest in IT: the culture was just not IT-oriented (this may be a feature of Continental firms more generally, as opposed to the Anglo-Saxon model). While financial systems at Carrefour are based on a common system (Peoplesoft, in this case), nothing else is. Some regional projects, for example in Asia, had led to local learning and convergence, but this was rare. The executive board at headquarters has recognised that Carrefour has fallen behind some of its rivals, and that Wal-Mart and Tesco, in their different ways, have a competitive advantage through the application of IT. A Chief Information Officer (Bruno Cabasso) was appointed in 2003 to lead convergence in key areas, with a strong team at the centre to lead projects. They have identified certain areas in which they need to catch up, have set clear targets, and outlined a road map to guide progress.

A constant theme running through any conversation with a Carrefour senior manager is the primacy of the customer. Cabasso describes himself – or perhaps the Carrefour culture – as 'paranoid about not getting too far from the customer'. Thus, even in IT projects, the first consideration is what benefits will flow to customers, and only then what value to the business. In general, the emphasis is very much on the business aspect, that is, the technology is not seen as interesting in its own right, but only as a way of improving the business.

Focusing on customers also means that Carrefour is deliberately not copying Wal-Mart in its IT development. Wal-Mart has a different business model, driven overall by low prices, and that drives their IT. Carrefour sees the customer relationship as primary, and local. Their road maps are therefore 'a bit complex – not 100 per cent centralised or decentralised'.

The major areas of concentration are:

▶ back-back office
▶ back office (assortment, communications, supply chain management, warehouse, logistics)
▶ front office (customer-linked).

Carrefour admits it is not yet seeing the benefits of its efforts, but is confident that they are coming. It recognises that mindsets do not change overnight, and that legacy systems cannot just be junked at once. There is a parallel effort to foment a cultural revolution. The IT community has, in the past, been conservative and technically minded, and it has to change to a more explicitly business orientation. This demands education – of technical people as well as operational managers – and this will take time.

The business advantages, when they arrive, will be first of all in efficiency, which will drive down costs (and interestingly, reflecting the concerns discussed below, the savings will be put back into prices, not profit). The other immediate benefit will be in supply chain management and negotiation with suppliers, where the speed and relevance of information are key.

It is fair to say that the foregoing is true above all of the hypermarkets, and especially of France. The supermarkets (acquired with Promodès) started some years ago on customer relationship management, and so are some way ahead. Spain and Belgium are also bright spots.

This leads us to a consideration of the format range and its place in the overall strategy. Carrefour was, and still to some extent sees itself as, a hypermarket company. It was the originator of the idea, and has done most to develop it. It normally enters a new country with hypermarkets: partly this is because it is quicker to achieve scale with 10–15 hypers, but it is also, Carrefour would admit, because 'we are a hypermarket company'. The large-format stores account for 59 per cent of sales, so are the core of the business.

The company sees itself as a retail innovator. For example, in 1997 it introduced the 'universe' concept, which it described as a revolution in hypermarket merchandising. All non-foods were split into four universes: culture and commercial; home, sport and leisure; body; and automobile. Improvements included better store decor and signage, advisers and sales staff with good product knowledge, facilities such as kiosks for listening to music, and 'in-store theatre' with performances and events.

In 1999, it tackled the food side by introducing MAGALI (MAGasin ALImentaire – food shop) to improve choice and inject theatre here too. In chosen stores, food was given its own separate entrance, and featured market stalls based on the famous Paris market Les Halles. Grocery was reorganised into four universes, based on consumption patterns not categories, each colour-coded: breakfast, meals and accompaniments, snacking, and ingredients. Other features were health and beauty as a shop-within-a-shop, and an in-store café.

Its latest flagship store, opened in 2002 in Carré-Sénart near Paris, has 14,000 sq. m. of space, with the ground floor devoted to non-food, and the first to food. Such continuing innovation fits into the Carrefour strategy of leadership and differentiation; although it competes on price it is not EDLP, using promotions to add excitement and difference.

Supermarkets appeared with the Promodès merger. They account for 18 per cent of sales, and operate under the Champion fascia in France. The brand is not global, and other fascias are used. They try to capitalise on local strengths, but also to transfer best practice between countries. They tend to be fairly small (up to 2000 sq. m.) with a restricted range of stock-keeping units (SKUs), only if there is no hypermarket within 45 kilometres will they build more than 2500 sq. m. The strong impression is that supermarkets are a useful fill-in, particularly where planning restrictions prevent a hypermarket being built. They seem to play an important but not central part in Carrefour's international strategy.

Hard discount is different. Dia was founded by Promodès in 1979 in Spain, and is now a prominent player in several countries. Carrefour aims to open one Dia a day around the world (compared with one Champion every three days, and one Carrefour hypermarket a week). In many countries, hard discount is the fastest-growing format, and both Dia and Ed (the Carrefour hard discount fascia in France) will profit from that trend. In China, for example, the group was aiming for 70 Dia stores by the end of 2003, 300 within five years, and eventually thousands. While hard discount brings in only seven per cent of total sales at present, this seems certain to increase.

Convenience stores operate under a number of fascias: Shopi (large 'superette' up to 900 sq. m.); Marché Plus (discount convenience); 8 à Huit (emergency shopping); and Proxi (small, up to 250 sq. m.). The various convenience stores account for 16 per cent of sales, and clearly fill a gap in the product range. On the other hand, their higher running costs lead to higher prices, and some fear that this could harm Carrefour's image.

And price, of course, is at the centre of Carrefour's current (2005) problem. All international retailers know that a strong – and profitable – home base is essential to provide the cash flow and profit to fund overseas expansion. In France, Carrefour came under sustained price attack from its main domestic rival, Leclerc, and hard discounters such as the German Aldi and Lidl chains from 2002 onwards. Daniel Bernard, the CEO, kept promising investors that he would reverse the trend of declining domestic sales growth. He launched the No.1 range as a fighting brand, and an international range known as PCI (Produits Carrefour Internationaux).

> One of the major events in 2003 was the launch of price leader 'No.1' products, priced below hard discount, and the development of global brand products at very competitive prices ...
>
> The 'No.1' line, with easily identified packaging and labelling, includes both food and non-food products, with a range of 1000 product items in 2004 available in supermarkets and hypermarkets. At the same time, an international line of products has been launched. Over 300 products, identical, presented in the same packaging printed in several languages and bearing the name Carrefour or Champion, are already on sale in the majority of the group's supermarkets and hypermarkets at very competitive prices in relation to hard discount prices. (Carrefour Annual Report 2003).

In the autumn of 2004, Bernard was forced to admit that so far, the new tactics were not working. The group seemed to be losing market share in France, and like-for-like sales in the core hypermarkets continued to decline (by 5.5 per cent in the third quarter). Moreover, market research showed that the public's perceptions of Carrefour were less than impressive. Despite the company's claims that it had achieved price parity with Leclerc, shoppers did not see it that way, and they rated Carrefour no better than second or third on the majority of other desirable attributes. Bernard had been under pressure for some time, but with the stock at an eighteen-month low, he began to look beleaguered.

It begins to seem that the whole hypermarket model in France may be under strain (see Text Box 3.3). Legislation, mainly the *loi Galland* and the *loi Raffarin*, dates from 1996, and limits both the physical expansion of the hypermarkets' space, and their ability to price some items below cost. This has had the odd effect of protecting margins, but depressing sales. Price deflation is common, and price wars contribute to that trend.

BOX 3.3

PRICE IN FRANCE

Florence Michel typifies the quiet revolution that the French food retail industry has undergone in recent years. Comfortably well off and married with two children, she is nevertheless standing in line at discount supermarket Ed in central Paris doing her main weekly shopping.

'Why should I pay €1 more for each of these when my children can't taste the difference?' she asks, pointing to her trolley full of drinks and snacks. 'I go to other shops and stores, sure, but for many things, the cheaper the better.'

Consumers such as Mme Michel are one of the main reasons Nicolas Sarkozy, French finance minister, brokered a deal last week under which large retailers, with the backing of their suppliers, agreed to cut prices by 2 per cent from September.

Finance ministry officials deny the deal is dirigiste, saying it is designed to improve confidence and spending. 'Consumers will see the difference in their wallets.'

But Mme Michel also highlights the reasons that retailers have mounted an increasingly hostile campaign against the current highly regulated market rules in France. Stores such as Ed, owned by Carrefour, the country's largest retailer, and Lidl of Germany have met growing success.

Analysts say the stores – known as 'hard discount' (using the English words) – have taken a share of about one-seventh of the market, and some surveys suggest up to 60 per cent of the French shop there at least once a year.

Their main advantage is selling own-brand products that heavily undercut the big-name brands. All this results from a 1996 law designed to protect small shopkeepers from the influence of large hypermarkets. Under the so-called *loi Galland*, retailers are forbidden to sell below cost price. Suppliers must also offer the same terms to all buyers

To get around this and use their formidable bargaining power, the largest retailers devised a scheme, known as *marges arrière*, where they themselves sell real or pretend commercial advantages to their suppliers – such as more shelf space – in return for rebates on the goods.

These margins are often between 25 and 35 per cent and have the effect of reducing the amount paid by retailers but also, perversely, of increasing the price for all stores as suppliers try to recoup their losses.

Leclerc, one of France's biggest hypermarket chains, launched an attack on the law earlier this year, saying in prominent advertisements that not only did it make consumers pay more, but that the government was playing down the rise in inflation because of it.

Leclerc, followed by Carrefour, introduced loyalty cards, which allowed shoppers to earn large discounts on many branded products bringing them closer to the level of 'hard discount' stores. Hypermarkets have also in recent years dramatically increased their own range of cheap and own-brand products.

Under pressure from the supermarkets, Mr Sarkozy felt obliged to act. He went about it quickly – his critics would say too quickly – and threatened retailers and suppliers that he would legislate if they failed to reach agreement within two weeks.

As well as the 2 per cent cut in September, the *marges arrière* should fall by 1 per cent in January. Mr Sarkozy has also set up a commission under the country's leading civil judge to examine the *loi Galland*.

But will it have any effect? Economists and analysts are sceptical. Mme Michel is more direct: 'With house prices and everything else so high, I want the basics cheap. They can cut the prices but I won't spend any more.'

Source: 'French shoppers resist moves to lift spending', by Richard Milne *Financial Times* 21 June 2004.

The question remains whether the hypermarkets will ever recover. If the *loi Galland* is repealed, the effect will be to intensify the price war. All the groups with hypermarket formats, such as Auchan, Casino and Leclerc, are in the same strategic bind – but consumers see Leclerc as the cheapest, and Auchan as generally the best quality operator. If a full-scale price war does erupt, margins will suffer. Daniel Bernard had said, 'Price is the key element' and pledged 'whatever is necessary' to regain price leadership. The group had already committed some €335 million to price reductions in 2004, and will presumably invest more (*Financial Times* 13 October 2004). As the group is already missing sales and profit targets, the effect could be severe.

One option is to compete directly with the hard discounters. Casino saw its hard discount fascias Franprix and Leader Price overtake its larger formats in operating profit in 2004. Carrefour has its Ed and Dia chains, but at present, they contribute only seven per cent of group sales. The company can also look to its overseas operations, which have increased their profits – but with 50 percent of sales and fully two thirds of profit coming from France, the international contribution is a drop in the bucket.

Carrefour's problem – and specifically Bernard's – was exacerbated by the influence of the various founding families. The Badin, Defforey and Fournier families had signed a pact with Carrefour after the Promodès merger, promising pre-emption rights on share sales, and consultation in the event of a bid. Even though the families own only 4.9 per cent of the shares, this was a useful bulwark, so it was uncomfortable when they refused to renew the pact in 2004 because they were unhappy with the shares' performance. Bernard had renewed a pact with the Halley family, who own 12.5 per cent, and the Spanish March family, who own a further 3.3 per cent, which gave him some protection. However, after the death of a senior Halley, the family appointed to the Carrefour board Luc Vandevelde, who had been CEO of Promodès before leaving to take the chair at Marks & Spencer. He is there to look after the Halleys' interests, and there was open speculation that, should the family continue to be unhappy with Bernard's delivery of the results promised, Vandevelde would be poised to replace him. The company, of course, dismissed such idle talk, and it was far from clear that Vandevelde, or indeed anyone else, could tackle the fundamental problems any better. The fourth quarter 2004 results were slightly improved (though the hypermarkets still lost share fractionally), so Bernard appeared to have some breathing space going into 2005 – but not much. The Halley and March families have bought further shares, and account for 25 per cent of voting rights. They have been unhappy to see their shares tumble from a high of €96 to under €40.

With hindsight, we could say that Carrefour made two related strategic errors. First, they continued their breakneck international expansion (13 new countries in the 1990s) into the new century with purchases of GB of Belgium, Gruppo GS of Italy, Marinopoulos in Greece and Norte in Argentina – many of them loss-making or even close to bankruptcy. They then faced multiple threats: earnings in Latin America collapsed as a result of currency devaluations, the Chinese government ordered them to stop their hypermarket expansion, and they lost sales in Spain when they re-badged all the hypermarkets there as Carrefour. Finally, with the added distraction of the Promodès merger, they took their eye off the ball in France, and missed the major swing to the discounters. They lost valuable time in reacting, and lost the price position that they are now struggling to regain.

In early 2005, the rumours around Bernard continued. The families had been ready enough to sack his predecessor, Michel Bon, in 1992. Possible successors being touted included – according to gossip – not only Vandevelde, but Jose-Luis Duran, the well-regarded CFO, and even Serge Weinberg, then CEO of Pinault Printemps Redoute (PPR), the retail and fashion group.

Finally, in February 2005, Bernard was forced to resign: after months of hard negotiation, the families' patience had run out. The new structure sees Vandevelde as chairman of a new supervisory board, with Duran as chairman of the management board and CEO. Joel Saveuse, the director in charge of Europe, and a long-term ally of Bernard's, was also forced to resign. Duran is highly regarded, especially in the financial community, for his exceptional grasp of the details of the group's business, and his articulate expression of his views. Vandevelde has a more mixed reputation, since his promising start at Marks & Spencer did not continue, and many thought that he had, in the end, failed to deliver. He is, of course, an experienced supermarket retailer, so may be better suited to the Carrefour position. The strategic challenges remain for the new team to face.

The ousting of Bernard, who had until recent years enjoyed a fine reputation for his success in driving Carrefour to number two in the world, shows that, in this highly competitive business, success must be maintained, and that perceived failure – even if only relative – will be punished severely. His view had been that some change was necessary, but not much; Vandevelde and the families disagreed. There was also criticism that the management structure at Carrefour was too hierarchical (not uncommon in France), so that change was slow to percolate through the organisation. How quickly the new team will be able to change that culture remains to be seen (shades of Sainsbury). Duran is thought to be more open, and will introduce his own people into critical positions. The next year or two will be crucial

To sum up Carrefour in early 2005, therefore, we can only say that the group has many strengths, but some serious weaknesses too. On the positive side, it has a full range of formats, considerable retailing skills, broad and deep experience in operating internationally, and leadership positions in more countries than any of their rivals. Their most serious problem lies in their heartland of French hypermarkets; beside that, other weaknesses in IT and in some of the countries they operate in seem comparatively minor. As the board is committed to regaining price leadership at home, they will have to scale back their international expansion plans. On a pessimistic view, they could be sidelined in the international game for several years, while their rivals catch up and overtake them. Their future will be decided in France.

4 Tesco: Chasing Hard

Nowadays it must feel at Tesco that everything they touch seems to turn to gold. But for many years, it was hard to see the company becoming even a sound British retailer, far less an international competitor of significance. The story of Tesco is one of astonishing and repeated transformation, of a company which began from the humblest of beginnings in London's East end, where the young Jack Cohen pushed his barrow round the streets of Hackney and Hoxton. It then survived periods of anarchic and indiscriminate acquisitive behaviour through the 1960s and 1970s by the skin of its teeth, fighting its way through to become a significant competitor in the UK retailing scene by the end of the 1980s. Checkout (1978) was a significant customer re-presentation and the basis of a company change programme, which put Tesco firmly onto the UK map and warned competitors that they now needed to be taken seriously.

Steady growth in market share, volume and profitability took the business into the 1990s, at which stage an economic recession and weakening sales caused Tesco to lose confidence and momentum. It looked as if growth had stalled, but once again, a further seismic shift in company performance was engineered, and this set Tesco on its way to become the dominant leader in the UK food retailing market today. This time the transformation was more widely based, a fundamental re-positioning of the brand and business range. New business development had begun, and this moved Tesco from its traditional UK food focus, to be a clear retailing leader. Alongside this, Tesco is now a force in several unrelated but important market sectors, hitherto untapped by most food companies – non-food categories, and financial services for a start. Tesco's capacity for change has thus seen few limits. It has shown sureness of touch and there are signs that further organic change is alive in the company today. It is a story of striking achievement, leaving this British company well positioned to continue to grow well into the long term.

It was not always so. The early years were eventful but Jack Cohen had no concept of business strategy and a deep hatred of consistency and focus in his dealings whether with suppliers or customers. Growth, however, he pursued with some success, often by acquisition (for example the Victor Value chain), but the business process remained confused. Such policies as he possessed were executed waywardly, and profits were poor and inconsistent. Tesco was famous for a buccaneering approach to business, for its reliance on Green Shield stamps as a promotional weapon, but most of all for its business adage 'pile it high and sell it cheap', which was both its founder's watchword and the customer's perception of his untidy but bargain-rich stores. However, he sailed far too close to the wind, and as his son-in-law, Leslie Porter, took control in the 1970s, results showed Tesco falling apart at the seams.

Porter sought to steady the ship, but it was his successor, Tesco's first marketing trainee, Ian (now Lord) MacLaurin who was to exert major influence on business performance. The catalytic relaunch of Checkout which MacLaurin and deputy David Malpas put together to stimulate pricing and revive sales has justifiably become a legend. It was an immediate success. More importantly, it provided an ongoing business platform from which Tesco could move forward and grow volume, share and profits through the 1980s. Progress was steady rather than dramatic.

There was nothing particularly clever about MacLaurin's strategy. He pursued it with energy and determination, building a united and progressive team, who knew their market, could exploit UK untrammelled free market growth, and gratefully rode the out-of-town supermarket boom. By 1992, they had arrived at a position where only Sainsbury stood between them and market leadership – a transformation of some magnitude from the harum-scarum Tesco of earlier days. Sainsbury was well ahead of course, as was to be expected from this formidable British institution. The Tesco approach was unashamedly to copy what Sainsbury did – after all, the model had been working for Sainsbury for more than a century so there was little case for re-invention.

But cracks in the Tesco approach were appearing. Recession and new price competitors emphasised the need for renewed competitiveness, and Tesco had allowed itself, in its lapdog emulation of Sainsbury, to become a higher priced grocer. This was not yet a problem for Sainsbury, who had food quality credentials of a high order and a powerful brand image to compensate its consumers. Tesco growth slowed. There was anxiety that Tesco expansion plans, bolstered by a market rights issue, might never pay off. The stock market marked Tesco down sharply. In the *Financial Times* Lex wrote (7 April 1993) 'the risk is that Tesco will have neither the brand image nor the price competitiveness to compete in a mature market'. The sure touch that MacLaurin's team had applied no longer seemed to provide answers. Where might they go next? Had Tesco a replacement saviour to do what he had done in 1978? Had it a strategy to answer tougher market requirements?

It did indeed. He had vision and strategy coming out of his ears – so it appears. Terry (now Sir Terry) Leahy had been made Marketing Director in 1992, while still in his thirties. He showed a mature appreciation of the problem, and set about confronting Tesco's slowing growth and slipping market share. He started to build a new and aggressive young team, rejecting the quick fix in favour of proper analysis – why were customers leaving their brand? Goodwill had been squandered and his 1993 Board recommendations showed perfectly clearly why this had happened:

► Tesco was seen as a poor second to Sainsbury whom it had been imitating
► Tesco now needed to institutionalise a process of listening to customers
► Tesco should build its development programme strictly on customer needs.

To summarise, Tesco needed to set about establishing, or maybe regaining, customer trust. Tim Mason, who took over marketing on Leahy's promotion to CEO, describes the new incremental approach to winning back customers as putting 'bricks in the wall'. Leahy wanted their new inclusive Tesco brand to be 'the natural choice for ordinary shoppers'. The claim 'Every little helps' was a frontispiece to the all-embracing position Tesco was to adopt.

The new strategy had practical implications. Tesco needed to compete again and more visibly on pricing. 'Value lines' were to provide this – alongside a new high-quality offering, later called 'Finest', which could take on important new top-end competitors such as Marks & Spencer, Waitrose, and, of course, Sainsbury. Tesco knew it had to make worthwhile improvements to service in store. The 'one in front' queue reduction offer was simple, recognisable and different. Most fundamental and important to long-term strategic advantage was the Clubcard introduction in 1995. Initially this was a simple loyalty scheme with a one per cent price discount, but with 10 million new members signing up quickly, Tesco found it had an innovation on its hands which its customers liked, which they began to trust and which, through time, created an element of information advantage on the customer base that Tesco was able to convert into meaningful advantage against all comers.

Confidence spread to the store pattern. Just as the Conservative Government reluctantly, and late to the game, discovered planning constraint, Tesco returned to the high street with its smaller Metro and Express store formats, a neatly timed strategy reversal from out-of-town only, which had been the previous approach. In summary, these important operational changes established the Tesco domestic recovery through the mid-1990s. With business acquisition – Hillards and then William Low were taken over and firmly integrated – Tesco was starting to grow again and quickly. It had emphatically, and for all time broken free from copying Sainsbury – a confident assertion of Tesco brand advantage was now available. It was no surprise when the company became UK market leader in 1995, a position from which they have never looked back. The Sainsbury hegemony had ended. Sadly for them, as the years passed, a steadily declining situation for this formidable institution went from bad to worse. Five consecutive leaders, two family members and three others, have failed to stem the tide (see Text Box: 4.1).

As one of a series of brief textbox discussions on success and failure among key potential international competitors (see also Text Boxes 2.2 and 6.2) the text boxes that follow are presented as illustrations of the way in which companies perform in today's global market. Of the three companies discussed – Kmart, Ahold and Sainsbury – each has at some time, in different parts of the world, appeared a formidable local and international competitor. Kmart was a discounting force in the US long before anyone heard of Sam Walton. Royal Dutch Ahold was once regarded as the most effective of a new breed of global food retailers and their CEO was bold enough to claim this for Ahold as recently as five years ago. Finally Sainsbury, doyen of a strong British food retailing industry, which it once led as of right, put down its international marker in the USA twenty years ago. Now it is gone from the global scene. Can it recover? Are there lessons to be learned from the demise of three powerful industry forces? We should consider them alongside the global winners – Wal-Mart, Tesco and – perhaps – Carrefour.

BOX 4.1

WHY DID SAINSBURY FAIL?

Not so long ago Sainsbury commanded a place in the future world leaders' column. Today it barely enters the 'also rans'. With sales approaching $30 billion (£15billion) and a leading position in the tough UK market, Sainsbury is still a significant force in the important UK market. It is astonishing how big and rapid the fall has been. After a century of steady growth and expansion Sainsbury appears to have completely lost its way. As an international force for the future it is no longer considered. Why did it happen? Can it come back? (See separate Text Box 4.2).

Sainsbury was founded in 1869 by John James and Mary Ann, the first family leaders, as a Drury Lane dairy shop. Its reputation grew steadily, the shops multiplied and the company developed a reputation for good fresh food, claiming to produce 'the best butter in the world'. By the time the second generation (Mr. John) handed over to the third (Alan and Robert Sainsbury), 'an empire of high class provision shops' was the *Financial Times*' description of this company. Patiently Sainsbury continued to expand, leading the UK's move to self-service with its first Croydon supermarket, building its knowledge and winning, in the process, the consumer accolade 'good food costs less at Sainsbury'. It didn't. Prices were high but the product was highest calibre. The post-Second-World-War years were good.

In 1969 came the fourth generation of leader. Once again, Sainsbury acted apparently with the surest retail touch. Mr, later Lord, John, took the company public in 1973, the share offer being 45 times over-subscribed. (Today the Sainsbury family still own 37 per cent of the company.) The following years were halcyon. Sainsbury led the market – it was the recognised gold standard. As out-of-town shopping came to Britain, Sainsbury had the best sites, food range and a high reputation brand. It seemed impregnable. Growth in profits always hit double figures up to 1990, when Lord John handed over to cousin David, another Lord Sainsbury. Everything still seemed set fair ahead.

Sainsbury, at that stage alone among British retailers, had not neglected overseas expansion. In 1983, John Sainsbury bought the strong Connecticut supermarket chain, Shaws, manifesting an early strategic intention on behalf of the firm to become international. The US was seen as the best geographic area for business expansion – many European retailers felt and acted the same – and Sainsbury followed its Shaw's investment by taking a sizeable stake in the important east coast Giant Foods company. Sainsbury was positioned to follow UK dominance with a strong international presence.

But cracks in the edifice had appeared. Sainsbury in Lord John's last years tried too hard to stretch its profits and underinvested in modernising its supply chain. It ignored non-food opportunities – the hypermarket had not come to Britain. Stores looked cluttered, drab and tired. The best new sites went elsewhere – often to Tesco. Its vaunted 'good food costs less' claim had become threadbare. Sainsbury marked time through the 1990s and watched first Tesco (what an embarrassment!) and then Wal-Mart's Asda, pass it in sales revenue, reducing Sainsbury to number three in the market. The first non-Sainsbury chief executives took over, first Dino Adriano, then Sir Peter Davis and finally, in 2004, Justin King. Sainsbury were ringing the changes fast, but to no avail. Retail competitive advantage was a thing of Sainsbury's past.

The results were all too visible, and they got worse. Successive management teams claimed to have the answer but it never materialised. Lord David, taking over from his cousin, spoke of 'consistent values and a passion to innovate'. Fine words, yet through the 1990s the decline worsened and became deadly serious. Sainsbury's once high-flying share price halved over ten years. In 1999, it sent for Peter Davis, former chief of Reed Elsevier and the Prudential, and marketing director of Sainsbury in its great years. Could he sort out the mess? He was personally keen to try.

After four years of effort and major investment in suply chain efficiency, which was one – but only one – of Sainsbury's business problems, Davis threw in his hand. An acrimonious departure followed. His relatively untried successor was Justin King, from Asda and Marks & Spencer, who took over the company. He blamed Davis for misapplying investment, taking his eye off the main consumer market where the company had to compete, and for allowing the competition to steal its clothes. However accurate this analysis, Sainsbury is now in parlous shape, albeit King may have stemmed persistent losses in share and begun to remedy the flagging shelf replenishment problems.

Through the decline Sainsbury had been forced to divest itself of non-core ventures, including a DIY position in the UK, and its international aspirations have disappeared. First Giant Foods was ceded to Ahold, and recently Shaws was sold to Albertsons. The UK's earliest, and initially strongest, global entrant has thrown in its cards. 2004 was a disaster year for the company. Sir Peter Davis's departure caused a boardroom rift over his severance pay. Virtually his entire team disappeared with him. The worst ever set of results, and a halved dividend, did not stop the rot. Any strategy for change is absent.

Why did this happen? Fundamentally, Sainsbury's problems were caused by arrogance and complacency at the centre of the company. What had been its strengths and key elements of competitive advantage – deep and searching knowledge of store performance, an efficient supply chain, but most importantly, a brand which epitomised food quality for a British market emerging from post-war years when quality had been non-existent – had been ceded to aggressive retail competitors (Tesco, Asda, Morrison) who used cost control, supply-chain edge, and pricing advantage to make Sainsbury's offer look tired and increasingly irrelevant. Sainsbury was a true retail institution, and is still an institution in Britain – but alas no longer a properly equipped or viable competitor.

As a UK leader and a potential international force, it can safely be ignored.

BOX 4.2

CAN SAINSBURY RECOVER?

Sainsbury is a long established company, operating in the UK for 135 years. Even today, as the third largest food retailer in Britain, and stripped down to its food retailing essentials in its home market, it accounts for £15 billion in sales. This is still a big global company. While it has lost all global presence, its UK revenues still place it among the top twenty world retailers. This is a worthwhile platform from which expansion is possible.

The UK market is an important world market. While returns may not match Continental European companies, performance statistics, for example store efficiency, are among the highest in the world. The record for innovative growth is powerful and accelerating as the quality of leading competitors – Tesco and Asda/Wal-Mart – improves as they go head-to-head against each other. Providing Sainsbury can keep pace with the best UK standards, which ironically it was instrumental in establishing, its recovery potential ought to be strong.

Alas however, there is no sign yet that it has the capacity to keep up with the best competition at home, even in food per se – which does not bode well for potential expansion either into non-food sectors, or indeed a return to international markets. Indeed, it is the length of time over which Sainsbury has now been a non-performer that is the first reason for doubting eventual recovery. Only divestment has kept the business afloat. 2004 was a year where no profit was made – an all-time low. The UK market has three committed and tough competitors – Tesco, Wal-Mart/Asda and Morrison/Safeway – all operating in the mainstream segment – 'decent quality at low prices' – giving Sainsbury little chance of a differentiated re-entry into the mainstream of the market. Each of them has more capacity to extend and develop their store base than today's Sainsbury which apart from some new high street 'local' stores, has done little.

A bigger reason for questioning Sainsbury's recovery is visible uncertainty over what strategy to pursue to make change happen. New management under King has stated that Sainsbury wishes to be a mainstream, that is, mid- to low-price player, and it has moved in this direction. The moves have been modest, made little customer impact, and 'the big three' have lost no sleep over them. Tesco and Asda persist in cutting prices themselves for their own reasons. An alternative strategy, 'best quality but at higher prices', has its adherents – the position traditional Sainsbury held, though John Sainsbury would not admit it. Today Waitrose and Marks & Spencer are well regarded high-price food stores. While they are small in size, it is not easy for Sainsbury to sweep these solid reputations away. For Sainsbury itself it would imply a much smaller business, at least for some years. Sainsbury is caught in a strategic dilemma and pursues neither strategy wholeheartedly.

Lack of strategy leads to lack of commitment to relevant innovation and business development. Sainsbury now lacks breadth, with a weak non-food position. Only banking represents success outside the core business. Its food quality has suffered; its brand lacks direction and relevant development. It is no longer clear what the thrust of the company's customer brand message is. With this uncertainty, the stores remain inadequately differentiated. This is worsened by poor shelf stock control, resulting in widespread customer dissatisfaction with what is available and where to find things. 'I can't find it' is a frequent complaint and this despite major investment in supply chain improvement, managed by Accenture consultancy.

Retail leaders must hold a fine balance between strategic company direction, and operating confidence that they can deliver the required advantage to customers in store. Sainsbury now possesses neither. Its management team is untried, and was still, in late 2004, blaming its predecessors. Confidence has ebbed as far too many changes at all levels take place, alongside persistent financially driven cuts to management headcount. Arrogance was never far from the Sainsbury culture. At times when the institution was impregnable, a top-down control ethic ensured operating standards and results were maintained. When competition woke up and matched them, this ethos became a millstone round Sainsbury's corporate neck. Sainsbury has sadly never appeared able to change to behaviour patterns where innovation and imagination could start to rebuild its great brand franchise. Today this looks as far away as ever.

So we see a company which, although Justin King puts a brave face on things, looks powerless to turn itself round and now relies on predatory bidders – of whom there are several – to effect a change to its fortunes and restore it to profitability and then growth. How are the mighty fallen!

A formative element in the recovery had been the way Leahy and his young team approached issues. Most companies know they are answerable to their customers. Many would attribute success to good customer research – to knowing what these same customers want. Tesco, certainly among the retail fraternity, perhaps more widely, have tackled this process with unique focus and determination. There had been continuous research and insights that had shown Tesco what it needed to do to restore customer confidence. Leahy drove and motivated his young team to use research and analysis to give Tesco a secure customer position – they never again wanted the experiences of the 1990s, where the Tesco leadership was seen to have lost its way as a team. They created a formidably robust customer learning base.

Having begun this way, the process became organic. Moves ahead were planned, using rigorous and regular customer research briefings, and these became a key element in company operating planning. 'Few weeks go by without us running customer research sessions somewhere in the country' was a remark Leahy made to one of the authors some years ago. The arrival of Clubcard gave an immense customer-centric impetus to the process. Management were able to see the effects of their plans quickly and clearly in the market. The ability to experiment and learn at limited cost, and in unique ways for a retailer, was enhanced. The company had at its disposal processes generating long-term market advantage, which perhaps inexplicably, competitors elected not to follow. Sainsbury, from its position of lofty eminence, at once dismissed the card as 'Green Shield stamps' in a new guise, although they later adopted their own (Reward) loyalty card. It built big momentum for Tesco.

Internal developments have been equally striking. From harum scarum beginnings, when Tesco shop managers were as renowned for their legerdemain and cavalier dealing as for their hostility to central policy constraints, MacLaurin's team instilled discipline into the company's operations, and the store manager has become an enduring company focus because of this. However, Tesco's store capabilities were still falling some way short of best practice, and the level of in-store support that Tesco offered its customers fell behind Sainsbury and Marks & Spencer, by some margin. Leahy could see that this needed to change. On-the-ground research and communications with store personnel provided the way forward. As usual, Leahy said:

> I would ask the groups what Tesco stood for. A typical response would be 'caring for customers'. Then I asked what they would like Tesco to stand for and they would use words like 'teamwork', 'praise' and 'trust'. These are part of our core values today. People want to enjoy being at work. The goodwill of the staff is the main productivity lever you have' (Harvard Business School case 9.503.036, 3 March 2003).

The programme of internal business learning that began with new zest in the mid-1990s broke new ground for Tesco, and has been a crucial element in the company's strength and its ability to expand out of its home market. Tesco behaviour places a unique and high level of focus on the store as the centre of the operation – it is in store that innovation is seen to work and developments are proved. Tesco had been given the desire to be a winning business during the MacLaurin years – from the 1980s on, the will to win was present. But it lacked a strategy to drive this through to competitive advantage – after all, 'copying Sainsbury', even doing this well, is not much of a battle cry for the troops. But now, in many ways, Tesco had struck out to occupy new ground, leading where others had not been before. This provided the critical self-belief and confidence that a real winning team required. Nothing so drives business performance as an unshakeable conviction, preferably held in equal esteem from boardroom to shop floor, that it has a winning formula that competitors cannot challenge. Tesco has laid its hands on this in the past ten years and has not looked like letting it go. This is now its primary asset.

Tesco itself believes that customer initiative has provided the key building block of today's formula. In his National Business Awards speech in 1993, Leahy was questioned as follows: 'What's your secret for making Tesco, Britain's number one retailer?' He answered in five words: 'We sell what people want', and went on to observe that 'the answer is usually greeted with bemusement. Can it really be that simple?'

He went on:

> Fast-growing companies cannot afford to have complicated processes, lots of red tape, long-winded decision-making processes. Simplicity must run through everything; its values, its aims, how it works, how it grows, how it does business with consumers, be they individuals or other companies.

Once again, business, big and small, understands this maxim – at a level of principle. However, too few observe it in practice. Tesco has absorbed the need to observe the twin requirements of *customer centricity* – having *all* business activity driven from a standpoint of real customer advantage; and of *process simplicity* – having retailing practice reduced to the simplest level of operation. The combination has become an irresistible force for business growth and management confidence, and appears now to be well rooted in day-to-day as well as strategic decision-making in the company. If this is the case, the transformation capabilities that Tesco showed at an episodic level, first in 1978, but later in the mid-1990s, might now become available to it on a steady and repetitive basis in the marketplace as a whole. It is the kind of organic process advantage that spells big danger for its competitors, wherever in the world they are encountered.

The Tesco recovery, which Leahy's new team had pioneered, bore fruit quickly and comprehensively. The first signs were evident from the firm leadership that Tesco began to cement in its home (UK) market for food, where growth in market share steamed ahead. There were other very good competitors in the market – Morrison and Asda for example – who were becoming major volume players, and who had a strong price-driven offer. But they, as well as less successful players (Sainsbury, Somerfield, Safeway) were swept aside by the Tesco bandwagon. Tesco was creating a mid-market franchise, and while attracting an increasing share of the quality-conscious shoppers, its offer was competitive with the continuingly big customer group who wanted low prices. By 2000, Tesco had a five point overall share lead against the second player, Sainsbury. As Sainsbury dropped back and Asda, bought by Wal-Mart in 1999, began to thrust forward, Tesco's lead widened further. Asda was known to offer the keenest market prices, and Tesco was prepared to see it hold this position, but it did not at any time inhibit Tesco's own progress. Additional large stores underlined their supermarket domination, but Tesco simultaneously spearheaded the move back to the high street. Tesco Metro paved the way where others followed. Tesco used a combination of organic growth, and acquisition to fuel this new source of high street, and petrol forecourt, growth.

The move from recovery to a strategy of all-out UK growth was helped by a determined push for penetration in non-food products. Tesco was some way behind the leader (Asda) in this field, so that the opportunity for the biggest operator in the market, with many more stores, was much greater. Asda had made a particularly strong point of marketing its clothes brand ('George') with help from designer George Davies, so that when Tesco had started to push its non-food drive forward, Asda's space allocation to non food in store was still 20 per cent greater than Tesco's. Other competitors lagged miles behind. A bigger incentive in the heavily investigated (by government bodies) UK market was that, with its food share pushing close to 30 per cent of UK sales, it had to diversify quickly into new untapped sectors – clothing, entertainment and financial services were all high on the list. Competition Commission authorities were waiting to pounce on what they saw as unreasonable market domination. Tesco discounts this opinion. Leahy is fond of quoting the figure of 12 per cent of all retail sales that Tesco holds as an indication of its relative 'smallness', and confirmation of its continuing capacity to grow at home. Its non-food share, at six per cent, remains tinier still.

Intrinsically, there seems no logical pattern to the sectors that Tesco enters. Many are certainly a far cry from the basic customer food basket, where few items sell for more than a pound or two. Thus Tesco has become a major factor in entertainment – CDs, now DVDs and books. Clothing has been an obvious area for growth, as have health and personal care, and it is clear that Tesco is just scratching the surface in these markets. Tesco will be happy to set up new services, such as opticians, in their bigger stores. Across the board, what is happening is a steady move to tap entirely new markets, where competition was slower and sleepier than in food retailing. Where volume was secured, it was at margins that often dwarfed food levels. And unlike, say, Virgin, who are willing to extend their brand indiscriminately, Tesco has been keen to move only when it saw that its offer was truly competitive with existing suppliers.

For the higher priced and bigger unit volume items, where space was an issue, Tesco was increasingly able, as time passed, to use its Internet selling capabilities. It had worked at tesco.com for many years before taking it national, but once it came it proved a fine way of servicing new markets at limited capital cost. Humby and Hunt (2003) note that 'in the first year tesco.com pushed its non-food lines, results were remarkable – in the run up to Christmas 2001, it sold 230,000 CDs and DVDs. Wine sales topped a million bottles ... ' Company policy was clear. 'The promise of customer care still applies' said Leahy. 'We develop a customer for whom a visit to Tesco is just part of running the household. Sometimes it's about buying a bike once a year ... [or] buying socks more regularly ... but it's also about buying presents quite a lot and buying food very regularly.' The (failed) American Webvan strategy of using food as a loss leader to get a foot in the door and drive customers to buying higher margin items has been firmly rejected by Tesco in its non-food approach. Indications are that customers like this, and find the Tesco brand an increasingly credible umbrella. Tesco is now recognised as an Internet shopping leader, on a worldwide level.

Tesco's push for flat-out growth took on a further dimension with the development and rapid expansion of services under the Tesco umbrella. It is this, along with its international capabilities, which clearly signifies the ambitions of the company, and its capacity to extend not just into markets contiguous with food, but far away from its traditional prime focus. Taken with dot.com expertise, it shows Tesco as a company with greater market breadth than any other British business, and right at the top of potential world leagues in the future. In 1997 Tesco believed it was ready to enter banking and was summarily rejected as a suitor by NatWest, at that stage one of the UK's big five banks. Tesco then set up a bank in partnership with the then smaller but highly professional Royal Bank of Scotland. Why banking? Leahy reduced the rationale to a typically simple proposition. 'This was the answer to a simple question, why do you need banks? Why can't you bank in a supermarket or on-line? A shop's till is effectively a bank. Money goes in and out. So why not allow customers to deposit money in it?' Tesco claimed it cost them barely 25 per cent of the banks' normal cost to sign up a new customer, and of course subsequent service advantage vis à vis conventional high street banks means they will have little difficulty in retaining this advantage. Tesco treats customer loyalty as a priority in a way that many banks barely comprehend. Its bank has accumulated more than three million customers quickly, and made a profit contribution from the start. Given its strong customer base and low acquisition cost, it can now position Tesco as a category leading instant access savings accounts.

Better still, the door has opened through the establishment of Tesco Personal Finance (TPF) to many new and established financial services products, in a market where the customer need for coherence and transparency has been ignored for too long by traditional providers. Loans, mortgages, travel and general insurance are all Tesco markets. The company has become the UK's fastest growing financial services company. 'We recruit financial services customers using our physical assets, brand recognition and loyalty', says Tim Mason; again a simple recipe for a market where complexity and obscurity had appeared to be inevitable. Of course, in some ways, Mason was selling himself short, since it was the Tesco advantage in customer information, generated from the Clubcard – not really a physical asset – which had given it the foothold advantage enabling the company to make secure and rapid progress with the TPF offer.

We hope that it will develop the offer to the customer by setting new standards of convenience, simplicity and value, and out of this we will generate some good demand and make some money out of it in the long haul (Leahy's words, emphasis added).

Tesco's young CEO was already by 1997 learning the gentle art of understatement.

The pace of activity in the opening years of Leahy's tenure – he took over formally as Chief Executive in 1997 – was staggering. Three major moves have been outlined. First, the move to dominate food retailing in the UK, well on its way before 2000 and accelerating thereafter. Second, the extension into non-food products where bigger share gains were available and at higher margins than in food. Third, the new presence of Tesco as a services company, beginning with financial services, but extending later into big new areas such as the mobile telephone market. 'Everybody at Tesco is more excited about the next few years than at any time in their career here', was the way he described things and one could see why and recognise the reality.

One major new area of strategy remains to be covered. International expansion has already proved important to Tesco in the few years it has been operating out of the UK. As time passes, and given the relative constraints of the UK market, international operations will become the bedrock of what could be one of a handful of significant global retailers.

By 1995 Tesco was perceived as a dynamic and profitable UK business, its food focus no longer being a limitation to future growth. But as an international player, it was a non-starter. There were doubts about whether the Tesco mentality could penetrate international markets. It was believed to be too homespun, too down-market, to be lacking in corporate gravitas and the scale and clout that created big worldwide corporate players. Worst or all for Tesco, it was starting the game far too late. Had not Sainsbury, its UK rival, invested heavily by buying Shaws in the USA as long ago as 1983? Was not Carrefour, its hugely successful French based rival, now with Promodès under its belt, and twice Tesco's size, miles ahead with its overseas operations in Europe, Latin America and Asia-Pacific?

Among the true world players – and ignoring both Ahold from the Netherlands, strongly placed in the US, and German Metro with strong positions in Europe and elsewhere – there was the mighty Wal-Mart. Wal-Mart, from 1999 its toughest local rival in its home market, was simply a worldwide phenomenon. The Wal-Mart brand is another very simple, down-to-earth offer – we price lowest. Nobody, certainly not Tesco, could argue that this was not a clear and believable customer proposition. Wal-Mart was then approximately eight times the size of Tesco. In one single good year, it could now build a company that would be Tesco in size. The worldwide struggle looked from a Tesco vantage point to be distinctly unequal. Could it, from a late start, even contemplate taking on Wal-Mart?

The first steps were faltering. The purchase of Catteau, a medium sized but feeble supermarket chain in northern France, did not produce the desired results either in growth or in margins. Squeezed by discounters and proper hypermarkets, by 1998 Tesco quickly decided to eat humble pie, and the chain was sold, at a loss. However, it did not simply beat a global retreat – quite the reverse. The next set of ventures was more promising, bought with clear strategic principles in mind. It set in train an approach that has now worked well for the company for a period of seven years. Beginning with the significant purchase from ABF in Ireland of a position that quickly gave Tesco leadership (overnight a 25 per cent share) in the Irish market, Tesco then put its mark down in two further and unexpected areas of the world. They were both logical, yet given the speed of execution, brave moves. With the Catteau fiasco still in their minds, and the time advantages that Carrefour, and many others, all enjoyed, Tesco knew they could not afford another false start on their planned route to becoming a world retailer. They also wanted to be somewhere where they could lead – quickly.

In retrospect, what they did made eminent sense. The first steps were towards Eastern Europe: Hungary in 1994, and later Poland, the Czech Republic and Slovakia. In each case, Tesco bought small thriving companies, reviewed, absorbed and integrated their managements, and set about driving the businesses to leadership positions. This was followed, quickly, by an emphasis on the fast-growing Asia-Pacific markets. Once again, however, they selected the medium-sized countries. Thailand, South Korea, Taiwan and Malaysia were targeted in the later 1990s, and effective operating local partnerships were involved. Tesco recognised that it needed to move fast. Hypermarkets were chosen as the best vehicle to adopt, a sign of open-mindedness, as this was not its UK format. Finally, in 2003 and 2004, Tesco began to 'bite the bullet', and has established initial partnerships in the two crucial Asian markets, Japan (2003) and China (2004). There is a business logic to this unusual and seemingly peripheral patchwork of expansion. Take the less critical targets first (Eastern Europe) and establish that you can make things work. Move to the fringe Asia-Pacific markets next, and again, in both Thailand and South Korea, show that leadership is possible and that you can achieve it with the teams assembled there. Finally, recognise the major challenges in Asia, where future growth will be fastest, where you must be present if you want to be a world-class retailer. While we can still only assess the early results of the programme, the policy is working admirably so far. Tesco's pace of development and growth is more than matching best competition in the regions it has occupied. On quality of achievement, if not yet in worldwide scale, Tesco is up with the best.

The company's overseas practice shows open-mindedness, a capacity to absorb best competitive international achievement, and its own strongly customer-driven on-the-spot operating. The business leaders have been the experienced David Reid, and now one of the new, younger tigers on the group board, Philip Clarke. They have known what they were setting out to do but also the way they wanted to do it. Theirs was not the traditional 'buy a position and then tell them how we do it from back home' approach. Leahy, quoted in the Harvard case noted previously, gives us a vintage Tesco summary:

There were no texts on how to be successful in international … it worked in our favour that we didn't start believing we had all the answers. How could we add value for us and our customers? We needed countries where we would be early entrants that were stable, with sufficient spending power and with growth potential. We recognised that our skill set involved opening networks of stores rather than integrating pre-existing chains. This led us to identify former Communist countries of East Europe and a few emerging overlooked countries in Asia.

A further indication of the essential humility, or willingness to learn alongside local partners and from local needs, was the adoption of the hypermarket as the vehicle, a style of operation more practised by Tesco's European rivals (Carrefour in particular) than itself. David Reid says, 'we did not have a ready-made international format. We had no hypermarkets in the UK … but it became obvious that it was the right format. It helped that tastes were more international in non-food than in food. It was also the right choice logistically … finally, it seemed to us that no matter how we started we'd end up opening hypermarkets so it made sense to skip the first step and open up hypermarkets to begin with.' A further advantage for the hypermarket is that, compared to supermarkets, you have to open many fewer stores, given their size and scale.

The big corporate players have tied themselves and their managers in knots for years about how to strike the best global/local balance in international operations. Strangely, this conundrum has not seemed to worry the parvenu, Tesco. In early 2003, Leahy noted that of 65,000 overseas people, Tesco had only 70 expatriate managers in – then – nine countries. 'They are trainers', he said. 'We've told the local managers they are to be the number one in their countries [that is, get on with winning] but we don't think of telling them how to do it. As a result, their enthusiasm is sky high.' This simple but persuasive mantra may be a lesson for some big and experienced multinationals who think they know better.

By early 2003, Tesco claimed leadership in six out of nine countries and profitability in eight from nine, with the combined contribution well over £100 million. There were signs that Tesco was the most profitable retailer in both Eastern Europe and Asia, a remarkable competitive achievement, given its late start.

In November 2004, *Retail Week* noted that Tesco, emulating Wal-Mart, were working closely with suppliers internationally to drive down prices. Leahy in 2003 had been keen to tell the authors how unimportant, relatively, he felt international economies of scale were, compared to growth and costs progress in the local markets.

What's important is not to lose any local economies of scale there. That's why it's important to be number one in a country and not just build (aggregate) sales across countries. The main advantage Tesco has, is to export our culture in the stores. Global brands won't be the norm in my generation. … after all, most of our customers think they are shopping in a local store.

He pointed out that it took companies – such as Unilever – a hundred years to get global brands to a world share of, say, ten per cent. Retailing will not be different, he suggests. The Tesco brand will accommodate differences, providing consumers want them. It is a beguilingly attractive philosophy. There is no question that Tesco believes in it, and it has the information systems, and the track record, to help it go in this direction. It is their chosen route, one where they have copied no one.

It is time to take stock of the Tesco position today, in early 2005, and assess where it is in the overall scheme of things, what its key achievements are, and how it is placed for the years ahead. The most compelling element of its performance has been noted – its dedicated allegiance to a simple, customer-driven philosophy of business. The Tesco Way, discussed below, sets out its approach to doing business, graphically, and embraces five elements: purpose, goals, values, principles and the steering wheel.

It proposes a way of working which is better, simpler and cheaper. We can observe the strong linkage between customer focus (way of doing business,) and internal focus. Core purpose is the single element allocated overall priority in its approach. 'Our core purpose is all about customers.' It is 'TO CREATE VALUE FOR CUSTOMERS TO EARN THEIR LIFE-TIME LOYALTY'. Few enterprises have managed to describe their *raison d'être* into a statement of such condensed and lasting import. It is a triumph of expression, and at the same time a mechanism enabling them to inspire and operate their business from top to bottom.

This level of policy and process assurance has been created in a short time – under ten years – and is accompanied by rapid growth and innovation in core activity, new market sectors and a dozen different countries. In turn, you find palpable confidence whenever you meet Tesco people on the ground. The authors have seen many of them over a period of twenty years and in many

Every little helps

Shopping Trip for Customers

The aisles are clear	✓
I can get what I want	✓
The prices are good	✓
I don't queue	✓
The staff are great	✓

No-one tries harder for customers

Every little helps

For our people

To be treated with respect	✓
A manager who helps me	✓
An interesting job	✓
An opportunity to get on	✓

Treat people how we like to be treated

different capacities – (supplier, advisor, author). Their cohesion is what sticks uppermost in the mind. They are happy about their company, which they think has found a winning recipe. They can state the principles, not because they have been drummed into them, but, one gets the impression, because they know principles matter and can help a business work. They are self-evidently turned on by the big part they have to play in things.

The result is a culture that is an unusual combination of confidence, desire to analyse and learn but, at root, humility about the scale of future challenge, alongside a recognition that Tesco can win where it plans the plays properly. Tesco managers might not state it this way but I sense they are frightened of nobody. This stems not from a US Marines-like bravado, but a mixture of thinking, learning and action that has generally produced results over wide expanses of business territory for some length of time. This is not a bad platform from which to look forward. It is worth looking in more detail at some of the components of the platform that have given rise to such assurance.

First, let us summarise Tesco group performance over the years from 1996. The most recent financial highlights statement shows group sales up by 18.7 per cent, year on year, underlying group profit up by 21.9 per cent, with Tesco now present in thirteen markets, the latest additions being Turkey and China in July 2004. Tesco profits have now, in 2005, passed the £2 billion threshold.

It is suggested that the specific components of advantage have been the following:

▶ *Human performance:* values and personal beliefs
▶ *Business processes:* leading to customer advantage
▶ *Store focus:* range and flexibility, including hypermarkets
▶ *Information utilisation:* integrated, business-wide, including dot.com
▶ *Breadth of Tesco brand:* Inclusiveness, reputation

which together produce broad-based sector and geographic advantage, and contribute a willingness to take on all comers and win. These are discussed briefly.

Where companies possess them, it is usually the human performance factors that can drive competitive advantage farthest; Tesco seems to have understood this. It works in a fairly pragmatic way, and by a process of managed evolution, being prepared to accept a great deal of trial and error as it has moved along. What is impressive is the way in which business learning takes place in the company; it can start virtually anywhere, but managers would tend to locate it most often in the store. Strategic members in the team would point to an inbuilt attitude to analytical, as opposed to intuitive, advantage, which demands 'we can do it' as a response, rather than just 'now we know this'. Dido Harding, working in Tesco's overseas team, was particularly clear about this, and critical of alternative company models. She felt these often lacked proper quantitative evaluation before being ritualised in corporate repertoires. Tesco did not need to do this: the store is its laboratory. It had the requisite measurement tools (information advantage nurtured and now in-built). There was company-wide recognition that, once evaluated in any one place, the best ideas could travel, and robust communication processes existed to make this happen.

You get the same answers in Tesco, virtually wherever you ask the questions. Knowledge is well disseminated, and there is a culture that allows people who start as young and inexperienced, quickly to get learning and expertise, invariably in the store, that builds corporate advantage. Thus, disciplines work well together – marketing/store/information, for example.

Overseas relates well to domestic, each with an understanding of its role in overall strategy. There is a good relationship between day-to-day operating factors and the building of longer term growth. Finally, Tesco have found the happy knack, so necessary in any institution, of getting the very best out of their people, and pushing them to levels of achievement in the company that they would have dismissed as ridiculous when they began their time there. (See Text Box 4.3)

BOX 4.3

'SPIRIT'* – CAN GRADUATES CATCH UP?

Tesco has through the years presented widely different faces to the world. It began with Jack Cohen, barrow boy and market trader. 'Keep your hand on the money and run', he liked to say. 'Pile it high and sell it cheap' linked Tesco stores for half a century, giving it *raison d'être*. Chaotic is the only way to describe Tesco in Cohen's and son-in-law Leslie Porter's years at the helm. After it went public, employees affectionately called the Board Room 'The snake pit'. Fifteen years of leadership by Ian (now Lord) MacLaurin and David Malpas instilled cohesion to the business and it began to grow profitably at last. The first signs of teamwork occurred after the 1978 success of Checkout. Tesco have not looked back and progress has been remarkable, such that Allan Leighton, long-time competitor (at Asda) wrote fulsomely in the *Daily Mail* (6 January 2005) of Tesco's excellent management processes as a reason for its success.

MacLaurin's era did in truth conclude with a distinct hiccup. After years of successfully slipstreaming Sainsbury, the dominant leader, Tesco simply ran out of steam. The viability of their strategy was questioned. Could their progress go on? A new team was waiting in the slips, led by marketing director, later CEO, Terry Leahy. These players – Leahy himself still in his thirties – young, untried but hungry, huddled frequently to address the issue. They needed, and found themselves, a dynamic, freshly crafted strategy. They promised each other (literally) not to let such a damaging 'hiccup' happen again. They created a hard-edged driving ethic at Tesco, which propelled the company to market leadership. It made customers top priority, and gave simplicity the role in delivering this. The new men had much in common, were ready to learn, patently liked each other and wanted to be best. They liked winning, and winning was something they got used to – in Britain and, later on, internationally.

Strategy, and the ability to deliver it to customers in the store, is at the root of Tesco's success. But people advantage is the other essential way in which the company have worked together to ensure they can win. Their company has moved from leading in the chaos stakes, during their early years, to an ordered set of methods that has turned them into a mature and intelligible corporation, able to work across a dozen countries with a management process that is recognisable and coherent wherever they are. Unsurprisingly, a simplifying influence for Tesco has been that the place they locate their operating advantage – the store – is also the place where they derive their internal communications policies. Each of Tesco's store managers is a personnel manager, and this element of his or her role is genuinely important. The simple shopping chart shown earlier demonstrates how neatly and naturally the twin requirements of customer advantage and Tesco people advantage fit with each other.

The company likes to say its leadership is not any one person, but 2000 leaders – store managers across a company. There is no doubting store primacy in Tesco's approach and the inevitability of the way they set out to organise human resources in it. You know if the responsibility was shifted away to a set of corporate headquarters, it would, for Tesco, be much less 'real' or important.

There are specific ways to ensure the process is live, one where everyone can participate, and things can change for the better – the 'Tesco Week in Store Together' (TWIST) is one example of this and the 'steering wheel' is a reinforcement. Some years ago one of the authors was quizzed at Tesco on the value of the established management-appraisal processes Unilever used for its worldwide managers. Tesco is an acquisitive learner. It listens and adopts best practice and it has done it with appraisal – it is in place and working as a significant element in management policy. It is aware that it needs to recognise the best 'coaches' and give them responsibility. Teamwork is critical in any big, winning company, and the retailer, who has stores open round the clock seven days a week, *must* recognise teams – it is beyond any individual or set of individuals to drive so complex, and always-on-show-to the-public, an enterprise.

David Potts is given great credit for the open-minded way in which these processes are encouraged. Team working, diversity and leadership are all elements he wants his store managers to study and enhance. In so driving an enterprise one is tempted to ask whether stress gets in the way. The answer is sensible and reflects how Tesco views this: 'We know people are going to work very hard, sometimes too hard. We want them to see their jobs in the context of their whole lives and we ensure that they have input to make sure they get this kind of "learning" or "context" regularly. We get a good response to this from our people so we keep updating it. This is a place expecting high performance but dealing with how to get it in a considerate and environmentally sensitive way.'

So people advantage is fundamental to Tesco strategy. The culture is, like its stores, classless and inclusive. Self-help and new ideas are a requirement. 'We can do better' is something Tesco people believe. The Board features committed professionals, practical leaders of their functions – Potts (store operations), Mason (marketing) and Clarke (information/international) for example. They recruit from anywhere talent can be found, now including a component of new country – Asian and European – nationals. One is struck by their enthusiasm, and their youth, but also by their long time in one company. An unusual feature in this 'university' age is the number of them who leave school at 16 but make remarkable progress thereafter. Leahy's reply to a comment on this was 'Well, you have to realise, ... the graduates – who arrive five or six years later – can sometimes find it difficult to catch up'!

* The authors are indebted to Lucy Nevill-Rolfe for this word.

The leaders of overseas (Philip Clarke), who also runs information, marketing (Tim Mason), and store operations (David Potts) would all be examples of this process at group board level, but there are many others. It is an achievement that began in the MacLaurin and Malpas era, when Tesco fostered a culture of 'try it and see', a style of encouraging people at all levels to innovate. Leahy, Reid and others can claim legitimate credit for continuing to see this as important and enhancing it, as the business has grown big and gone international in the last ten years.

People and mentalities come first, but effective processes are not far behind. Here too Tesco has come a long way and developed its own proprietary model of success. Thirty years of international business taught the authors the need for the 'dog-eared' plan, turned to by management when questions of direction arose. (The plan that lies untouched in the desk drawer is not worth the paper it is written on.) David Potts was an eloquent proponent of this truth when discussing Tesco's approach to business planning. Of course being Tesco, the plan is the *customer* plan. Unashamedly, the early initiatives are centrally agreed, strategic choices outlined, with clear top-down budgets – an evolutionary change, David said, from the MacLaurin era. Thereafter, however, the process becomes deliberately communicative and inclusive, and through a series of 'town meetings', a consensual set of agreed operating plans are put together, endorsed and embarked upon by entire teams. Through the year at regular intervals, the same communicative process ensures that plans are delivered and necessary changes made. There is awareness in the ambitious Tesco community of the need for trial and error. There is recognition of the need for incentives, and these are widely spread through the company.

David Potts described the balanced store card by which Tesco assessed its own performance – the four quadrants of the steering wheel at Tesco.

It would be possible to assess individual components of success, say customers only, or profits only, but the consolidation of four key elements was a business strength as he saw it. 'We get better at this every year', he said,

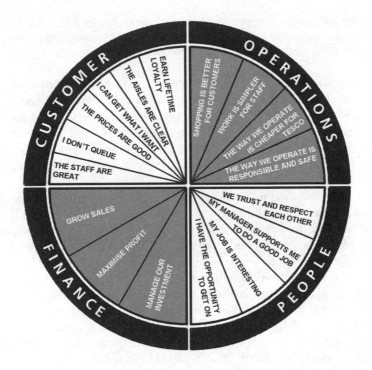

'better' in this instance meaning 'simpler'. 'It's more than a straight maths game', he went on: 'If it were simply this we'd be … [nowhere].' The word he actually employed was a lot stronger. Whatever the level of management, passion was necessary to drive the process forward – 'the battlefield had better be in the bloodstream, and of course most of the time it is.'

The third element in the armoury is the concentration in Tesco on the primacy of the store and its operations to business success of the whole. Tesco has been described as being 'obsessed with stores' (Harvard Business School 2003), and they might not deny it. Maybe it is a deeply held understanding of this that makes the company reluctant to build itself a steel and glass corporate HQ as most £30 billion plus companies like Tesco would have done years ago.

Whatever it is, there is no doubting that it is a universally held belief. The TWIST 'Tesco Week in Store Together' programme is an endorsement of the idea and is practised by everyone in the business. It requires participants to work on a specific store task, understand it and, where possible, seek to improve how it is performed. Philip Clarke spent a week stocking shelves. Leahy had, among other things, worked a cash register. He said:

All our 1000 managers do it – a week in a store is a great morale booster for all concerned, and a makes everyone feel part of the team. Also, it produces some great ideas. Next time you buy sandwiches from us look for the barcode. It was on the back because the designer thought it spoiled the label, but when sandwiches were reduced, we had to put stickers on the front and back. The person on the checkout had to check front and back of the pack – this took time. We sell a million sandwiches a day. Someone who was TWISTing noticed this and suggested we put

the price and barcode together on the front of the pack. The saving from that – £½
million. All these savings mount up – last year our drive for simplicity and efficiency
made us £230 million. To coin a phrase – every little helps.

Nothing has been more striking in the recent transformation of Tesco
from a successful but primarily operations-driven UK food retailer to a
strategic world player in a range of markets, than the primacy of information
in effectively supporting key changes in policy. Having begun the early
1990s with a succession of focus groups with consumers and seen what
consumer-driven changes could achieve, Leahy and Mason's marketing team
were early converts.

MacLaurin had used information through the early periods for the orthodox supply chain, replenishment, and logistics roles and they had built world-
class systems, or so they reckoned, that Philip Clarke, today's information
head, accepts were the backbone of the company. But over the past decade,
things have both spread in application and profoundly accelerated. The
company has begun to develop its own proprietary software and has departed
from the standardised technologies retailers are adopting. Where they need
bespoke systems for competitive advantage, the UK business has access to
them. Speed, simplicity and lowest cost are the drivers, geared to making sure
customers get the benefits, but staff are of course the facilitators of advantage.

Philip Clarke believes that Tesco now lead against all comers in customer,
and related store information processing. He can see the development of
comparable systems-driven benefit for the international and services
businesses. They are confident enough now to sell some of their basic learning in information systems to competitors such as Safeway Inc. and Kroger
in the USA, thus opening up potential wider partnership avenues for the
future perhaps. Philip presides over a formidable informations team at Tesco
of 650 people, a clear indication, in a company that eschews empire building, of the priority the company attaches to analysis-driven advantage and
where this has taken them.

Clubcard and the Internet are discussed more fully in subsequent chapters,
but they must be noted briefly here since they have both been important
building blocks in the process. It is the use to which Tesco has put the
customer information base it created that has been crucial. In 1997, the
company established the Customer Insight unit to identify and propose new
store and range development hypotheses and strategies for customer advantage. Tim Mason said:

These people were geographers, statisticians who had spent lots of time
understanding how customers would behave. They could crunch through ... Clubcard,
see the patterns, and help the management ... understand what was going on, and
point to what might be done with it. They had ... to find and present the data in a
way which was stark and clear.

The key partner was Dunn-Humby, in which Tesco have now taken a
controlling interest, and with them Tesco learned as they went along. Simon
Uwins summarises the process well:

We moved from being intuitive to analytical. This is a much more complicated business than it used to be. Better data led to better thinking ... and gave us the confidence to ask the right questions. You can have all the data you want but the key is to use them to ask the right questions.

Alongside Clubcard must be ranked the tesco.com approach and its leadership position in home shopping markets. Phillip Clarke described how the Internet caught their attention well before the dot.com frenzy began. Exploring its potential took a long time, and six stores carried the responsibility for learning for three years. There was, again, lots of trial and error. Fainter hearts would have lost faith, but Tesco managers realised that there were customers who would, ultimately, die for the idea, so they persisted, using technology and common sense to simplify the system. Leahy says:

Today your online order is received by the nearest store, where we will push a specially designed trolley with a scanner, around the store. The scanner will tell us how much of each product the customer wants and where the product is located ... several orders can be completed simultaneously. The process is simple though the technology is not. The orders will be placed in one of our vans ... we developed clever route planning systems.

The description is typical of the Tesco approach to an issue. If the customer wants it, we'll let them drive and appraise it, and keep things as simple and low-cost as possible. It is a lesson that the proponents of the American Webvan operation failed to keep in mind when they were putting together, at the same time, their large and expensive warehouse-picking home-shopping system. Where is Webvan now? Today tesco.com is the largest grocery Internet operation in the world. Ninety six per cent of the population have access to it and 110,000 orders are placed on it each week. From small beginnings ...

Finally, let us consider the Tesco brand. It is no accident that Tesco has been run for 25 years by two chief executives whose formative experience was in marketing – a rarity in British business. The Tesco approach to the brand changed markedly over these years. No serious attempt to challenge Sainsbury brand supremacy took place until Tesco had become market leader – to assault a seemingly impregnable Sainsbury citadel, standing for good food at decent prices would not have paid off; Tesco's credentials were inadequate. However, as innovation flourished and direct challenges to Sainsbury began to work, Tesco had the product and knowledge to formulate its own brand policy. It sought to be an inclusive brand, making an appeal to a middle market, and establishing a broad framework into which its range of innovations and market extensions could fit. Fitting the 'bricks into the wall', each move helps to make the whole building a shade stronger. The phrase 'Every little helps', which has fronted brand communication for many years, nicely evokes the approach.

The importance of customer loyalty to Tesco, and the use of simple straightforward language, make the brand and company identifiable and accessible to customers. It has become an object lesson in down-to-earth consumer branding – short on the manipulative wizardry and buzzwords esteemed by advertising agencies, rooted in offering a visible result to the shopper. Tim Mason says:

> [Our] brand has been transformed over time from being cheap, downmarket and distressed to that of most admired. We aimed to provide the 'best shopping trip for everybody'. We recognise Sainsburys' attempt to justify higher prices by being aspirational, Asda … has low prices but … are perceived by many as a bit too cheap. We hope that no one can complete the sentence 'I don't shop at Tesco because …'.

Tesco knows that its brand is the company and its company is the brand – as it should be.

We have tried to delineate the components of Tesco's strength over the past ten years, accounting for its strong market position as dominant UK food leader. It also has exceptional growth prospects in further sectors, UK non-food, services, notably financial products and Internet shopping. Thirdly, international expansion, initially in Eastern Europe and more importantly Asia, now provides a significant and fast-growing third leg to the company.

Are there potential Tesco weaknesses to consider alongside these three strengths? Tesco is internationally small, less than half Carrefour's size, and about one-sixth of Wal-Mart's. It is grouped quantitatively with (a sinking) Ahold, and (a distinctly different) Metro in the second global division. It has become global, very late – 30 years after Carrefour and ten after Wal-Mart first left their home markets. Though it now moves fast and confidently across national boundaries, the capital required for international expansion is a constraint, despite imaginative measures being taken to raise funds. Tesco's entire dependence on long-run cash and profits from UK food and now non-food is a vulnerability. Wal-Mart could, in principle, choose to depress Tesco UK earnings through cutting prices further. Some believe the Government appears anxious to put brakes on Tesco share growth. Tesco is an increasingly high visibility target for anyone who wants to attack the industry. It knows this but it is still a fact.

A further weakness is the big area of the developed world Tesco has not entered – USA and Continental Western Europe are the missing pieces. Since these have characteristically been leading growth and high-margin markets, if it wishes to be at the top of the world league, Tesco must find a way to fill these gaps. This is neither cheap nor easy. It may require a volte-face in the acquisition policies Tesco has been pursuing, and this may be enough to challenge the essence of the Tesco culture, nurtured so impressively by Leahy and company over a decade. The Tesco brand, so neatly and broadly formulated, can sometimes appear anodyne, even anonymous. Perhaps it is susceptible to frontal attack on points of quality or price, although, in a market with several strong competitors, there has been no sign of this so far.

Finally, as with all major and fast growing retailers in developed markets, and given its expansion plans and ambitions, Tesco is vulnerable to the interest groups that want to limit its increasing consumer power. This is a well-rehearsed litany in Britain now – Joanna Blythman's recent book *Shopped: The Shocking Power of British Supermarkets* (2004) expresses the point of view clearly, and the view has many articulate followers. (The issue is discussed more fully in Chapter 9). Meanwhile Wal-Mart's American consumerist problems have not gone unnoticed at Cheshunt. Tesco in Britain, with its 12 per cent retail share, is as vulnerable as Wal-Mart in the US with, say, eight per cent, and British pressure groups are no less well armed or articulate. There are, in summary, many pitfalls ahead on the path to becoming a world competitor.

The cares of state do not yet weigh too heavily on the Cheshunt team. Leahy's 'Future' approach to challenge ahead, begun some years ago, shows the way they respond. He says:

'Future' was about the means of delivering change. All our managers, me included, 10,000 of us in all, went through this. They had to retrain to learn new skills. It was time to stop people doing what was unnecessary and bring a lot more focus to everything we do. Changes are tested to make sure they work. Change is made easy to understand. Work is planned so that people are not asked to do more than they can manage. The team is trained.

This is a down-to-earth and evolutionary process in which everyone can participate.

An enviable combination of operating confidence, small-town humility, and the Scouse self-mockery, so easy to find in the streets of Liverpool, will stand them in good stead for the big wars ahead. They appear to fear no one and, as Leahy patiently reminds us, 'There are other ways of doing business than Wal-Mart's.' It may look to outside observers like a David versus Goliath struggle, but that is not the way that Tesco leadership reads the game. 'We can tackle Wal-Mart around the world, and are stronger than when they arrived in the UK', was another summary. 'Wal-Mart are not market wreckers' was a further viewpoint encountered – although there might have been just a hint of wistfulness in the statement. 'Our information systems are put together differently and have more direction and flexibility than theirs', was a legitimate claim of product advantage. At every turn now you find Tesco people thinking actively about how to become the best in the world, and for many years ahead there will be room for both these potential juggernauts to survive and thrive. Tesco will look forward to the challenge with its usual mix of excitement at what's new, and equanimity at knowing how to deal with it when it meets it.

5 The Contenders

While we are clear that 'the big three' (Carrefour, Tesco and Wal-Mart) are the major players internationally, there are several other companies that have made significant progress – indeed, some are in many more countries than anyone except Carrefour. Some may become global players. Here, we describe them briefly and assess their chances.

Casino

Casino was, for much of its life, a big but strangely unconvincing player in the French market, with almost no overseas interests. Its origins, though, make it one of the most senior of all major current food retailers.

The group traces its history to the end of the nineteenth century, and gained its name from the site on which Geoffroy Guichard started his business in 1898: it had for many years been a casino (and rather a disreputable one at that). Casino the food retailer opened its second branch in 1898, and continued to expand. In 1901, it launched its first own-label products – surely a first. By 1929, it had 20 factories, nine distribution centres, 998 stores and 505 concessions. In 1948, it opened a self-service operation in the original premises, again surely a first. A supermarket followed in 1960, and the first hypermarket in 1970. By 1971, it had 2575 outlets.

Despite its mainly French focus, Casino opened a chain of cafeterias in the USA in 1976, and bought a cash-and-carry (C&C) chain there, Smart & Final in 1984. Apart from those adventures, it stayed firmly at home.

In France, it operated hypermarkets, supermarkets, discounters and convenience stores, but by the 1980s seemed to lack ambition. Promodès, a major competitor later taken over by Carrefour, took a large stake, and Casino seemed likely to disappear.

In 1996, it came to life, stimulated principally by the Galland and Raffarin laws, which further and more severely restricted loss leading in the French market. As a result, Carrefour and Casino in particular were able to strengthen their inherent position and their returns substantially, in a relatively oligopolistic market. Casino embarked on two new strategic thrusts, internal and external. Internally, it restructured its buying department and invested heavily in logistics. Externally, it began to develop a serious international presence. There had been a tentative foray overseas with a hypermarket in 1995 in Réunion, an island in the Indian Ocean. The expansion proper opened first in Poland, then moved quickly into five countries in

South America, and into Taiwan. In 1999, it acquired 66 per cent of Big C in Thailand, and continued to expand outside Europe (Reynolds and Cuthbertson 2004 p. 107). In 2002 Casino acquired a substantial increase in capacity by acquiring stores from the failing international elements of the Dutch Laurus company.

By the end of 2003, Casino operated 8900 stores in 15 countries: 311 hypermarkets, 2363 supermarkets, 992 discounters, 4825 'supérettes' (convenience) and 246 restaurants. Despite the overseas growth, fully 80 per cent of turnover still comes from France itself (but almost all recent sales growth is from the international side). Although a member of the founding Guichard family is honorary president, the active management is in the hands of a younger generation of professional managers. The Director General (CEO), Pierre Bouchut, is highly regarded and the group clearly has a strategy: to leapfrog its competitors in Western Europe, and grow business in countries at the stage of economic take-off. It often acquires a good business that it can develop, or takes a minority share (it describes its international development strategy as 'reasoned, ambitious and lasting'). The vehicle, like Carrefour, is mainly hypermarkets, but the hard discount format will also be important. Several others have the same idea, of course, but it seems certain that Casino will be one of the handful of players internationally.

Auchan

Auchan is another French, family-owned company (see Text Box 5.1) that has a presence in many countries. Its name derives from its first location in the Roubaix district of France, which was called Haut-Champs – hence Auchan. The Mulliez family control 84 per cent of the shares, and provide the chairman, vice chairman, a further two members of the supervisory board and a director. The family has extensive other interests, including Leroy Merlin, a French DIY chain and Decathlon, a sports goods retailer present in 23 countries in five continents.

BOX 5.1

FOUNDING FAMILIES – A NICE LITTLE EARNER?

Across the retail world, the importance of a group of founding families can be seen in building strong national retail companies, many of which have in time become significant internationally, often with the original families still playing a significant role. Some of those who have 'stayed for the ride' have, as we shall see, continued to exert an influence and become enormously wealthy along the way.

Nowhere has this been more common than in the heartland of the continent – George Bush's 'Old Europe' has many families who have had a huge say in retailing development right up to today. In Germany, for example, there is Tengelmann, a century-old company that has twice, through world wars, lost control of much of its asset base, but has been able to re-group and remains a top-twenty global player today. Tengelmann still answers to the great grandson of the original founder and has remained a force internationally, purchasing the once great A&P company in the eastern US, and Superal in Italy as part of its post-war expansion. The enormously strong Metro company now has a full-time operating CEO, Hans-Joachim Koerber, who speaks eloquently for Metro's global strategy. However for many years, right up to the mid-1990s, Metro was 100 per cent owned by a legendary German individual, Otto Beisheim, who presided over many years of profitable international expansion.

These two companies pale into insignificance in global terms when compared to Aldi, a third formidable German company. The Albrecht brothers, Theo and Karl, built Aldi, dividing the company in two – one running northern and one southern Germany – over the post-war years and gaining a unique reputation for tight cost control and even tighter prices. Their cleverly marketed appeal to hard-pressed Germans in the post-war years has not diminished, as these consumers have become some of the wealthiest in the world – nothing seems to make them want to stop chasing Aldi's renowned promotional prices. The Albrecht brothers have been great negotiators, highly competitive, very secretive, and finally, very, very rich – the family fortune has been estimated at around $27 billion.

Across the Rhine, several French families have exercised comparable influence over the highly profitable development of the French hypermarket industry. The Badin, Defforey and Fournier families at Carrefour have only recently started to relax their personal control over the strategic development and financial controls at Carrefour, allowing Daniel Bernard, as their chosen CEO, to begin to manage the company on the same basis of 'free market enterprise' as his Anglo Saxon and American rivals have done for many years (the Halley and March families continue to exert their influence, as we saw). At Auchan, the Mulliez family still have a big say: while in the unique franchising operation at Leclerc, the family again continues to call the shots.

The way in which retailing has developed in mainstream Europe has unquestionably been affected by the desires and policies of handful of families, who have succeeded in maintaining a high degree of influence over government policy, which, while taking early initiatives to cap national expansion, has nonetheless provided an intelligible, not easily penetrated, platform in both France and Germany, which has been effective in deterring new external entrants.

In Britain family influence has been less prominent, although until the Sainsbury company, at the time a dominant supermarket leader, took itself public in

1973, the two related arms of the Sainsbury family provided a powerful holding influence on company policy, and the family continued to provide the chairman and chief executive for a further quarter century thereafter. Today, while their holding has absolutely declined, as the business has weakened, Sainsbury's are still numbered among the richest and most influential of British families.

Finally, in the USA we have the astonishing story of the Waltons, shareholders of the Wal-Mart company which Sam started in 1962, with Sam's children owners of 39 per cent of the world's largest company today. These four, second-generation Waltons are all included among America's ten richest individuals, an indication of how profoundly Sam's legacy has changed the US financial scene overall. Nonetheless, as befits children of the humble Rogers, Arkansas founder, they keep a low profile, though their joint fortune is greater than that of Bill Gates and Warren Buffett's combined, and is 117 times greater than Teresa Heinz Kerry's – whose Heinz-derived wealth came in for comment during the 2004 US Presidential campaign, sometimes to John Kerry's detriment.

The Walton children have discrete roles but act as a collective where their fortunes are concerned. One son, John, concentrates on philanthropic ventures, a second, Jim, manages the – separate and newer – family holdings outside Wal-Mart, a third, Alice, the only daughter of Sam, pursues her own family interests, mainly to do with horses, while the fourth, Rob, is the Wal-Mart board chairman. Rob has made good relationships with Sam's executive successors, Glass and Scott, who both speak highly of his interest and expertise, notably in legal and real estate matters. The four's current dividends – around $800 million annually – do enable the family to live well, but alongside their huge and growing wealth, they are beginning to recognise growing community responsibility, for example in education. The new Wal-Mart foundation will be a powerful future benefactor in the US in the years ahead, able to be ranked with Ford and Gates and therefore significant also in international terms.

So even in the world's biggest and fastest growing market, the long hand of family influence persists!

The Auchan group consists of hypermarkets, supermarkets, a bank and a commercial property developer. Hypermarkets have been, and remain, the major contributor, with 78 per cent of turnover.

International expansion began early, with the acquisition of Alcampo in Spain in 1981. Hungary followed in 1988 and Italy in 1989. The group entered the supermarket field with the acquisition of Docks de France in 1996. Like other groups, it then expanded mainly in Europe, both within the EU and in Central and Eastern Europe. It entered China in 1999, and is currently in 12 countries: eight in Europe (including Russia), and China, Taiwan, Argentina and Morocco. France still accounts for some 60 per cent of revenue.

Firmly established in the hypermarket and supermarket formats, Auchan has noticed the rise of hard discounters, and is experimenting with two models. Les Halles (after the famous Parisian food markets) is a hard discount hypermarket, while Au Marché Vrac (bulk buying market) consists of small stores with no fresh food, aiming to price 30 per cent below rivals. Its main formats are also positioned firmly on a low price platform.

The family is very clearly in control, and has shown both an interest in operating internationally, and the ability to do so. It has the stated aim of increasing the number of outlets by 25 per cent by 2005, but seems unlikely to do this by organic growth alone. Like its major French competitor, Carrefour, Auchan has made two ultimately abortive forays into the US. It chose bravely and entered the highly competitive urban Houston and Chicago markets in 1988/89, but by 2003 this ended in ignominious failure, and it has not repeated the experiment. In Europe, it has been willing to work through joint ventures (for example La Rinascente in Italy), and through franchising, so this may be the path it follows. It wishes to continue to expand abroad, but has said that this expansion will be in Central and Eastern Europe and China; it will enter no new countries in the short term. It will continue to be a competitor to Carrefour and Tesco in the markets they work in, but may not become a true global player as long as the family remain in the driving seat.

Metro

Until the merger of Carrefour and Promodès, Metro was the biggest retailer in Europe. It is hard to grasp as a single, unified company, as it is a retail and trading conglomerate with six main divisions, only some of them of interest to us in this book. Like Casino, its origins lie in the nineteenth century: one of the firms that eventually formed part of Metro was founded in 1879. The modern Metro, however, really started in 1964 when Otto Beisheim opened the Metro Cash and Carry in Salsund, and it is on the cash-and-carry business of Metro and Makro that international expansion has been founded.

The six divisions are: Metro C&C; Real hypermarkets; Extra supermarkets; MediaMarkt (consumer electronics); Saturn (music, consumer electronics, new media, telephones and so on); Praktiker (DIY); and Kaufhof (department stores).

The group as a whole has a presence in 28 countries, but by far the most international is the C&C, which is in 26 (the other food businesses are in only two outside Germany – Poland and Turkey). Metro C&C has outlets in 21 countries in Europe, and Morocco, China, India, Japan, and Vietnam. It accounted for 47 per cent of group turnover in 2003, and three-quarters of its sales are abroad. The stated objective was to achieve over 50 per cent of total group sales from overseas, concentrating on Eastern Europe and Asia: that was achieved in the third quarter of 2004. Admittedly, this was partly caused by very weak domestic trading by the company in the cut-throat German home market.

1 Wal-Mart supercenter

Source: Wal-Mart

2 Sam's Club

Source: Wal-Mart

3 Asda, Harlow, UK
Source: Asda

4 Letñany, Prague
Source: Tesco

5 Wal-Mart Neighborhood store, China
Source: Wal-Mart

6 Carrefour, Wuming, China

Source: Agence Rapho

7 Carrefour, Guanghua, China

Source: Carrefour photo library.

8 Dia, Beijing opening

9 Tesco HomePlus, Yeong Tong

10 Champion, Beaune, France

Cash and carry is an attractive way of entering a country with a pre-modern food retailing infrastructure. There will be thousands of existing retailers, mainly small. Even when western multiples such as Wal-Mart or Carrefour enter, they will account for only a small proportion of the market. Indeed, their entry will present such a challenge, particularly in pricing, to the locals that they will find the C&C offering even more enticing. It will take many years before these markets arrive at the concentration levels seen in western countries, so that C&C will have a healthy future. Operators such as Metro will of course have the option of introducing their hypermarket or supermarket formats when they deem it appropriate.

Hans-Joachim Koerber, Metro's CEO, is not short of confidence regarding the future of his group, nor is he reticent about its forward strategy. He regards the international base as well differentiated, and is particularly insistent on the credibility of Metro's approach to the staffing and management of its overseas operations. Contrasting Metro's successful – in his view – entry into Eastern European and Asian markets with Wal-Mart's clumsy and mishandled entry into Germany, he attributes Metro's performance to clear operating principles, a culture that genuinely seeks best international practice, and a management that promotes locals and relates strongly to the local community. While there are elements of apparent rigidity in Koerber's approach, it does have the virtues of clarity of purpose and of execution. Meanwhile, despite the very wide range of activity and the price and cost challenge in Metro's German trading achievement, there is no doubting the drive they are making in key overseas markets – a further 12 C&C outlets were opened in China recently, to add to their existing 21 sites.

For Metro, there are crucial questions of ownership and stability over the years ahead. It seems unlikely that they can hang on for much longer to their unusual range of diversified domestic operations. Their supermarket performance has not been strong and in recent years, Real and Extra have both experienced volume losses. They are apparently unable to constrain the relentless drive of Aldi and Lidl's stripped down, low cost/limited range stores, and it could be that Metro may one day wish to divest itself of its supermarket operations – there would surely be a queue of likely buyers, despite the difficulties of German trading – thus enabling the group to position itself clearly, once and for all, as the world's leading C&C exponent. In late 2004, they sold a quarter of their German supermarkets to Rewe, and closed more than 20 others; this may be a sign. This could be a highly attractive and focused strategy for growth.

Aldi

Aldi, a hard discounter, is an extraordinary phenomenon in its native Germany. It sells a narrow range of purely own-label products, but is visited by 90 per cent of German food shoppers in a year. As a result, its founders, the Albrecht brothers, are comfortably the wealthiest people in Germany with some €15 billion each in assets (*Financial Times* 5 October 2004).

This is the result of over 50 years growth from the first shop in 1948. Its stated aim is 'to provide customers with the products they buy regularly – ensure those products are of market leading quality and offer them at guaranteed low prices'. In practice, this means about 700 items of the most frequently bought grocery products. To add excitement, it offers 'Surprise Buys' of non-food items at bargain prices; the offer changes every Thursday, and lasts until stocks run out. This trading recipe has certainly caught the imagination of German shoppers rich and poor, who await these weekly price specials with real interest and then pursue them avidly.

Consumers appreciate the overall offer, and voted Aldi their favourite business in 2004.

> The retailer was awarded 86.6 out of 100 points. A source from Forum (who conducted the survey) comments that the 'reputation of Aldi for offering particularly favourable prices places it at an advantage when the economy is weak' (Financial Times 19 October 2004).

Furthermore, despite its maturity as a trading approach, recent years have seen rapid growth for Aldi and Lidl, the two leading discounters. Discounter share nationally in Germany has grown from just seven per cent in 1980 to approximately 35 per cent today. Their price advantage against conventional stores, including hypermarkets, is perhaps 20 per cent or more and their cost advantage on an admittedly spartan product range is about 30 per cent. This is surely a durable customer recipe and engenders competitive advantage in Germany not dissimilar to that earned by Wal-Mart vis-à-vis its conventional supermarket competitors in the US. One can see how in Germany the failure of Wal-Mart's entry is to some degree a case of 'the biter bit'. The difference of course is that in Germany, low capital costs – compare US Wal-Mart – are matched normally by high labour costs; but here the discounters can again look to a significant advantage versus the German norm. Hence, the big two discounters' return on capital, though not disclosed, is estimated as a highly worthwhile 20 per cent.

Aldi's international expansion has been mainly in Europe, where they operate in nine countries, but they have penetrated the American market successfully with 700 stores, and recently entered Australia. As a privately owned (and very private) company, they release few details about relative profitability and future strategy. In some countries, they make little headway: in Britain, for instance, they have a market share of only one per cent. Even in Germany, their sales growth has recently stalled, and in 2004 they had to increase advertising spend and cut prices.

Nevertheless, the formula is proven and slickly run. Aldi knows how to cut costs and keep them low, a significant element in the Wal-Mart approach to business. The markets that are receptive to the hard discount format appear to be growing in number and significance – note China's massive significance – so Aldi has the potential to continue to grow internationally.

Lidl

Lidl, like Aldi, is a German-based hard discounter. Founded in Schwaben 30 years ago, it started to expand internationally in the 1990s. It has confined itself to Europe, but within that area is in an astonishing 21 countries from Ireland to Estonia and Norway to Greece.

It is the second biggest discount retailer in Germany but possibly Europe's fastest growing food retailer, achieving a turnover of €36 billion ($48 billion) in 2004. It is a family business, still controlled by one man, retail tycoon Dieter Schwarz. It has a workforce of 150,000 people. Highly secretive, Lidl opened ten per cent more stores in 2004, and registered a sales increase of 17 per cent. Commonly known as the Schwarz Group, it is based in Neckarsulm in Germany, and is now challenging the successful Aldi, by registering bigger increases in Europe, while adopting the same limited range, rock-bottom price model to Aldi.

While the two groups are highly similar and directly competitive, it seems they are capable of growing together. The consumer predilection for low-cost discounter models is a benefit to both companies and is hurting conventional supermarket competitors more than alternative discounters. The conjunction of weakening economies in Western Europe, alongside the rapid opening up of Eastern European markets, are both beneficial trends for Lidl. The firm majors on the discounter format, but it also owns hypermarkets and superstore divisions and it opened fifty larger format Kaufland stores in Germany in 2004. Its discounter modus operandi is to rely on sites of 3–10,000 sq. m., with limited amounts of car parking space. Shoppers familiar with Lidl stores say the chain sells virtually anything, many items under its own Lidl brand, for prices at least 20 per cent lower than average cut-price supermarket chains.

Lidl's aggressive cost-cutting stance does not please everyone. Germany's biggest trade union has accused it of subjecting employees to 'degrading working conditions', and in an echo of the resistance to Wal-Mart's low US wages, Verdi – the union concerned – have published a black book accusing Lidl of creating an atmosphere of fear among its employees. 'Economic success goes hand-in-hand with miserable working conditions', a Verdi executive told *Financial Times Deutschland*. Workers have to work hours longer than contracted, for which they are unpaid. They are routinely suspected of stealing and toilet breaks are frowned upon as a luxury, she said. The management of the Schwarz Group have responded by accusing the union of a defamation campaign and point to their outstanding record of job creation.

Like Aldi and Wal-Mart, Lidl seems well placed to use its tried and cost-effective model to ride a growing discounter wave present in Europe and the US simultaneously. In Europe, Lidl's focus may allow it to grow more quickly than Aldi who has a worldwide position to defend. Its approach is uncomplicated: *'Wir sind total uncompliziert'*, they claim proudly (www.Lidl.de). Although they have strong shares of eight to ten percent in Germany and the Czech Republic, they mainly reach only one to three per cent.

Privately owned like Aldi, it seems likely to continue on its current path, and stay in Europe.

Ito-Yokado

Geographically, Japan's Ito-Yokado is one of the most diversified international retailers, present in more than 20 countries, usually through licensing
arrangements. Superstores form a major element in the company's domestic
portfolio, but the sluggish Japanese economy has slowed growth badly and
over many years. This is not so in the convenience store market where the
company has a powerful and growing presence, based on its well-recognised
7-Eleven brand. The Dallas-based 7-Eleven company is the premier name
and the largest chain in the convenience retailing industry and has stood up
well to increased US big store and discounter competition. Ito-Yokado has
therefore highly complementary strengths and in two big and very different
markets. First, it owns the leading convenience store brand in the US,
backed by steady, if undramatic, expansion into a range of European and
Asian markets with this format. Around a quarter of Ito-Yokado's growth
has come from the US and related market convenience stores.

The majority of revenue is, however, in Japan, and here the company, as
the incumbent player, has the full range of trading formats and a good own-
brand presence. Responding to increased international competition in Japan,
and cheap food imports coming across the border from China, Ito-Yokado
has introduced the concept of 'Everyday fair prices', a description that indicates that the company knows from whence its key future challenge will
come. It has divested its discount portfolio and strengthened superstores,
and the home base will be crucial to company long-term success. As evidence
of progress, Ito passed ¥100 billion profits in fiscal 2004/5 for the first time,
marking 26 years of consecutive profits growth.

In summary, we can say that Ito-Yokado is a significant long-term international player because of its successful convenience store brand and policy
married to a big country Japanese base. For it to become a leading overall
competitor ahead, it needs to sustain its leading position in Japan, and hope
for better domestic economic trading conditions. It resembles German Metro,
although much smaller. They both operate in a becalmed domestic base, but
with historic strength, bolstered by command of a growing minor segment
(cash and carry for Metro, convenience for Ito-Yokado). Each represents an
interesting strategic position as mainstream competition intensifies.

Tengelmann

A long established family business, Tengelmann has been in the family's
hands for four generations. It appeared on the IGD (Institute of Grocery
Distribution) summary of global retailers in 18th position in 2003, down
from 2002's 16th position; in 2004, it ranked 25th among all retailers in the
world. It operates in 11 European countries and in the USA, China and
Canada. Eastern Europe and Austria feature prominently – usual areas for
German expansion (it has 400 stores in Austria). However, many of these
overseas stores are 'OBI', its DIY brand.

International development has been key to its strategy as there is little room for home expansion. This is because its mainstream supermarket business – Kaisers/Tengelmann – is increasingly uncompetitive. As much as 56 per cent of sales are outside Germany, but the overall results of its international strategy are not impressive. Disappointing results at home and in the US account for this judgement. It may even be that divesting its grocery interests may now be on the cards. It has pulled out of Holland and Hungary recently.

Its US acquisition, A&P, is a big factor in this assessment – it is, and has long been, a basket case on the east coast of the USA. It was the number one on the east coast in volume terms for some time, but is now not really a contender. Wal-Mart is killing it where they interact on the east coast and this can only get worse as Wal-Mart accelerates urban expansion in this region.

Tengelmann has a soft-discount brand (Plus) as well as the main fascia. It is also in DIY. Plus did very well in 2002, 20 per cent growth in turnover in Europe. Its restructuring programme seems to focus on Plus and DIY at the expense of mainstream supermarkets. Germany and USA are the 'strength positions in food' it wants to defend. It intends to maintain international at around 50 per cent of turnover. It also intends to convert the US supermarkets to a discount format to compete better with Wal-Mart.

In summary, Tengelmann is a weak performer, and is probably going to get a lot weaker. The conversion to discounting may be following market trends correctly, but it also may be too little too late.

Aeon

Japan's Aeon is the 26th largest world retailer, with 2002 sales of $25 billion. Like several other groups, it covers many different retail markets. Outside Japan, it operates in China, Hong Kong Special Administrative Region (SAR), Malaysia, Thailand, UK, USA and Canada.

The core business of the Aeon Group, Aeon Co., owns or franchises nearly 3900 stores worldwide. It operates about 460 JUSCO superstores (mostly in Japan), and 2600-plus Ministop convenience stores. It is also Japan's largest supermarket chain, with about 665 stores. Aeon also runs a number of specialty chains, including The Talbots and Laura Ashley stores in Japan. It has a joint venture in Japan with Sports Authority and owns about 60 per cent of the women's clothing chain The Talbots. Additionally, the firm operates the 1900 outlets of the Welcia nationwide drugstore chain. Other Aeon operations are shopping centre development and credit card services.

There are other small groups operating internationally, but where they are in fewer than six countries, we have ignored them. It is worth mentioning some regional players who may have some impact in the future. Shoprite, for instance, is a South African company that, since the end of apartheid in 1994, has expanded rapidly and is now in 16 countries in

Africa, from its home in the south up to Egypt. In late 2004, they opened a branch in India. These are all poor countries, so Shoprite sells a limited range of goods at low prices.

Two bigger firms are both located in Hong Kong SAR. Dairy Farm operates convenience, discount, supermarkets and hypermarkets, as well as foodservice, DIY, drug and specialty stores. It is in six countries in South-East Asia, and ranks 146th among world retailers. Hutchison Whampoa, one of the leading groups in Hong Kong SAR, owns AS Watson. It is in eight countries in South-East Asia, and seven in Europe (though in many of these it is the drugstores, not food). It is relatively small compared with our leading players (ranking 170th in the world), but it clearly does not lack ambition. These companies, and others like them, will present possible challengers in the future.

6 Issues in Going Global

Since global retailing is still at an early stage of development, we should not expect to see established patterns, of entry, development or models that confidently predict success. Rather, we should envisage a series of individual experiments, carried out over time by the leading protagonists, and gradually a corpus of core learning being acquired by those companies. This is what has happened. So far, however, we are a long way from seeing orthodox or established patterns. It is not possible to detect best practice either of market entry or business development. It is only latterly that individual business development models have started to collide with each other, producing markets where the international players are beginning to compete in a serious way. However, through the decade from 1990, and certainly through the first years of the 21st century, we can now see the interplay of competitive approaches, and we can certainly see the beginnings of winning entry strategies for some players. Additionally, the market has offered us some big losers, companies that have not merely had to exit from experimental entry in an international venture, but in some cases companies whose entire international strategy has collapsed, causing re-appraisal of the company's capacity to compete globally – anywhere. The battle is now joined. There are twenty companies who see themselves as international competitors in food retailing in the years ahead, and half a dozen whose positions look for the moment reasonably secure.

Location focus is changing, of course. Everybody used to beat their way to America, convinced that this was the home of best supermarket practice and also of an enormously affluent shopping fraternity. Now, the east is as attractive as, maybe more than, the USA. The first important variable for any company seeking to compete outside its home market is the choice of market to enter. There are still limitless opportunities today, even if one wants to concentrate on the top ten or a dozen countries where prospects look attractive. We have observed that a precondition of venturing abroad is the need to lead, perhaps dominate, the company's domestic market. This has been an invariable rule for the successful players – broken significantly only by Wal-Mart, which, although not a dominant US leader when it began its international adventure, possessed a strong and growing revenue and profits base in the US when it extended into the adjacent NAFTA countries in the early 1990s. The rationale is obvious: if expansion starts to threaten home investment and a growing revenue stream, it is unlikely in the early years to produce compensating returns, and the strategic rationale for expansion disappears. This is something Carrefour may be experiencing now. Equally, it is unlikely that any retailer who has not succeeded handsomely at home will have the confidence or the management resources to compete away from home.

There are many reasons for establishing an international strategy. First, in many cases, home-market growth may be inhibited by market factors, or – more often with European companies – by legislation limiting further expansion. This was the experience in France and Germany in the 1970s, and the mid-1990s saw further national statutory extensions and tightening of legislative restrictions across Europe, including for the first time the UK.

A second motivation for food retailers – and the factor applies in non-foods too – has been the lack of market growth as consumer spending priorities move from foods to more exciting areas such as travel, technology in the home and entertainment. In developed markets food as a percentage of the spending budget is firmly in decline. Thirdly, and this is a key factor in Western Europe, population growth has slowed dramatically. What has been called the 'fear factor' – watching one's competitors beginning to invest and learn while one is stuck at home fighting painful domestic market battles – is a growing element. It must worry the big American supermarket companies right now. On the positive side can be cited the absolute size of the international market opportunity – estimated by the Institute of Grocery Distribution, UK, at $3.5 trillion. Finally, and significantly, there is a natural wish to be first mover, to gain competitive knowledge and market experience which can translate into strength in overseas markets, long-term advantage and sizeable permanent profit streams. The acceleration which might then come from international economies of scale, where these are available, simply adds to the inherent attractiveness of the equation. Carrefour has been the past master in adopting this approach.

There is a range of ways in which a market entry can be effected, and the choice will depend on the resources available to the company, the degree to which international expansion is critical to its strategy, and the amount of risk it is prepared to take. Obviously, the big, developed markets offer the most opportunity: the consumer base is there, and there will be major common factors that can be applied across national boundaries. It is worth observing, however, that retailing, and particularly food retailing, has been a market which has developed with strong national models and even idiosyncrasies – as might be expected in a market where food and consumer taste is concerned, and in an industry where detail has always been an important operating element. A further influence establishing national differences has been the propensity of government – nearly all major developed-country governments – to intervene at some time in the food-retailing process, and in the case of some countries, France for example, frequently and trenchantly. There is something essentially visceral about government's attitudes to consumers and food that makes them behave in proprietorial ways in their home market. This has occurred in Europe for decades, was fundamental to the course of US market development, and is now happening in Japan, India and notably in China. When governments intervene, international companies usually have to dance to their tune, if they want to succeed.

Smaller size markets offer the advantage of smaller risk, the investment may be more welcome, and the level of competition lower – through lower visible market potential. Entry into smaller, emergent markets may provide the requisite confidence for the new international company to learn what is different from operating at home, to work out where it must be flexible, and to build up management confidence, both in its home team and with new local managers and employees. Similarly, the scale of entry can be managed to contain risk when this is required. Most of the international players have wanted to begin in a handful of stores. Some, Auchan for example, have found it difficult to scale up at all from this. In the early days, this did not seem to matter very much as competition was not moving fast, and in most cases not at all.

Today the situation is changing. Organic growth at home is now – certainly for European firms – probably too slow to get meaningful business learning or competitive advantage except in the least-sought-after internat-ional markets. A more common approach recently has been to look for an efficient and developable partner in the entered market. The low-risk approach is then to take a small stake, and to begin to build it only when joint process begins to gel and the new team begins to work. At this stage, a bigger share of the company may be acquired or, where available, full acquisition completed. In some of the most significant markets, there are signs that the partnership route will be the only strategy permitted by the host government. China appeared to follow this approach but there has been considerable relaxation recently, and signs that the Chinese model of market development has freed up substantially. Equally, there are significant players who have adopted the partnership route to international expansion, and have been happy to see it as an enduring limited risk strategy.

Finally, there is the committed frontal approach: to designate a selected country as a key growth area, to search for the most appropriate and avail-able local company and to make a full bid, hostile or otherwise. Where markets are free this can work, but except for companies with the highest cash capacities, this is high risk in mainstream markets. Even where cash is not a constraint, it is still a big risk, since a failed full-scale acquisition puts the company's trading reputation at risk, not only in the entered country, but probably elsewhere. This will affect the home market stock rating, and may bid up the cost of future expansion moves. While twenty years ago such moves were rare and unnecessary, the pace of expansion in some countries today – notably Latin America, and leading Asia-Pacific countries – make the case for flat out acquisition, where it can be found, more attractive.

A further key variable is the format the company chooses for market entry. Given the high degree of variability across countries, this is a critical issue. For a long period, the choice seemed to be relatively simple, and became a matter of food only (supermarket) or food and non-food (hypermarket). The Continental European model had traditionally been the hypermarket – in France and further south, but not in Germany, which had its own very particular approach – whereas both the USA and the UK traditionally favoured the supermarket model. The two coexisted happily across the world until the 1990s. Since then, however, choices have multiplied. Formats which had always existed on some scale, such as cash and carry, or convenience stores have gained in importance as they have been adopted on a world scale. Warehouse clubs have become a significant feature, especially in the NAFTA region. Finally, the steady, and now quickening, rise of the discounter businesses, whether massive as in the Wal-Mart supercenter, or small and limited-range, like the Aldi store, have provided a range of further entry options internationally. America now has both, and Dollar stores have also been growing fast. The summary truth emerging from this profusion of retail formats is that choice has made entry strategy more delicate and, even when the initial format has been selected, in competitive countries the strong likelihood is that multi-format approaches will be necessary if the new entrant wants to sustain its growth into the longer term. Such has been recent experience.

With this background, we can list an enormous number of international moves, many of which amount to very little in the end. Several European companies were establishing supermarkets under their own brand name in adjacent European and US markets during the 1960s and 70s. It became the fashion for leading European operators to take a US stake. Even small European market operators, from Belgium and Netherlands, bought US chains. The Germans and French were the most active and several big moves were made. German Tengelmann early on acquired the highly significant – at the time – A&P chain, while British Sainsbury bought Connecticut Shaws in the early 1980s. Neither profited. There was little traffic in the other direction, and Asia was at that time not a factor of any importance. The big moves were made initially by Carrefour, which had a clear strategy as well as the necessity to generate international growth, its hypermarket expansion being limited by the French *loi Royer*, passed in 1973.

Carrefour took the view that its ability to have a leading retailing presence was going to be determined by international expansion, and it began its moves before the end of the 1970s – well before any other international player in today's market. It is enormously to this company's credit that, having espoused the vision, there was no backtracking, although there must have been times when Carrefour wondered why it was ploughing so lonely a furrow with so few travelling companions. The Carrefour family investors early on set themselves the target of opening three new geographic markets a year, and they regularly achieved this, becoming, by the early 1990s, the mature operator in the field; the company with whom the new entries of the 1990s normally had to compete. Carrefour used its French hypermarket model and it proved a winning formula for them. Its strategy, described earlier in Chapter 3, shows determination and maturity – a genuinely internationalist view achieved ahead of its time in this industry.

Carrefour believes in the hypermarket format, in which it was a pioneer, and it is one it knows well. It invariably places its stores in the centres of population density, and then on the fringes of big cities. Its policy has been to be first, and therefore position itself as an international leader. It also aims to be a leader in the individual markets it enters. It has a strong central policy function, and appears to want to manage the brand from Paris. In international terms, to the extent that any one company can be said to have set a pattern for others to follow, Carrefour has done this.

The Ahold approach was very different and, although the company has abandoned its growth strategy and is now fighting for its life, it merits consideration since until two years ago it appeared to be carrying all before it, and its international policies were in many ways unique. Ahold adopted a high-risk strategy, being prepared to buy companies in quick succession in target markets to boost its presence. It adopted the supermarket format, and its drive to find leading brands and 'bundle them in' was used to great effect, especially in the US, where Ahold's acquisitions took it to a position of recognised market leader in the Eastern states of the US. It was a rollercoaster ride – Ahold kept moving; not willing to settle down and digest its acquisitions, it preferred to allow local managements, usually innovative and successful teams, to continue to press for local market growth. This policy appealed to Americans, who – until the foodservice crash – liked what they saw in the company, and felt Ahold had more room to expand. Ahold was voted Retailer of the Year by its supermarket peer group in 2000 – a big achievement for the Dutch company. It had in the process stolen a march on many European rivals who had bought positions in the US over the 1980s and 90s (Delhaize, Sainsbury, Tengelmann, Auchan and so on). Cees van der Hoeven went on record to claim that Ahold could become the 'world's best, most successful food provider.' Then hubris struck with a vengeance. (See Text Boxes 6.1 and 6.2)

BOX 6.1

WHY DID AHOLD FAIL?

Royal Dutch Ahold was a top three world food retailer in 2002, with a turnover of $67 billion. The IGD's global index, which takes into account 'international competence' factors, ranked Ahold behind only Carrefour, and above Wal-Mart and Tesco. Ahold operated in 27 countries in Europe, Asia and America, and was strong in the US, several smaller European markets, and Latin America. A mere 17 per cent of Ahold sales came from its home market (Netherlands). Its global strategy, begun in US as long ago as 1977, pursued 'thoroughbred acquisitions', that is, leading regional companies, turning over above $1 billion, with strong brands, good managements and innovative cultures. For ten exciting years to 2002, Ahold grew spectacularly, by 20 per cent plus per annum. It appeared to be on course to deliver its promise to become 'the world's best and most successful food provider', with a strong and diverse retail, food service and Internet offer.

The accepted rationale for Ahold's dramatic reversal attributes the problem directly to the detection of major accounting scandals in the company's US

Food Service unit. There is no question this was a major catalyst, and no company could have escaped the consequences of dereliction on this scale in a major market, particularly at a time when accounting irregularities were claiming many sizeable US victims (Enron and World Com for instance). However, the truth of Ahold's demise is more complex. While accounting scandal brought corporate inadequacy into the open, it at the same moment opened a Pandora's box of related issues which would inevitably have caused the company big problems ahead, had the accounting scandal not occurred when it did.

The scandal quickly claimed a number of prominent scalps, including both the Chief Executive, Cees van der Hoeven, the highly articulate Dutchman who had led the company's advance for many years, and Michael Meurs, Ahold's Chief Financial Officer. Anders Moberg, the financially experienced (formerly Swedish IKEA) executive who replaced van der Hoeven, at the princely salary of $10 million per annum, described his role as 'family doctor, here to stop the bleeding', and recorded that Ahold required 'radical surgery to restore the patient to health'. He later went on to admit that the company's problems were 'not just fraud ... Ahold had showed tendencies before [the fraud] that showed the company was heading in wrong directions'. Moberg knew Ahold was a mess.

Ahold had indeed followed a high-profile and iconoclastic strategy for many years previously, which in retrospect now looks highly adventurous, much though its European, and some US, investors liked it at the time. The high-quality, branded acquisitions that it took on were very much allowed to fend for themselves after purchase. Ahold showed no intention of seeking to integrate the marketing fascias of companies it acquired that were close to each other – for example along the eastern seaboard of the US, where it owned at least six retailers. It even rejected until quite late in the day the opportunity to take synergies from rationalising these same companies' back-office operations. In time, this unusual strategy would have proved costly and uncompetitive.

There was little attempt to produce a coherent long-term business strategy either. In retrospect, it was brave for a company with Ahold's limited world experience and modest US business exposure, to assume a business platform which embraced supermarkets, food service and the Internet all at once. Next, van der Hoeven was content to allow the quality and performance of his newly acquired companies, around the world, to continue to provide growth and profitability on a sui generis basis. 'Let 100 flowers bloom', while appealing to investors in the short term, might have worked less well once Ahold had become – as it did – the world's third biggest retailer. Finally, the combination of this cavalier operating philosophy and an absence of corporate direction created the inevitably 'loose' backdrop against which foolhardy risk taking and ethical weaknesses are likely to happen – as they did at the big US Food Service unit.

Ahold's weaknesses therefore were a great deal more broad based than the reports attributing major reverse simply to the accounting issue have led us to believe. Company credibility is not yet restored, and Moberg's team have been inhibited in their desire to put the company back on a proper investment footing by the threat of major class actions against the company in both US and European courts. There have been sensible and positive actions taken to resolve the financial constraints on the company: the $2.5 billion rights issue in 2002 and the steady progress of asset sales, culminating in the sale of US Bi-Lo and Bruno at the end of 2004, have achieved their stated targets. But the end result is not today an attractive-looking or even coherent proposition.

What is left is a pale shadow of a once far-reaching global retailer. Iberia, Latin America, Asia, and much of the US business have all gone from its portfolio. Sales, according to the latest quarter figures, appear to be running at a bit more than half pre-scandal levels. The company made a significant trading loss in the latest quarter. Worryingly, the flagship US retail units – Stop and Shop and Giant Foods – are hitting discounter competition and a weak dollar. The uneasy partnering of a supermarket and a food service company for the moment remains. From the ashes of a big and adventurous global company, a constrained and much smaller business may still emerge, but what it will eventually look like, and how its strategies for growth might develop won't be known for some time.

BOX 6.2

AHOLD – NO WAY BACK?

Ahold's current business publicity still likes to describe itself as the world's third largest retailer. In truth, it is nothing like this any more. The surgery which Anders Moberg and his new board have had to undertake has been dramatic and powerful, but has produced a much smaller and straitened enterprise, and one with inevitably limited international aspirations. The statements sometimes go on to claim that the year 2004 – following a directionless 2003 and a cataclysmic 2002 – was a 'transitional' year for the company, one in which all the necessary actions to put the company back on a sensible trading platform, with its strategy and operations recognisable once again, took place. This too is a long way from the whole truth. Ahold is still some way from a survival plan.

It has been forced to sell its strong positions in much of the US, Latin America, and some of Europe (Iberia), and weaker positions elsewhere (Asia). It looks likely that the need for focus to restore what remains to profitable trading will soon force the sale of the sizeable US Food Service company, number two to US Sysco in this worthwhile market.

The strategy which Moberg set himself listed several key targets:

► A rights issue ($2.5 billion)
► Asset sales ($2.5 billion)
► A minimum of five per cent annual sales growth
► Margin restoration – five per cent being the overall target
► A decision on the viability of food service.

True, a number of these have been achieved, although not those which reflect on the success of current and future trading, nor, yet, any decision on the crucial area of food service. Alongside the problems with operating, which have been experienced everywhere in the geographic portfolio, it is with issues of company reputation, trust and credibility, where management still makes little headway. This combination of trading problems and stakeholder mistrust even came together at one stage in the company's home stronghold, the Netherlands, where consumer and shareholder joint anger produced a boycott of company stores.

Recently, attempts have been made by the new board, now containing a number of Moberg's former colleagues at Swedish IKEA, to present the company to investors on a 'normal forward trading' basis. Investors however remain unpersuaded by this naïve approach and note the 'continuing lack of transparency in spite of Ahold's pledges to rebuild internal controls and restore investor trust' (*Financial Times* 'Ahold looks beyond road to recovery' 12 November 2004).

'They still didn't answer the questions we wanted' said one analyst. The problems now stem from margin declines across the entire US market affecting all conventional US supermarket operators, and caused by the steady advance of discounter trading in the US – Wal-Mart included – and reducing supermarket profits. So far Ahold has few answers, and the problems of digging its way out of the liquidity crisis, while restoring profitable growth, appear well beyond the company. Hannu Rypponnen, CFO, says Ahold have made '70–80 per cent of the changes necessary to regain trust among investors', but admits that so far this perception is not shared by the shareholders themselves.

Continuing operating problems in the remaining US supermarket units are, however, the main reason for Ahold's inability to meet the agreed, pretty minimal, business targets which the new team set more than one year ago. Operating margins have continued to decline, falling to 1.9 per cent from 4.2 per cent in the US and well short of the goal of five per cent. In Europe, where the remainder of Ahold's volume now is, the company has held its ground better. Ahold's new team are taking a more orthodox line than its predecessors where cost management is concerned. Integration of back-office units at US supermarkets is at last being pursued and there is even an intention, prior to settling whether Food Service is retained, to seek synergies between retail and food service units. Not before time perhaps. This represents major change, but it may be too little and too late.

Investor confidence and operating performance at US units are both areas where it is difficult to see meaningful recovery for the new company. The biggest brake on progress is, however, the experience of the new management team now put in place. It seems doubtful whether Moberg's predominantly Swedish corporate leadership team has the knowledge or retailing competence to rebuild growth in US or possibly even in Europe. To achieve momentum will require a reconstituted retail leadership, clear where growth will come from, and with a competitive strategy to differentiate Ahold from the many well-heeled competitors it now faces. Discussing this recently, Anders Moberg commented that he 'had started thinking about strategy', and indeed that he 'had a few ideas'.

Investors will be hoping that this outline intention will become more specific and competitive over the period ahead. Until it does, and until Ahold shows that it has the strength to compete effectively in markets outside its tightly managed home base, any thoughts of global recovery look distinctly premature.

As if to underline the fragility of the enterprise, judges in Amsterdam ordered a new Ahold investigation in January 2005, responding to nine claims by VEB, the Dutch shareholders' association, alleging mismanagement over a five-year period from January 1998 onwards. The suggestion is that previous investigations have left questions unanswered, and that Ahold executives should have spotted the US fraud a lot sooner than they did. Ahold is far from out of the wood.

The jury will for ever be out on whether Ahold's quick-fire, high-flexibility, 'stimulate-local-entrepreneurship' policies might have succeeded in the long term. Ahold made precious little attempt to harmonise or create coherence between its alternative brands or fascias, of which it had many, even when they were physically close to each other. It had recently embarked upon the task of creating appropriate back-office synergies, but even here it is not clear how far it had gone. Its principal achievement, in retrospect, was the high level of initiative it took with its acquisitions.

We can now turn to Wal-Mart, who began to expand out of the US alongside Ahold, and through the 1990s went on to become a formidable international player. Wal-Mart's big advantage is that it can address international issues with unique focus and commitment, and the relentless growth in US profits and cash generation is sufficient to make even significant forays outside the US little more than a rounding error on the parent company's results. There is a native mid-western hunter's simplicity to Wal-Mart's approach and message wherever it trades; at its best, this represents strength where others find the company's performance difficult to match. At its worst, its trading style looks gauche, even naïve, and it does not appear to have the capacity, internationally, always to learn quickly from its mistakes. This is a harsh accusation for the world's biggest and perhaps most successful company, but its record does show this. Wal-Mart intends to export its American culture and message to the major markets of the world. Its implicit belief is that the trading strength represented by its high-level command of every day low pricing will be a high enough consumer and business systems priority for it to establish a leading market position wherever it trades. So far, against this admittedly high standard, it has not quite succeeded.

Wal-Mart has been prepared to 'play all its cards' once the opportunities were there. Thus, it has taken stakes in overseas companies, prior to then increasing its holding. It has used organic growth, trading under its own name, when this seemed right, it had time, and there was nothing available to acquire. It has bought significant players outright when this was warranted. Wal-Mart's initial moves into adjoining NAFTA markets were highly successful. It was able to create a strong position in Canada, bolstered by non-food sales, but it was in Mexico that Wal-Mart was especially success-ful and this country is a pinnacle of international performance for Wal-Mart today. It has become, in one decade, a major company in the Mexican economy, starting from scratch through acquisitions and expansion, and now has a large range of successful trading formats including its mammoth supercenters.

The advent of the supercenter, and its ubiquitous success in the US, has prompted Wal-Mart to look at its overseas operations as a principal oppor-tunity to drive growth through this format wherever it trades. This has not always been possible, notably in Europe, where space constraints and trading restrictions have combined to make this difficult, for example in the UK or Germany. This has inhibited the speed of growth of the Wal-Mart machine. (In the UK it has built double-decker stores as a response to space restric-tion.) However there were other deficiencies in Wal-Mart's approach to its German entry that made matters a great deal worse: the company made little effort to understand the iconic German consumer and trading philosophy, and ignored its government's bewildering range of trading restrictions. Finally, its approach to management, relying on a heavy dose of US imports to drive its message home, was clumsy. Failure has resulted, and there have been few signs since, despite Wal-Mart's open admission of failure, that it has found the right way in to this important country.

In the Far East, Wal-Mart has avoided the problems of Germany, but it has not yet created Mexican-level success nor even the British achieve-ment – where Asda has made steady progress since Wal-Mart acquired it in 1999. In both Japan and China, the indications are that Wal-Mart is treading warily. It has endeavoured to stimulate growth in Seiyu, and raised its stake there without, as yet, creating significant growth. It has been contemplating a bid for Daiei, Japan's third biggest chain, but will not be the only prospective purchaser. Little confidence exists that it really knows its way forward. In China, ostensibly an ideal market for the super-center development, Wal-Mart is pushing these ahead, having had a business base in China for several years. So far, it has barely scratched the surface of economic opportunity, and the indications are that its mix is not yet profitable. Importantly, however, it is there with its principal trading format, and providing it can make its kind of EDLP attractive to the Chinese consumer, and pilot a negotiation route through tricky and multiple government constraints, it ought to be well placed.

Wal-Mart has been recognised by China's policy makers as an appropriate business catalyst for Chinese retailing. Once again, one suspects that it is the cultural challenge that Wal-Mart is finding most perplexing. Wal-Mart is well placed to offer multiple trading formats – it has a huge range at home from which to draw. It is economically strong enough to compete with defined discounter stores. Finally, it has huge faith in its company trading approach and the Wal-Mart brand name, and it uses this, without question wherever it trades – even Sam's Club in the US can be regarded as a derivative of the original US brand.

At this stage it is worth reviewing the distinct policies of the main protagonists. Carrefour have been first, have the best geographic coverage and have concentrated on the hypermarket format, but covered the discounter position when necessary. It has moved quickly, but taken limited risk in the biggest markets and has retired when it did not find the winning recipe (US, Japan). Given home-profits growth, not by any means a certainty, it is well placed, with a portfolio diversified across Europe, Asia and Latin America. Competitiveness in China, Asia-Pacific and Latin America is now an issue.

Ahold has promised much but finally delivered little. For ten years it appeared that its high-risk acquisition policy was paying off, and for a period Ahold had good positions in Europe (home market), USA, Asia and Latin America. Its policy was emphatically to encourage local branding and development and it worked handsomely in the US for a period. It looks as if the end position, however, may be only a small country home base, and if it is lucky a few 'cherry-picked' positions elsewhere. It will seek to maximise the strength of its Stop and Shop/Giant base in the eastern US but its status as a mainstream player has been lost.

Wal-Mart has been prepared to take most risk, to tackle exclusively big markets, and, where available, to grow rapidly by acquisition, using the Wal-Mart name. Its preference has veered towards setting up supercenters on the US model but this has not always been easy. So far, its unqualified successes have been confined to Mexico and probably the UK. Unlike its US experience, it is clear that Wal-Mart as an international operator has a great deal to learn – life is not as simple as it had imagined. It is using China as an important future learning base and has been at its most flexible there.

By comparison, the remaining players have confronted market entry in a range of different ways. Metro, Ito-Yokado, and Costco have chosen a retail format enabling them to operate in a segment of the market which has been smaller, lower opportunity and lower risk, but has generated learning, a developable strategy which they could defend, and a worthwhile profits stream.

The issue for each is whether genuine scale can ever be built in these fringe formats, and then whether they can confront competition and move towards the mainstream market. There is no precedent for this happening, yet.

Of the others, Auchan has moved relatively slowly and while it appears anxious to pick up the international pace, it looks as if it has not the domestic strength or enough good overseas platforms, to achieve this on its own. Casino has understood this problem and has moved, usually with the help of local overseas partners. It too is picking up speed internationally as indicated by the Laurus acquisition in Holland and its flexibility is evident, for example in the formats chosen – Casino has built its Leader price brand into a strong and complementary discounting property to the mainstream Geant and Casino operations. All the above are strategies that are capable of keeping the companies concerned in the retail game internationally, but without any real suggestion that they have the capability to join the leading big three.

Within this big three, Ahold is now unquestionably replaced by Tesco, who has entered the big leagues in spite of a late (1997) start. Tesco's policies are worth considering in their own right, given the handsome returns they have offered. Once it became clear to the new management that Tesco was beginning to generate strong UK profits, it tried, and then abandoned its attempt to enter northern France, and instead focused not on the biggest and visible markets (compare Wal-Mart, Ahold and even Carrefour), but on the emerging markets of Eastern Europe. Perhaps surprisingly, since it was not a format the British managers had ever used at any significant level, it elected to use the hypermarket model, until then regarded as the preserve of Continental operators. It chose its position and timed its entries just as free-market conditions were beginning to loosen up a swathe of markets in Eastern Europe. It applied a method – buy into an effective local operator, learn with him and then push in the extra investment to move towards market leadership – which was timely and highly effective. It contained the financial risks until it became clear that it had a winning formula, but once this had happened it then moved decisively. Within three years, Tesco knew it had a series of successes in the former communist satellite markets of Eastern Europe. It was ready for the next move – logical evolution from what it had achieved in Europe.

With a series of market leading positions in East European markets being secured, Tesco moved to establish similar positions in the emergent markets of Asia-Pacific. Initially it eschewed the very biggest countries (contrast Wal-Mart), and concentrated on Thailand, Malaysia, South Korea and Taiwan. Only later did Japan and, latterly, China enter its sights. Again, it seems that the policies have worked: Tesco has secured rapid growth in share; has built up a series of good market positions, using local partners; has developed good local joint ventures, for example Tesco/Lotus in Thailand; and seems to have achieved a sound balance between ensuring the right level of brand and quality control while encouraging local managers to lead its Asian operations. (Tesco has remarkably few expatriate managers in all its international businesses – a total of one in one thousand is quoted – a matter of legitimate pride to the HQ team which feels it creates confidence in Tesco's capacity to move further and quickly into new markets.) In each of these situations, Tesco has had to compete with international players who have usually got there before it, but it has had a strong enough management approach and product mix to succeed. Many of the ideal features of international expansion have been adopted in Tesco's moves to secure its base in Eastern Europe and Asia-Pacific from 1997 to 2004. We examine these later.

But there is one further feature of recent Tesco moves that deserves mention and which may prove strategically significant in years ahead. The expertise achieved in the UK company using the Clubcard, and through time developing in-store detailed information systems to create a leading position in e-commerce in the UK, has enabled the company to establish a partnership with Safeway Inc. in the US. Under the terms of this arrangement, Tesco has taken a stake in Safeway's e-commerce company, licensing its technology to Safeway in the process. It is a remarkable partnership and may yet afford the means of entry for Tesco into the US market, which would be very costly through more orthodox means.

To summarise the key parameters overall therefore:

1. Companies seeking international expansion have clear choices regarding the *degree of risk* they need to take to ensure success. Low-risk routes include organic growth and limiting store numbers in the early stages. More risk is involved in making local acquisitions, although this has increasingly been accepted as normal in an era where many governments seek to protect their local retailing companies from foreign takeover. The biggest risk is to make full-scale acquisitions of existing companies and the leading exponent of this mode has, unsurprisingly, been the company prepared to take most risk – Wal-Mart. There are some examples, but not many, of on-going partnerships being adopted for market entry.

2. Companies have a *choice of market* to be tackled, and over three decades there have been a variety of approaches. Once again, market selection involves varying degrees of risk. The market leader in process terms has been Carrefour, which has steadily pursued a policy of global expansion, generally tackling big markets and initially concentrating on those most akin to its home market in Europe. Thereafter, the policy was to make significant international moves in all continents, latterly including Africa, so that a world presence has been built. This approach to market selection – go where you know most and tackle the big markets – has been adopted by most of Carrefour's followers, of whom Wal-Mart has provided exclusive focus on big markets.

   Tesco has pursued a contrarian approach, tackling 'second level' markets first, and building success in these before moving to the biggest countries.

3. *Format strategies* have also been diverse. The first mover, Carrefour, chose to focus on hypermarkets, and has only latterly adopted the discounter format to build further share. It now has more than one retail brand, therefore. Tesco has followed the hypermarket choice. Wal-Mart has chosen a range of format approaches, but clearly prefers wherever possible to build supercenters. As one would expect, companies have backed existing expertise – whether it be discounters (Aldi, Lidl), convenience stores (Ito-Yokado), cash and carry (Metro) or warehouse clubs (Costco). This has enabled them to build segment dominance and discourage competition from entering.

4. Finally, *policy choice:* how far do we intend to centralise our approach, and how much local discretion will we give once the enterprise is fully owned? Carrefour's approach might be described as a 'middle way', establishing the format and fascia and making expertise and operational knowledge available to the international business, which was invariably led by Carrefour management, but allowing elements of local discretion in range, trading practice and so on. Wal-Mart is the best example of strong central control: clear operational policy based on EDLP, and driven, in most cases, by Wal-Mart expatriate management – at least until success is achieved. Ahold, while its global flag flew, was the least dictatorial, allowing acquired companies to continue with their own brands and operating philosophies, and even harmonising back offices only slowly. The Tesco model appears to recognise local expertise and build on it, and its policy appears to be a careful blend of local experience and central policy direction.

What has worked? Is there best practice we can discern from these diverse patterns? Becoming first mover, (Carrefour) has created a long-term vision and consistent advantage. Learning and limiting risk before tackling the big market challenges has paid off – (Carrefour and particularly Tesco.) Hypermarket channels have worked better than most other formats for most players but, more importantly, companies have succeeded where they have adopted differentiating formats which they knew about in advance, and where they possessed inbuilt advantage (Aldi, Ito-Yokado, Metro, Costco). Tackling adjacent geographic markets has created winning situations (Carrefour, Wal-Mart, Costco, Metro.) Partnerships can limit risk and create distinct positions at low cost (Casino, Tesco). A blend of central policy control and local management effectiveness works best (Tesco, Carrefour) but too much or too little central direction has sometimes limited success (Wal-Mart, Ahold). If success is elusive, and the model is not working, the best players cut their losses and move on (Carrefour in the US and UK, and Tesco in France.) As international markets have become more competitive, flexibility matters increasingly – develop new trading formats and cover the growing discounter threat. This can be with a distinct brand (Carrefour, Aldi) or under the main brand (Wal-Mart, Tesco).

A more honest summary might be, however – many routes have been tried and, so far, there is no clear single winner. There is, perhaps, an emerg-

ing pattern of hypermarkets and hard discounters as the winning formats –
but even there, we would not rule out the growth of supermarkets and
convenience stores in some markets where, for whatever reason, the leading
choices are not suitable. Competitive strategies will no doubt continue to
build on existing strengths and, as the key markets are now increasingly
occupied by a majority of the leading companies, there will be fewer easy
pickings, and fewer obvious winners than hitherto. The retail 'shake down
cruise' is just beginning, internationally.

7 Information and Technology as Competitive Advantage

It is a commonplace that information and communications technology (ICT) has caused a revolution in business methods. This is true, not only of hi-tech industries, but also of seemingly humble retailing.

Consider the nature of the task facing a multiple food retailer. The company will have a range of formats, spread over hundreds or thousands of outlets, dispersed over hundreds or thousands of miles. The smallest store may have only 700 stock-keeping units (SKUs), the largest up to 100,000. Many are fresh food, with a shelf life of a few days, and the need to replenish shelves daily or several times a day; others may be consumer durables, and they are sourced from all over the world. Yet the retailer aims for – and the best consistently achieve – over 95 per cent availability. Customers soon notice if items are missing from the shelves, and go elsewhere. Supply-chain management therefore becomes a core competency for a retailer.

To manage this consistently, and at an acceptable cost (or better, a competitively low one), would be impossible without sophisticated ICT systems. Lessons from Japanese lean manufacturing systems (such as just-in-time delivery) can be applied to supply chains, but demand accurate and timely information, and coordination and cooperation within the chain – what is where now, what is needed when and where, who will deliver and how? Although retailers had been working on their systems for decades, the innovation that kick-started progress was barcode scanning. This enables managers to track both at the pallet and case level, and at the checkout. With information flowing up and down the chain, the system can minimise stock at each level, and assure continuity of availability.

All this begs the question of what it is that is being made available. The factor that adds to the complication is the shift from supply push to consumer pull – the idea that it is consumer demand that pulls stock through the system, rather than manufacturers and retailers deciding on what we should be able to buy. Dell has built its whole business, and taken over leadership of the PC market, on this idea. By building only to order, and ruthlessly minimising inventory levels, Dell typically has only four days' stock in the entire operation, compared with rivals' thirty days. This is a clear competitive advantage, not only reducing costs, but also freeing up space for more production lines and allowing more rapid reaction to changing markets.

Retailers must apply the lessons, and the leaders have done so. Wal-Mart is often seen as 'the best supply chain operator of all time' (Abell, http://www.

computerworld.com/industrytopics/retail/story/0,10801,74647p3,00.html).
Sam Walton explored the idea of using computers to handle inventory early in
Wal-Mart's history, but the system was primitive until barcodes arrived.
Although barcodes were invented in the 1960s, and first appeared in the
1970s, it was not until the 1980s that enough packaged goods were barcoded
to enable them to be used in inventory control. Wal-Mart invested in point-
of-sale terminals that made use of barcodes in 1983, and four years later
installed a massive satellite system linking all stores to headquarters – thus
providing real-time inventory data.

If this were one major step, the next would be equally revolutionary. Wal-
Mart realised that cooperation with suppliers would be essential, and began
to share its data with them. This ran counter to the prevailing culture in the
industry, where all parties guarded their information jealously from each
other, and relations were adversarial. This new partnership approach is
crucial in optimising throughout the chain, rather than just in that part
within the retailer's control. It can lead to the collaborative planning, forecasting and replenishment (CPFR) programmes that most companies have
been developing in recent years. For Wal-Mart, it delivered a cost of goods
some five to ten per cent lower than competitors – a valuable competitive
edge. As important, its early lead left rivals struggling to catch up: Wal-Mart
has been able to stay ahead, and continues to innovate.

Tesco was also early to start applying the lessons from Japanese manufacturing. The famous book on Toyota and its methods, *The Machine that
Changed the World* (Womack, Jones and Roos 1990) publicised the approach
in the west, and the follow-up, Womack and Jones' *Lean Thinking* (1996)
apparently became required reading at Tesco. The company had started to
invest heavily in modernising its supply chain in 1983 with the adoption of
scanning. Between then and 1996, it introduced centralised automated
ordering, centralised distribution, automated warehouse control and EDI
(electronic data interchange) with its main suppliers.

> As a result, lead times to stores came down from 7–14 days to two days ... and
> Tesco was able to reduce its stock holding from 4.4 weeks to 2.5 weeks. At the same
> time, its range increased from 5000 to 40,000 food SKUs and average service levels
> rose from 92 per cent to 98.5 per cent (Jones and Clarke 2002).

Since then, it has continued to build a world-class system, one which is
certainly recognised as second to none in Europe – and which Tesco itself
would claim to be the equal of anyone's, even Wal-Mart's. It says that inventory levels are now 17 days or less overall, and ten days for food.

The motivation behind this early, and continuing, effort stems from
Tesco's culture. It started from dissatisfaction with the status quo, and
reflects what one director described as 'our restlessness, our determination
to improve', a characteristic that, revealingly, it shares with Wal-Mart.

Continental European retailers have been relatively slow to follow these
leads. If one reason was the differing cultures in French and German firms,
another was their respective business models and therefore organisation.

Carrefour, for example, sees its relationship with customers as essentially local: it has therefore been fairly decentralised, and this has hampered the sort of IT developments seen at Wal-Mart and Tesco. Carrefour's culture could have been seen as not IT-oriented: it claims, for example, that it had less need of a centralised IT system than, say Tesco, because its hypermarket model allowed it to make profits in a way that Tesco, with its supermarkets, could not (the British firm, not surprisingly, dismisses this idea).

Whatever the reason, it seems to have woken up rather recently to the strategic importance and benefits of IT. In 2003, the Executive Committee set up a central IT function, led by someone with both and IT and store management background, with a small central team to drive change throughout the business. The team has identified clear goals and a road map to reach them. It realises that change will not be immediate: there are legacy systems that cannot be just thrown out, and there are mindsets to change. Given that its approach is still local, it does not see one monolithic system dictating from the centre, but it is working on convergence. It sees customer focus as central to its operations: the first test of a proposed new system is what customer benefits it will deliver, and only second what benefit to the business. Bruno Cabasso, Chief Information Officer, says Carrefour is 'paranoid' about not getting too far from the customer.

In looking internationally, it is instructive to compare this approach with the other two leading players. Both have superbly efficient systems developed centrally. Both have made acquisitions abroad, and therefore have had to cope with legacy systems (and cultures). They both try to apply their central system as soon as possible, since they know the hard benefits in costs and efficiency that they can gain – and will forgo for as long as the systems do not converge. Tesco provides its foreign subsidiaries with 'Tesco in a box', the minimum core of the process and system; additional layers and modules can be added as the market and company gain in complexity and confidence. They aim to converge to the world's best processes so as to deliver improved assortment, reduced stock, reduced waste, increased productivity and better availability. While being sensitive to local markets and cultures is a key skill, IT is perhaps an area where these considerations do not apply ('They're all just shops', as Phil Clarke, head of both IT and international at Tesco, puts it).

The other contributors to successful supply-chain management are, of course, the suppliers. We noted how Wal-Mart began to develop partnerships very early on. Its famous collaboration with Procter & Gamble is symptomatic. As the relationship progressed, P&G located managers from many functions actually in the Bentonville headquarters of the retailer. This allowed them to work together on reducing inventory, forecasting demand, and managing categories to their mutual benefit.

Other companies, affected by the difficult economic conditions of the 1980s, also saw the benefit of cooperation. The Efficient Consumer Response (ECR) initiative was set up in the USA in 1993: it aims to bring together all the parties in the supply chain, and work publicly on driving out inefficiencies and reducing costs in the system. The idea spread to Europe in the following year, and there are now 22 European countries with ECR initiatives. Farther afield, there are now ten national schemes operating under the aegis of ECR Asia (Hong Kong, Singapore, the Philippines, Indonesia, Taiwan, Thailand, India, Malaysia, Korea and Australia). Estimated savings from ECR run to billions of dollars, and participants believe that they are achievable.

The need to work together in this way led to the recognition of the central place of standards: if suppliers, intermediaries and retailers in many countries are trying to communicate with each other in the most economical way (that is, using ICT), common standards become absolutely essential. This recognition led to the Global Commerce Initiative (GCI), which is working on establishing these standards. The fact that the co-chairmen of GCI are Lee Scott and Antony Burgmans, respectively CEO of Wal-Mart, and Dutch co-chairman of Unilever, suggest how important it is.

For outsiders, the actual workings of the various projects seem to take place in an impenetrable thicket of acronyms, of which GTIN, EPC AND GDS are just the most important. The projects aim to conform to EAN.UCC standards; the EAN.UCC system standardises barcodes, EDI transactions sets, XML schemas, and other supply-chain solutions for more efficient business. The GTIN, or Global Trade Item Number, feeds into the Global Data Synchronisation (GDS) network, while EPC (Electronic Product Code) feeds into the EPC global network. The nature of the information overlaps, but is different. The EPC data are more detailed, and are often collected by RFID tags (see Text Box 7.1).

BOX 7.1

RFID

The next big thing in supply-chain management is, and has been for a while, the Radio Frequency IDentification tag or RFID:

Radio frequency identification (RFID) has been around since the 1980s and is already widely used to identify vehicles and track livestock.

A basic system consists of an antenna or sensor, a transceiver with decoder and a transponder tag that is electronically programmed with unique data. The antenna/sensor, transceiver and decoder can be packaged together to make a reader. They can be placed on a production line, in a doorway or a tollbooth for example to establish an electromagnetic field and receive tag data from objects passing by.

The range is about 2.5cm to 30m, depending on power output and radio frequencies used. Passive tags get their power from the reader; more-expensive active ones have an internal battery and usually have a read/write capability, with a memory of up to 1 megabyte.

RFID's advantages over older technologies such as barcodes include a read capability that does not depend on contact or line of sight and a speed of reading that is less than 100 milliseconds (Financial Times *Special Report, Information Technology, 12 May 2004*).

While most applications so far are outside the retail supply chain, it is here that there is considerable excitement (or hype). Wal-Mart carried out a pilot in Texas, and told its 100 biggest suppliers to attach RFID tags to all pallets and cases by January 2005 (so much for partnerships, say some). Tesco and Metro have also asked suppliers (more gently) to adopt tagging at case level. The benefits are obvious, in that each item tagged can be tracked in real time. At present, costs are such that they are worth using at case level, but only for a few high-value or easily stolen products at item level (razors are a common first item to try). If costs fall sharply, as with similar electronic products, then their use may become widespread.

There are other problems:

Ask Colin Cobain, IT director at Tesco Stores – the UK's leading food retailer – when he thinks item-level radio frequency identification (RFID) tags in store may transform retail activity, and he raises a hand to scan a metaphoric horizon: 'It's decades away,' he says, 'the technology doesn't even work with the bulk of our product assortment.' (Financial Times *23 June 2004*). *Where they are used at item level is in non-food, especially high-priced merchandise such as suits and fashion clothing.*

There are some privacy concerns: in theory, retailers could use the tags to track behaviour in ways that consumers would resent. Marks & Spencer makes the tags easily detachable. In fact, most consumers do not seem to be too worried, but it may become a sensitive issue within the context of generally increasing concerns about privacy.

What it all means is that there should, eventually, be a seamless web of standardised, unambiguous descriptions of most SKUs and a common language that all parties, wherever they are, can use electronically. This in itself should increase efficiency and reduce costs.

At the other end of the chain – or perhaps at the front, if consumers are really driving supply – is the understanding of what customers want. Retailers have vast amounts of data from scanning – but making sense of it is a challenge. In *The Grocers*, we listed the skills that we believed would discriminate between future winners in food retailing and the rest of the pack. First on the list was 'the skill to use customer data to understand the market at increasingly fine levels of detail, and find new ways of segmenting and serving customers' (Seth and Randall 2001 p. 316). It is not clear that many have yet achieved that.

For all the claims made about data-mining techniques, the only concrete example of applicable results from basket analysis is the placing of disposable nappies (diapers) next to beer (presumably because the new parents could no longer go out in the evening) – and even that may be apocryphal. There may of course be many other real examples, but if so, retailers are keeping them quiet so as not to give too much away to competitors. One of the problems is the sheer volume and complexity of the data. Finding patterns, even with the most sophisticated analysis software, is very difficult.

Traditionally, retailers felt that because they were 'close to customers', they did not need market research (Marks & Spencer, notoriously, thought that it did not need marketing at all). The company that has, in our view, made the most progress, is Tesco. That stems from the crisis in the early 1990s when growth stalled, and it is significant that the reaction was to go back to customers and study in detail where Tesco was falling short. This was led by Terry Leahy, then Marketing Director and now CEO, and the company has continued to use research and analysis to guide strategy.

While scanning data have their uses, the big breakthrough came with the introduction of a loyalty card in 1993/4. Tesco staff had studied loyalty schemes running in the USA several times, but had always concluded that they were too expensive, with limited benefits. What had changed was the availability of huge computing power to analyse the data: loyalty cards are, after all, as important as a source of customer data, as they are as a promoter of loyalty. More interestingly, the Tesco team saw from the beginning that, by using that data, they could use the card to reward loyalty in a more targeted way than simpler schemes (for a detailed history of the Clubcard and its associated data analysis, see Humby and Hunt 2003).

What is fascinating about the Clubcard story is that, from the beginning, analysis of trial results showed Tesco management things that it did not know, or even suspect, about its customers. One striking fact was that a small proportion of customers accounted for a massive part of profitability. This is well attested in other fields (and is known as the 80/20 rule or Pareto effect), but neither store managers nor head office marketing people had suspected it here. Practitioners of direct marketing will see immediately how allying card data to direct mail campaigns would allow tight targeting of promotions, and the measurement of their effects, and this too was a revelation. When the team first presented the results of all its analysis to the board, the directors listened in silence. At last, Sir Ian MacLaurin, chairman, said, 'What scares me about this is that you know more about my customers in three months than I know in 30 years' (Humby et al., op. cit.).

It is easy to see that simple analyses can produce useful and actionable results, for example what departments customers visit (and, as important, which ones they do not). Beyond simple patterns, things get very complicated. As anyone with any familiarity with marketing data will know, research often produces results that are trivial (people who buy gin also buy tonic), or already well-known to people in the field. Finding new knowledge is harder. Working on huge data sets is both a blessing and a curse: trying to use all the millions of bits of data at once is often likened to drinking from a fire hose. Many associations that appear are hard to interpret correctly, and multivariate statistics can be a minefield for the uninitiated.

This leads to perhaps the most important conclusion about customer analysis: it is the people who carry out and interpret the analyses who are central. 'It took us two years to identify the sort of people who were good at analysing Clubcard data. You have to use intuition and creativity as well as statistical know-how, and you have to hope that you have identified the right things to test' said Tim Mason, now Marketing Director of Tesco (Humby et al., op. cit.). He might have added 'business sense' as a criterion, as any application has to have a business benefit. Some of the best analysts have advanced degrees in mathematics or mathematically based science, together with an interest in business and a practical grasp of business issues. Given the nature of the work, they are often found in specialist companies.

An example of the issues can be found in segmentation studies. There is some disagreement among retailers as to whether segmentation is desirable or necessary for a company aiming to satisfy the mass market. We assume that it is a valuable part of understanding the market: there are many different types of shopper and shopping occasions, and the retailer who understands these differing needs and preferences best will win against those who do not. Tesco has moved through several phases in segmenting its customers, starting with what it calls 'buckets'. These were subsets of all the products in the baskets, selected from the 8500 lines that account for 90 per cent of all sales. Using cluster analysis, it was able to identify 27 discrete segments that made sense, for example some bought a lot of high-value prepared food, others bought large quantities of convenience food, and so on. As an example of how to use such results, when the company wanted to introduce selective price cuts to combat Asda, it identified a product bought by the most price-sensitive segment (in this case an own-label value margarine). Targeting such products rather than something that everyone buys, such as bananas, should change price perceptions and have a disproportionate effect for a relatively low cost (Humby et al., op. cit.).

Tesco subsequently refined the model with a second-generation segmentation using a typology of the sort of products in the basket ('needs preparation' against 'ready to eat', or 'adventurous' against 'unadventurous'). It produced 'approximately 15 segments, amalgamated to six high-level segments' (Crawford Davidson, quoted in Reynolds and Cuthbertson 2004 p. 317).

We have spent some time on Tesco for two reasons: we believe that it is ahead of the game, and it has been open about what it does. Of course, other retailers carry out data analysis and market research. There are different ways of being close to customers; what we have described shows the rich possibilities available from the huge amount of data that retailers routinely collect, but do not always use.

There are two further areas where technology has had an impact on food retailing: online shopping, and the in-store experience. We are all familiar – perhaps over-familiar – with the hype of the dot.com bubble. Some commentators foresaw the demise of conventional retailing, with superstores becoming darkened hulks dotted around the outskirts of our towns. We have seen the bursting of the bubble, with almost all the dedicated online grocery projects having failed. Some were spectacular: in the USA, hopeful punters invested £2 billion on just two ventures, Webvan and Streamline. Webvan, the most ambitious of all, reached a stock-market valuation of $8 billion. Its sophisticated model was based on very large, highly automated warehouses – but it never attracted and retained enough customers, and went bankrupt in 2001.

Meanwhile, some of the more modest entries worked quietly away, building up a steady business. The most successful has been Tesco, which started in 1997 in a deliberately simple way. Indeed, many in the industry thought its operation laughably simple, with online orders faxed to stores for picking and delivery. It has continued to use store picking, although the whole operation is now highly sophisticated, with computers on the trolleys (carts) to guide the pickers through the store. It expanded rapidly in the UK, until it was the biggest online grocers in the world. By 2002, it achieved annual sales of £356 million, and claimed to be profitable. By 2004, it could report 24-week sales of £307 million, an increase of 27 per cent, and profit of £15 million – an impressive 95 per cent jump. The offer has increased far beyond food, although that still accounts for the majority of sales. The tesco.com site offers the major categories, apart from groceries, of: finance and insurance; telecoms; wine; electricals; DVD, video, CD and games; flowers; and books. In November 2004 it announced that it now offered mortgages, and music downloads.

Many were sceptical in the early days, but Tesco showed tenacity, and belief in its approach. There is still argument in the industry as to the relative merits of store picking and warehouses. The advantage of the Tesco way is that it can start with low capital costs, and still have the option of building warehouses if and when it needs them. Its success was recognised in a groundbreaking move in 2002, when Safeway (the US chain) entered a joint venture with it. Safeway had previously tried twice to launch an online service, but had failed both times. It is possibly the first time that the USA has had to look to a European company to help it with an Internet business.

Other firms have also been active. Wal-Mart was early in the field, starting in 1996. It had some teething problems, and had to shut its site down briefly in 1999 for a re-design. It also had a dispute with Amazon, who had poached several of its IT executives; this was settled in 1999. Wal-Mart is coy about its online sales. It appears to offer its whole range on its website, and, like Tesco, has entered the music download market. It ships rather than delivers, so looks more like Amazon than Tesco. We must conclude that its operation is successful, but probably that it forms a minor part of its total sales.

An alternative model was Peapod, which started in 1989 and went online in 1996. It partnered with established food retailers such as Safeway and Krogers. Later, Ahold bought a majority, then the entire business. Peapod has survived, and works with Ahold's US businesses Giant and Stop and Shop, operating in Chicago and seven states.

Carrefour has been more tentative. It has its Ooshop online offering, but only in three regions of France: the Ile de France (around Paris), Greater Lyon, and around Rouen. This lack of enthusiasm may reflect the French adoption of the Internet in general, which was held back for some years by the existence of France's own proprietary telephone information system, Minitel (see Internet penetration figures below).

Casino has taken a different route. Its 'cdiscount' online subsidiary gets over the geographical problem by offering delivery by post or courier services. It can do this because the range offered is mainly non-food; the food range is wine, a limited number of fair-trade products (tea, coffee and so on), and specialised packaged foods such as health and slimming foods. It looks more like Wal-Mart than Tesco or other home-delivery services.

The international spread of online shopping is, as Phil Clarke of Tesco points out, dependent on:

▶ A high level of Internet penetration
▶ High population densities
▶ Customers who actually want the benefits offered.

To that we would add consumer confidence in buying online (which is still low in many countries).

Penetration rates in the top 22 countries are shown in Table 7.1.

The results are much as one would expect. Leading countries are the advanced Asian countries such as Hong Kong SAR, Singapore, South Korea, Japan; USA and Canada; the Nordic countries and other leading economies in northern parts of the European Union; Australia and New Zealand. France does not make the list, as penetration there has not reached the 50 per cent cut-off (the figure was around 40 per cent in 2004).

As a result, outside its home base, Wal-Mart offers online shopping only in Mexico and the UK; Tesco only in Dublin (Ireland), Seoul (South Korea) and – through its Safeway joint venture – San Francisco and San Diego. Future expansion seems certain, but will depend on all four criteria, not just the availability of the Web. While there was certainly too much hype about dot.com start-ups, there has also been some cynicism at the other extreme about the feasibility and profitability of online food shopping. Food alone would not be profitable, but the companies under discussion have a wide range of non-food products and services to offer online. The economics depend on attracting and keeping a large enough customer base, and reducing costs. The two main cost areas are picking and delivery. We have noted the argument about warehouse against store picking; put simply, warehouse picking has lower variable costs, but a high up-front capital cost, while store picking offers an economical way to start, but may run into problems with congestion if it is too successful. Home delivery, which seems central to a true home grocery-shopping concept, has various solutions. Attended delivery, that is when the customer is at home to receive the goods, is expensive when many deliveries have to be in the evenings and at weekends (since so many couples are both out during the day). Alternatives that have been tried are various sorts of individual boxes in customers' homes, shared boxes, and collection points. These reduce the delivery costs, but increase investment (and often prices charged). Successful online grocers will experiment, and use whatever is most suitable to the different territories in which they operate.

Table 7.1 **Internet penetration rates**

Top 22 countries with the highest Internet penetration rate				
#	Country or region	Penetration (% population)	Internet users Latest data	Population (2004 est.)	Source and date of latest data
1	Sweden	74.6	6,722,576	9,010,700	Nielsen//NR Aug/04
2	Hong Kong	72.5	4,878,713	6,727,900	Nielsen//NR Aug/04
3	United States	68.8	201,661,159	293,271,500	Nielsen//NR Aug/04
4	Iceland	66.6	195,000	292,800	ITU – Dec/03
5	Netherlands	66.5	10,806,328	16,254,900	Nielsen//NR Aug/04
6	Australia	65.9	13,359,821	20,275,700	Nielsen//NR Aug/04
7	Canada	64.2	20,450,000	31,846,900	C.I.Almanac – Dec/03
8	Switzerland	63.5	4,432,190	7,433,000	Nielsen//NR Aug/04
9	Denmark	62.5	3,375,850	5,397,600	Nielsen//NR June/02
10	Korea, (South)	62.4	30,670,000	49,131,700	KRNIC – July/04
11	Singapore	61.0	2,135,000	3,499,500	ITU – Sept/04
12	United Kingdom	58.5	34,874,469	59,595,900	Nielsen//NR Aug/04
13	Liechtenstein	57.6	20,000	34,700	CIA – Dec/02
14	Germany	57.1	47,182,668	82,633,200	Nielsen//NR July/04
15	Bermuda	54.2	34,500	63,600	ITU – Dec/03
16	Japan	52.2	66,548,060	127,853,600	Nielsen//NR July/04
17	Croatia	52.1	2,318,240	4,453,700	ITU – Sept/04
18	New Zealand	52.0	2,110,000	4,059,900	ITU – Dec/03
19	Taiwan	51.1	11,602,523	22,689,300	Nielsen//NR June/01
20	Faroe Islands	50.9	25,000	49,100	CIA – Dec/02
21	Finland	50.7	2,650,000	5,231,900	ITU – Dec/02
22	Norway	50.0	2,288,000	4,577,500	C.I.Almanac – Dec/03
TOP 22 in Penetration		**62.1**	**468,840,669**	**754,384,600**	**IWS – Sept 30/04**
Rest of the World		**6.1**	**344,090,923**	**5,582,313,287**	**IWS – Sept 30/04**
Total World – Users		**12.7**	**812,931,592**	**6,390,147,487**	**IWS – Sept 30/04**

Notes: (1) Countries with a penetration rate higher than 50 per cent qualify for this list. (2) Internet penetration statistics were updated on September 30, 2004. (3) Demographic (population) numbers are based on the data contained in *gazetteer.de*. (4) The most recent usage information comes from data published by *Nielsen//NetRatings*, *ITU* and other research sources. For definitions please read the surfing guide.
Source: www.InternetWorldStats.com

As the population becomes increasingly at ease with computing and Internet use (as today's young people grow up), then online shopping will grow. If the current leading food retailers do not offer the service, then independent competitors will. Such operations exist, for example xpressgrocer.com and freshdirect.com in New York or FoodFerry.co.uk in London. These will always remain small, as they cannot compete against the mass-market operators, with their scale and established brand, but they offer a specialised and worthwhile service in city centres. The conclusion must be, therefore, that any company wanting to be a major player will need to offer the service in those countries that are ready for it, and continue to roll it out as other countries mature.

The final application of technology is in the store itself. So far, most applications have been mainly for the benefit of the retailer: scanning, just-in-time deliveries, and so on. Such efforts will continue – with greater use of radio frequency identification (RFID), for example – as the search for efficiency is unending. More recently, companies have been looking to improve the shopping experience more directly (developments such as scanning, loyalty cards and data mining have, it could be argued, led to indirect benefits to customers). Some innovations are already available in some stores: self-scanning to cut down checkout times, kiosks offering targeted information, for example. Others are being tested in projects such as Metro's Future Store in Germany. This brings together a large number of partners, mainly technology and software firms such as Intel, SAP and IBM, but also brand owners such as Coca-Cola, Gillette and Henkel. It aims to help both the retailers and consumers; for consumers, its goals are to make the shopping individualised, reliable and comfortable. The website (http://www.future-store.org) gives examples:

More Individuality

The consumers display quite different shopping behaviors. Some customers like to take time when choosing products, compare prices and obtain in-depth information on the goods. Others are in a hurry and want to do get done with their shopping as fast as possible. The Future Store uses technologies that meet the expectations of both types of customers alike.

Even upon entering the Future Store, the customer is greeted individually – by the Personal Shopping Assistant, a handy small computer the customer receives for the loyalty card. With this device, the customer is able to recall an own shopping list composed of the purchases of the last few weeks. Self-scanning of products is also possible with the Personal Shopping Assistant. This saves time at the check-out because long lines are thus avoided.

More Reliability

The innovative RFID technology used in the Future Store increases the reliability of many processes in the store and improves customer service. For example, employees recognize faster when products on the shelves are running low. They are thus able to refill the shelves earlier than today and avoid out-of-stock situations. The benefit for the customer is a more reliable product availability.

There is also a wealth of new possibilities of customer information. So-called Information Terminals, for example, provide detailed information on specific product lines such as meat or wine – an important measure to gain the customers' confidence in the goods offered.

Reliability also means excluding mistakes in price labeling. In the Future Store, this is done electronically. An integrative system ensures that the prices indicated on electronic displays are identical with the prices stored in the check-out system. If a price changes, it will automatically and simultaneously be indicated on the shelf and in the check-out systems.

More Convenience

Looking for a certain product in the store – a piece of cake in the Future Store. The Personal Shopping Assistant shows the customer at the touch of a button in which section and on which shelf the desired goods can be found. New technologies such as this one help to make shopping a faster and more pleasant experience for the customer.

The so-called intelligent scales also offer more convenience: The customer does no longer have to memorize numbers, as the automatic scales recognize fruit and vegetables on its own.

The payment process in the Future Store is also a lot faster and more convenient than in conventional stores. The customers can pay with the Personal Shopping Assistant and do not have to empty the shopping cart any more. Or they just make use of the self check-out option – without requiring a cashier.

These innovations show the directions that the industry is looking in, and there are other examples, such as Carrefour's innovation centre. As with online shopping, the speed with which such innovations spread internationally will depend on the readiness of each country. This is not only a case of technology, but infrastructure, consumer acceptance, and probably the competitive necessity of investment for differentiation.

To sum up, the efficient and creative use of information and technology will be first, a core competence for retailers; and second, offer the potential to be a competitive weapon. No one can afford to fall behind, and the leaders may draw further ahead. At present, Wal-Mart is world leader in supply-chain systems, with Tesco close behind. Carrefour is taking up the challenge, but is some years behind; while some leapfrogging may be possible, it may suffer some disadvantage until it is in touch – and it desperately needs costs savings in its vital home territory. In consumer understanding, we believe Tesco has done more, and progressed further, than anyone. It will be hard to catch it up in the short term. Wal-Mart is driven by a different, EDLP-based model, and seem less bothered by the need for deep customer insight, except what it gains by close contact on the shop floor. Carrefour, like Wal-Mart, sees itself as close to customers, but has not done the years of data analysis that Tesco has. As markets around the world develop, and the leading players find themselves in direct competition more and more often, these competences will become more important.

8 Global Advantage: Theory and Practice

We live in an increasingly international world, so the surprise is not that retailers should go international, but that they took so long to do so. In one sense, of course, they have operated internationally for ever, since they have always bought their goods from around the world – though that has also increased in recent years. In ideas, too, they have for many years been willing to borrow from successful retailers in other countries: European retailers copied the self-service idea from the USA, for example. In other senses, they have lagged behind manufacturers, some of whom have been establishing their presence abroad for over a century.

Now, European retailers especially are operating on an international scale. Table 8.1 shows the international turnover of the largest 30 retailers, and their relative 'international-ness'. Given their enormous home market, US retailers have felt less need to go abroad so far, although several are not far off many of the Europeans. Companies from the smaller European nations are the most likely to look abroad for opportunities.

This suggests one of the main reasons why some retailers venture overseas, and others do not. Table 8.2 summarises the push and pull factors influencing the decision. We could deduce that Wal-Mart has been pulled abroad, by the desire to export a formula that works well in the home market, its company skills and strengths, and its corporate philosophy to become an international business. European retailers are much more likely to have felt pushed, by mature, crowded markets and regulations restricting store building and corporate takeovers.

Conventionally, in business textbooks, food has been thought the least international of products, because it is the most 'culturally grounded': tastes and habits differ widely, and how people buy, prepare and eat food is very much influenced by culture (in its widest sense). Moreover, there are plenty of local shops whose owners know the market, and local produce is freely available. In this context, it is hard to see that the large mass-market retailers have any great competitive advantage, unless they buy an established large chain (as Wal-Mart bought Asda in the UK). What is certain is that, to succeed, they do need a competitive advantage that works in each country in which they operate.

In return, what do they get? The theoretical advantages are opportunities for growth, economies of scale, transfer of learning, geographical diversification of risk, possible first-mover advantage, and ability to exploit a brand, product or know-how.

Table 8.1 **International sales of the largest retail companies**

Size rank	Company	Country	MCap, 01/07/02 (US$million)	International turnover as % of sales	Integrative measure of globalization*
1	Wal-Mart Stores	US	241,973	16	1.2
2	Carrefour	FR	38,794	51	2.2
3	Tesco	UK	26,350	15	0.4
4	Ito Yokado	JP	20,614	34	0.7
5	Ahold	NL	19,281	92	5.2
6	Costco	US	17,177	18	0.2
7	Sears Roebuck	US	16,505	10	0.1
8	Hennes & Mauritz	SD	14,796	89	1.9
9	Pinault Printemps	FR	14,429	55	3.7
10	Safeway	US	14,016	8	0.1
11	Marks & Spencer	UK	13,727	15	0.7
12	Metro	BD	11,151	42	0.4
13	Sainsbury's	UK	10,815	21	0.2
14	TJX Companies	US	10,326	11	0.3
15	Castorama Dubois	FR	10,067	69	1.7
16	GUS	UK	9,380	26	1.3
17	Staples	US	8,939	7	0.1
18	Aeon Co.	JP	8,938	11	0.2
19	Boots	UK	8,838	9	0.2
20	Casino	FR	7,952	25	1.9
21	Kingfisher	UK	6,559	46	1.1
22	Dixons	UK	5,797	14	0.1
23	Office Depot	US	5,086	15	0.2
24	Tiffany & Co	US	4,961	51	0.0
25	Next	UK	4,702	3	0.1
26	Delhaize	BG	4,341	85	2.7
27	Karstadt Quelle	BD	3,000	10	0.2
28	Signet Group	UK	2,584	71	0.7
29	Michaels Stores	US	2,551	4	0.0
30	Esprit Holdings	HK	2,256	87	3.2

Source: Oxford Institute of Retail Management, reprinted from Reynolds and Cuthbertson 2004 with permission from Elsevier
* The integrative measure of globalization is a composite of: percentage of sales abroad, number of regions, and relative concentration (see Reynolds and Cuthbertson 2004 p. 100)

Opportunities for growth we have already noted. Companies are always looking for growth, and new countries are just like new segments and new markets opening up domestically. The company must evaluate the various options in terms of risk and reward, and allocate resources to the most promising. Our retailers still have to decide how much to spend in their home market, against each of the opportunities abroad; as we have seen, for

many, particularly the Europeans, other countries will look a better bet. The
more mature and concentrated the home market, the more attractive expansion overseas becomes. A company based in the USA, China or India can see
plenty of opportunity at home, and would be less tempted. Conversely, the
firm starting from a small country – Belgium, Hong Kong SAR – is likely to
run out of headroom at home before the company based in a large economy.

Table 8.2 **Push and pull motives for international development**

Push	Pull
Mature markets, few opportunities	Growing population in host country
Intense competitive pressure; declining market share	Economic growth; growth of consumer spending in key groups
Saturation or impending saturation in floorspace provision	Presence of niche market; desire to export a formula that works well in home market
Slow economic growth	Removal of barriers to entry
Low population growth, changes in demographics	Strong product brand
	Fragmented competition
Regulation restricting store building, especially large store formats	Company skills and strengths
Regulation restricting growth via corporate takeover	Corporate philosophy to become international business
High operating costs	Opportunity to learn about international retailing/establish base for further expansion

Source: Oxford Institute of Retail Management, reprinted from Reynolds and Cuthbertson 2004 p. 102,
with permission from Elsevier

Economies of scale in service businesses are not the same as in manufacturing. In buying, there are of, course, theoretical advantages to buying on
a larger scale. There is a story of Lee Scott of Wal-Mart being furious when
he found Asda, the UK subsidiary selling an item for $21 that Wal-Mart was
selling in the US for $5.95, even though the items were identical and came
from the same factory in China. Economies of scale in buying are very prob-
able in non-food. In grocery, the advantage may or may not exist, depending on the product: for packaged, standardised products, it may; for fresh
food, perhaps not (though Carrefour, for example, has run an international
promotion for melons). While precise figures are not made public, our
leaders all claimed significant savings; one quoted a range of 10–15 per cent.
Using electronic exchanges such as GNX also brings economies. There are,
of course, some extra costs – in communication, coordination and administration – in buying for several countries. It can be done only with a wholly
or partly centralised buying function. This in turn must reflect the
company's overall strategy on local adaptation of product ranges. Currently,
global sourcing is in its infancy in most retailers, but seems certain to grow
in importance.

In services generally, there may be economies of scale in back-office
systems, and this may also apply in retailing. We noted in Chapter 7 how
Wal-Mart has applied its back-office systems to Asda in the UK (and presumably elsewhere); Tesco, similarly, installs its systems rapidly in new countries.

This not only brings efficiencies, but also brings the subsidiary up to speed far faster than could be done by designing tailor-made systems. Carrefour is only at the beginning of this road.

Transfer of learning in international companies often starts as a one-way street: headquarters transfers all its wisdom to its grateful subsidiaries. Later, for the less ethnocentric managements, it is possible to see learning of all sorts in many parts of the network. Wal-Mart, for example, has transferred the George clothing brand from the UK to the USA; Tesco has transferred learning from central Europe, Korea, and Thailand to other countries. This, too, may be expected to become more of a feature – and a greater source of potential competitive advantage – as the firms mature as international organisations.

Diversification of risk may be an important aim of strategy if some parts of the world are volatile. This may be economic volatility, which has not yet been abolished even in advanced countries, or political, or a combination of the two. Carrefour made extraordinary profits for some years in Latin America, but sadly many of those countries have had a very bumpy ride in recent years through the interaction of political and economic crises. Carrefour has been able to balance the downturn in its Latin America business with gains in other regions. As we noted in Chapter 1, countries such as Russia may be very attractive, but they also carry undoubted risks. The wise retailer will try to balance growth opportunities against risk to achieve a reasonable spread.

The idea of first-mover advantage is an attractive one: if you are first in a market, your lead should be permanent. Cees van der Hoeven, CEO of Ahold before the disaster, certainly expressed that view when he said that Ahold wanted not only to enter international markets, but to be first in each new country. Unfortunately, the truth is slightly more complicated. Many of the instances of apparent first-mover advantage look only at the firms left in the market, rather than at all those that have taken part from the beginning. Not many people remember, for example, that the first portable computer was made by Osborne, not by Toshiba (let alone Compaq or Dell); or that the first civil jet airliner was made by De Havilland, not Boeing. If we redefine it as 'first-mover opportunity', then perhaps we are on safer ground. The first to arrive in a growing economy that does not have a modern retailing system has the opportunity to organise the market and gain an early lead over competitors. Good management should secure that lead, but it is not inevitable. It may be better to be a fast follower, allowing the pioneer to take the risk and establish whether a market really exists. Judging exactly when to jump in will be testing: too early, and you share the risk; too late, and you may never catch up.

Finally, there is the ability to exploit a brand or other asset over a wider field. This, again, is a seductive notion, and one that has driven many international strategies (Coca-Cola, McDonald's ...). For a food retailer, given the issues of cultural and market differences noted above, it is worth examining exactly what asset may be exploited internationally. Do shoppers want to know that their supermarket is part of an international brand? Is it motivating for them? With brands such as McDonald's, that has been the case: consumers in many countries flocked to the iconic outlet, eager both to sample its food and to share its American-ness. Wal-Mart may benefit from the same effect although, as we saw earlier, anti-American feelings could dilute that effect. When Carrefour entered Japan, the local consumers had a clear idea that it was French, and of what that implied. The fact that Carrefour did not initially meet their expectations led to disappointment.

The retailer needs to know, therefore, what image, if any, local shoppers have of the source country, and of the brand itself. Do they know that Tesco is British, and, if so, what attributes does that carry with it? In some regions, British-ness might suggest modernity, but might also carry overtones of past colonialism. It is doubtful if it brings the image of wonderful food.

The potential benefits of being a multinational with a standardised brand will also depend on the competitive structure in a country. The market conditions and positioning of the home country may not be transferable to a new and different setting (for example, the positioning of McDonald's in America is quite different from that in emerging economies, where it is a luxury purchase). For a food retailer, it may, in the end, be less a brand, or a set of formats, but expertise – systems, skills and knowledge.

We should perhaps add a benefit that may flow from an unacknowledged motivation in going international: massaging the managerial ego. People who get to the top of large companies necessarily have a considerable personal self-belief, and a desire to conquer new fields (we may call it the Alexander the Great syndrome), that may drive them to seek new territories to invade, whatever the objective business case. Certainly, there have been some odd choices of countries in which to establish a branch. It is the board of directors' job to keep such excursions in check.

To sum up, the theoretical benefits of international expansion are clear. It does offer opportunities for growth, although not, so far, very profitable growth. Economies of scale will be available, but so far are not huge; they will grow, but may conflict with other strategic factors. Transfer of learning is certainly possible, and the well-run company will actively look to increase it. Diversification of risk is also an opportunity; some fine judgments will need to be made. First-mover advantage does not always materialise, and on its own should not override other considerations: overall market attractiveness, fit with strategy, competitive situation, and likely profitability. The ability to exploit products and know-how is a definite benefit; whether the brand also fits in this category will vary.

9 Social Issues: Who Loves Global Retailers?

Food retailers, like any other business, live in society – or, for the international operators, in many different societies. They affect, and are affected by them. Only if they can be seen to contribute to the society as a whole, rather than damage it in the selfish pursuit of profit, will they flourish. In this chapter, we will discuss the main challenges to international food retailers: anti-globalisation (anti-Americanism and anti-capitalism); attacks on multiple supermarkets in general; problems of food safety and quality; health issues, particularly obesity; reduction of consumer choice; effects on suppliers, both large multinationals and small, local firms; and the way that governments respond through legislation and regulation.

As the last century drew to a close and the new one opened, the so-called anti-globalisation movement gathered strength. There were spectacular, and violent, demonstrations in Seattle, Prague, Genoa and hundreds of other cities around the world. Quite what all these people were protesting about was not always clear. In fact, the movement brought together protesters against environmental damage, third-world debt, child labour, multinational companies, genetically modified food (genetically modified organisms (GMOs)), harm to animals, unfair trade, capitalism, and many other issues. The movement gained intellectual support not only from populist (and extremely popular) books such as *No Logo* (Klein 2000), but also from works by serious economists such as *Globalisation and its Discontents* (Stiglitz 2002). The title of one book by a Cambridge academic is suggestive: *The Silent Takeover: Global Capitalism and the Death of Democracy* (Herz 2001). Whole forests have been felled in the ensuing debate, which we will not rehearse here (except to mention the most cogent rebuttal of the anti-globalisation arguments by Wolf 2004).

The events of 9/11 and the subsequent wars took much of the wind out of the movement's sails. The huge, violent protests have disappeared, but a widespread feeling of scepticism about business has remained. Much of it stems from the powerlessness that people in many countries feel when confronted by the seemingly unstoppable march of American economic and military might. The support expressed in France for José Bové, an activist turned farmer who destroyed a McDonald's outlet under construction, is symptomatic. Roads in rural southern France bore the twin slogans 'Libérez José Bové' and 'Non aux OGM' ('organismes génétiquement modifiés' or GMOs). Partly this is a resistance to inevitable change, but partly it is a genuinely felt fear of losing a much-loved way of life. The easiest scapegoats to blame are the multinationals, especially the most visible ones: Nike, Coca-Cola, McDonald's, Starbucks – all American.

It is possible to argue that such protests are not representative of the population as a whole: McDonald's, for example, has been very successful in France, and now has over 1000 restaurants there, so quite a lot of French people are 'lovin' it'. Nevertheless, criticism has been so pervasive – stoked by corporate scandals in the USA and Europe – that many businesses have responded. Corporate Social Responsibility (CSR) has grown into a whole new industry, and few large companies do not at least pay lip service to it.

It is striking that Wal-Mart's 2004 Annual Report (http://investor. walmartstores.com) is devoted almost entirely to showing what a warm, caring, responsible company it is. The strap line on the cover is 'Good Jobs, Good Works, Good Citizens'. The contents page lists the sections: Good Jobs, Good Careers; Building Lasting Relationships with Suppliers; Neighbors Helping Neighbors; Raising the Standard of Living; Good Investment; and Supporting our Service Men and Women. A charitable non-governmental organisation (NGO) could hardly do better. Wal-Mart is easily the biggest and most visible retailer, and this is a response to the sustained attacks on it over the past few years. These include class action lawsuits from employees, allegations of the use of illegal immigrant labour, and popular rejection of proposed new stores (see Text Box 9.1). Wal-Mart maintains its innocence, of course, and again the interesting question is how representative the attackers are of the population as a whole. Until now, its sales growth has shown that most people like the product, but there were signs in late 2004 and early 2005 that some, at least, were not spending as freely there as they did. Whether anti-American feeling resulting from the Iraq war will have an impact on sales in its overseas branches remains to be seen.

BOX 9.1

WAL-MART – THE DARKER SIDE

The emergence of Wal-Mart as America's (and the world's) largest company in sales, and its central place in American life, were marked by an academic conference dedicated to it in April 2004 (Lichtenstein 2005). Its triumphs had already received due recognition. McKinsey's analysis of productivity gains in the USA in the period 1995–2000 had pointed out that half that growth was in retailing and wholesaling, and that Wal-Mart alone had caused the majority of that through its leading-edge practices. It was *Fortune* magazine's most admired company in 2003. *The Economist* ran a laudatory article on the company (April 17–23 2004). The conference, however, also threw some light into the darker corners of the legend (see Head 2004, on which this note draws).

Some of the charges have been described in Chapter 2. The first major area of criticism is the treatment of the workforce. The US government has issued 60 complaints against Wal-Mart since 1995 at the National Labor Relations Board, but the law seems to have little effect. (That the company has accepted a union in China reflects both the power of that country's attraction, and the fact that all unions in China are government bodies; no independent unions are allowed.)

One result of this relentless focus on keeping costs down is that employees in the USA are paid very little. In 2004, a sales clerk received $8.50 an hour, or about $14,000 a year, $1000 below the government's definition of the poverty line for a family of three. Fewer than half Wal-Mart's employees can afford even the least expensive healthcare packages offered by the company. According to a report by (Democratic staff of) the House Committee on Education and the Workforce (2004), Wal-Mart's low wage levels mean that many employees qualify for government assistance under the federal welfare system (which would not be regarded as generous in many countries in Western Europe). The report estimates that for a 200-employee store, the government (that is the taxpayer) is spending $108,000 for children's healthcare, $125,000 a year in tax credits and deductions for low-income families, and $142,000 in housing assistance (Head 2004).

Another reflection of the intense pressure on management to keep costs down is the way that stores are consistently understaffed, and that employees are monitored continuously. An imaginative result is the invention of the crime of 'time theft'. Any time spent not obviously carrying out the allotted tasks, such as associates (as Wal-Mart employees are known) talking to each other, is stealing time from the company, a punishable offence. Another result is the very high staff turnover: 50 per cent of Wal-Mart's workers left in 2003, compared with 24 per cent at Costco.

A potentially even more serious allegation is that the company discriminates against women (see Chapter 2).

Critics argue that the company's employment practices are not just bad in themselves, but that they have a deleterious knock-on effect on other companies. When Wal-Mart was planning to enter California, the incumbents, Safeway and Albertsons, tried to lower their employees' pay and benefits, which led to a strike. The companies won that battle, but it may be seen as symptomatic of the 'race to the bottom' brought on by the fiercely competitive Wal-Mart approach.

The firm has also been accused of using sub-contractors who employ illegal immigrants, and of importing cheap goods made by sweatshop workers in developing countries. Wal-Mart always defends itself against these allegations. As it is so visible, it is a tempting target (as was Nike with similar attacks). Nevertheless, there is no doubt that some of its business practices are questionable. They are so embedded in its culture that it may find it hard to change: when low, low prices drive low, low costs, few compromises are possible.

Wal-Mart took out a double-page ad in the journal in which many of these allegations were brought together, *The New York Review of Books* (7 April 2005, pp. 6–7). The ad, headlined 'Wal-Mart's Impact on Society: A key moment in time for American capitalism', took the form of an open letter from Lee Scott, CEO. Its counter-arguments can be summarised:

▶ Wal-Mart's Every Day Low Prices policy raises living standards by passing on savings to consumers, particularly those from middle- and low-income families. These may amount to some $100 billion a year.

▶ Wal-Mart's average national wage is around $10 an hour, competitive with comparable retailers. Retailing generally pays lower frontline wages than some other industries.

▶ Of Wal-Mart's associates (employees), 74 per cent work full time, compared with 20 to 40 per cent at comparable retailers. Wal-Mart therefore spends more broadly on health benefits than some competitors.

▶ Critics fundamentally misunderstand the nature of the industry. Wal-Mart earns a profit of just 3.6 per cent of sales. If they either raised wages or increased prices, they would harm either shareholders (many of them associates), or consumers. 'We believe that offering good jobs at fair wages and benefits with unparalleled opportunities for growth, while also delivering world-class savings to over 270 million customers, is the best way to do right by all our stakeholders.'

Readers will draw their own conclusions.

Anti-Americanism has certainly grown in the early years of the 21st century, not only in Muslim countries but also in many of the nations where majorities opposed the Iraq war. It was fed, too, by actions such as the rejection of the Kyoto treaty and the International Criminal Court, the holding of prisoners without trial in Guantánamo Bay, and the scandals of Abu Ghraib prison, leading to a general sense that the USA was increasingly acting solely in its own interests, without consulting or thinking about its allies and the wider community. The question again is, how widespread is that feeling? It may be confined to the *bien-pensants*, the chattering classes, the intellectuals, and not shared by the great mass of people. Where US retailers arrive in a country for the first time, they are usually welcomed with open arms. They are, of course, still relatively small; perhaps when they and their western competitors come to dominate a market, local people may feel differently. There have been indications in some markets of a return to local loyalties, for example in PCs in China and some consumer products in Russia. Certainly, the ready acceptance that Wal-Mart, Carrefour, Tesco and the others have received in most countries suggests that anti-globalisation will not affect them for some time yet, if at all. Where they have met resistance, it is because they have been insensitive to ways in which the local culture differs from their own.

As to general criticism of supermarket multiples, they have not so far been accused of contributing to the drug problem or the rising number of births to teenage single mothers, but they have been charged with many of the other perceived ills of modern society. As Sir Terry Leahy of Tesco put it, 'we all know that supermarkets come in for a fair amount of stick. Here are some of the things that are said about us: We destroy corner shops. We tear the heart out of local communities. We concrete over fields and cause millions of people to sit in traffic jams. We squeeze our suppliers and are bad for British farming. We encourage people to eat unhealthily. We are responsible for an epidemic of obesity. And that's just the more polite things' (quoted in *The Observer* Business Economics 5 December 2004 p. 3).

To clear some of the ground, then, we should note that, as throughout history, some individuals hanker after the 'good old days', and resent what they see as the failings of the society they live in. Whether it is crime, speech patterns, spelling and punctuation, manners, traffic, or the taste of bacon, someone, somewhere is complaining about it.

We can identify some of the changes that have happened in most developed nations, and for which supermarkets cannot in fairness be blamed. These include car-borne shopping, a desire for convenience, different family structures, and less formal eating patterns. In wealthy societies with widespread car ownership, most shoppers prefer to drive. Even a government enquiry in Britain into the effect of large food stores on town centres concluded that people decide first on mode of transport, then on where to shop; mainly, they want to use their car (DETR 1998). In the USA, it is estimated, people will walk for only 200 yards: anything further, they drive. Before Europeans feel too smug, a very similar figure is used in planning shopping centres in Europe.

This habit may be bad for our health and the planet, but it has happened, and will continue. Supermarkets built on the edge of or outside town centres have taken advantage of this trend, but they emphatically did not create it (we will return later to the question of whether they actually increase overall traffic, and if they have destroyed town centres). If people still shop frequently, and walk or take public transport, then the supermarket model does not appeal. That applies at present to many developing countries (and perhaps, to an extent, to Japan). Will western supermarkets change these habits when they enter a country? It is difficult to see that the adoption of the driving habit will follow a radically different path from that in the west, and supermarkets will contribute to the trend, perhaps, but not drive it on their own.

A related question is that of convenience. It is a truism that modern life is faster, that everyone is busier, has more choices and more to do – and so has less time. Therefore, there is a general desire for convenience: anything that saves time or hassle is welcome. Again, supermarkets have profited from this by offering one-stop shopping (as others have: for example drive-through banks or fast food outlets). They also offer more and more semi- or fully-prepared food. While there are critics of this, as we shall see, there is no doubt that a segment of many societies consists of individuals who work long hours, possibly also commute over long journeys, and are only too pleased to pay someone to do some of their domestic work for them. Time is precious to such buyers, and they want convenience. Supermarkets did not cause this development.

Another very visible change in the developed world is the range of family and household structures. The old situation where the average family, and household, consisted of a married couple (a man and a woman), and just over two children, no longer exists. Single-parent families, same-sex partnerships and smaller households are common. Supermarkets cater for these new consumers and, to be fair, not even their harshest critics accuse them of creating them.

An allied trend, however, that the supermarkets are accused of aiding and abetting is the disappearance of the family mealtime. Where once the whole family traditionally sat down to eat at least one meal a day together, nowadays individual members graze and snack, eat individual portions of different foods, and rarely, if ever, come together in a socially-binding ritual. Once more, this may or may not be deplorable, depending on your point of view, but we cannot blame the supermarkets for it, or for catering to it.

In all those cases, supermarkets are just reacting to changes in their customers, which is exactly what they should be doing as well-run businesses. There are, however, charges that can legitimately be brought against them, and we will examine these in turn.

The first is the undeniable effect they have had on small shops. In every country that did not have draconian protective legislation, such as Italy or Japan, thousands of small shops were destroyed by the rise of the supermarket multiples. In the UK, a typical example, the number of independent grocers fell from 116,000 in 1961 to 20,900 by 1997 (DETR 1998), and the decline has continued. Other independent food shops – butchers, fishmongers, greengrocers, bakers – also suffered. Small shops simply cannot compete on price with a large multiple and its enormous buying power. Even voluntary combinations using a common fascia, though they helped, were not enough.

Leaving aside the purely economic argument for the moment, it is here that the car-borne shopping argument comes into clearest focus. Small shops are usually on a high street (main street in the USA), or in a local shopping area. Such is the volume of traffic today that, in most of these, parking is forbidden. Parking nearby may be difficult to find, and will normally have to be paid for. Given the choice, most consumers will drive, and therefore make a longer but easier journey to a supermarket, where they can park free.

There is still a demand for local, convenience stores. Increasingly, the major multiples are trying to fill that gap too: many of them have one or more formats of small stores in town centres. They can pay higher prices for the sites than the independent, and still charge lower prices for the merchandise (at least on some products if not on all).

What have we lost by this mass destruction? Here we have to distinguish between mere nostalgia and real loss. Yes, it is pleasant to be greeted by name, and have one's order anticipated. Certainly, some independent shops offered real expertise and high quality. But many did not. In the affluent suburb of southeast London, where both authors lived at one time, it was possible to buy better bread at any of three supermarkets than in some of the local bakers. The only remaining fishmonger closed, at least as much because it was badly run as because of a lack of custom; it was also impossible to park outside it. Where small shops survive, they are offering something that customers want: specialist knowledge, a particular range, high quality. In France, good, independent specialist shops are thriving even in the face of competition from supposedly rapacious multiples (though legislation does, as we have seen, limit the large stores).

A serious charge is that this process has led to the disappearance of shops from certain areas, notably villages and town centres in some countries. The effect of Wal-Mart on small towns in the USA has been well documented (see for example Ortega 1999). One small retailer after another cannot compete with the out-of-town superstore, and closes. As supermarkets extend the range of their products and services, they force more specialists out of business. The town is hollowed out, with large stores in shopping centres and malls in the suburbs or outside, and nothing is left in the middle. The same has happened in the UK, and to a lesser extent in other developed countries. Only highly restrictive planning and zoning laws have prevented it, although the food and shopping culture also contributes. As the government report (DETR 1998) referred to earlier stated, some town centres remain lively and prosperous even after the supermarket moves out. The size of the hinterland, and energetic town centre management, can overcome the loss of major destination shops.

We must also recognise the impact of other changes in retailing, and in society. In the centre of the small market town where one author grew up, there stood The George hotel and pub, with a dignified eighteenth-century front. In fact, the building was considerably older: a tavern had operated on the site continuously since 1359, and it had been named The George by 1467. It is now a shoe shop, a branch of a national chain. The rest of the main street features charity shops, banks, a few local stores, a Boots and a Woolworths. Although the town has doubled in size, the three cinemas that used to entertain us have all disappeared. There is a large Asda in the shopping mall, and a larger Tesco on the fringe. Most main shopping streets in British towns and cities are populated almost entirely by national multiples; local, independent stores have been driven out by high rents and taxes. We may regret this, but it is the result of economic forces and government policies (or rather lack of any coherent policy), not solely the depredations of supermarkets. The comparison with a country such as France is striking: there, the town centre normally offers a range of specialist shops, including high-quality food retailers of all sorts. This is the result of government actions as well as local food culture. The French government is traditionally more interventionist than many others, and the French population is tolerant of, and even expects, such policies. It is difficult to imagine them in the USA, and we shall have to watch with interest how countries in Central and Eastern Europe, in Asia and elsewhere react to the incursion of multiple retailers.

A particular issue in some countries has been the claim that there are 'food deserts', especially in deprived inner-city areas and some (often equally deprived) rural locations. Supermarkets were accused of shunning such neighbourhoods as unprofitable or too difficult, and there seemed plenty of anecdotal evidence that 'the poor pay more', and that the under-privileged found it more difficult than their better-off peers to buy a healthy diet. Interestingly, the Competition Commission found no evidence of this phenomenon in Britain. 'In fact, the proliferation of supermarkets was higher in the poorest areas than elsewhere ... Some multiple retailers have also been actively involved in opening up areas that historically offered less good access to the range of products available to consumers elsewhere' (Competition Commission 2000). On this charge, anyway, the supermar-kets can plead innocence.

If supermarkets alone are not the only culprits behind the disappearance of many small independent shops, they must still bear their share of responsibil-ity. As they widen the range of products and services, they compete with more and more local outlets. Their food range is now very wide, and they usually have counters offering (or, critics would say, simulating) the craft skills of butchers, fishmongers, delicatessens, and what the French call *traiteurs* – preparers of fresh dishes. Their non-food ranges cover not only clothing, elec-trical goods, videos, and books, but also a huge assortment of other goods and services (see Text Box 9.2). As one critic put it:

> There is not a provider of goods and services whose business our large supermarkets aren't after. The newsagent, the florist, the garden centre, the chemist [pharmacist], the bookshop, the beautician, the off-licence [liquor store], the dry cleaner, the health food shop – any retail outlet, independent or chain, is fair game. Our largest supermarket chains have become multi-tasking retail monsters with voracious appetites, looking for larger and larger stores to accommodate a higher proportion of non-grocery items. The sky is the limit. (Blythman 2004 p. 294)

BOX 9.2

PRODUCTS AND SERVICES IN A LARGE SUPERMARKET

- ► Marriages
- ► Birth registration
- ► Mortgages
- ► Insurance (pet, car, house, travel, life)
- ► Post office
- ► Wills
- ► Internet service
- ► Flu jabs and other medical services

► Eye testing, spectacles
► Nail bar
► Nutritional advice
► Alcoholic drinks
► Coffee bar
► Newspapers and magazines
► Banking
► Crèche
► Bureau de change
► Flowers and plants
► Videos
► Jewellery
► Food supplements
► Books
► Hairdressing
► Garden equipment
► Tools
► Carwash
► Photo development
► Dry cleaning
► Domestic phone services
► Kiosks for downloading music
► Cigarettes
► Electricity and gas provision
► Travel agent
► Stamps
► Paint
► Key cutting
► Glass hire
► Body mass index testing
► Petrol

Source: adapted from Blythman 2004 pp. 294–5

As the hypermarkets and supercenters spread, they will endanger an ever-wider group of specialist local stores, the friendly shops that give colour and individuality to an area. They have to: it is in their business model, their DNA, to grow at all costs. Although in an expanding economy, growth need not be a zero-sum game, in which one winner necessarily means equivalent losers, the trend is inevitable. Supermarket chains will grow at the expense of local independents.

Should we be bothered about this? Supporters of supermarkets argue that they bring efficiency, and that that is good for everyone. McKinsey even claimed that the British economy would be more efficient if planning laws were relaxed, so that large chains could put even more small, relatively inefficient retailers out of business (McKinsey 1998). If we counter that this will lead to a reduction of consumer choice, such critics say that consumers are choosing – and they are choosing the supermarkets. Most shoppers like what the chains offer. The very detailed analysis of the industry in Britain carried out by the Competition Commission found:

> A high degree of consumer satisfaction with the supermarkets' grocery offer. In terms of overall value for money, 24 per cent of respondents rated their regular supermarket as 'excellent' and 57 per cent as 'good'. [A]n 'excellent' or 'good' rating was given by 90 per cent for ... quality, 89 per cent for its product range and 86 percent for its service (Competition Commission 2000).

It is hard to dismiss such evidence, and it seems likely that similar satisfaction levels can be found in other countries.

Are shoppers idiots? Some critics seem to think so, arguing that supermarkets are fooling us with clever ruses. They pretend to offer what we want to buy, but actually, they are stocking what they want to sell. This will hold only for countries with a weak food culture. Where food is seen as an important, indeed central part of life, spending time and money on high-quality produce is worthwhile, and normal. Retailers therefore have to respond to the demand, and cannot get away with substandard offerings. France typically stands for such a culture; so could Japan. In countries with a weak food culture, shoppers cannot discriminate between good and poor quality in food, so they will accept what they are offered as long as it looks attractive. Britain can stand for such a culture (although anyone older than 40 has seen a huge, and mainly beneficial, change in the food bought and served there). There are many other countries with a similar culture, including the USA.

Is it supermarkets' fault? The chains themselves would say that they have done a lot to educate consumers about the various product ranges, with helpful labelling, shelf cards and recipes. The determined critic will have none of it. 'These kindergarten classification schemes make no attempt to educate or really inform consumers about the tastes or properties of food' (Blythman 2004 p. 43). This seems rather akin to expecting schools to instil discipline in children, when the parents do not. Only consumers can learn about the tastes and properties of food, and ideally, they should start doing so at home, as children.

There is a certain chicken-and-egg aspect of the food quality question. Do consumers not know much about food because supermarkets offer them only a narrow range, or do supermarkets offer a narrow range because that is all that shoppers will buy? The argument rages especially fiercely about fresh produce. Critics, and some suppliers, claim that the chains will buy only certain varieties that fit their demands – and these demands are more about shelf life, handling and appearance than about flavour. Apples are a good example: suppliers and campaigners constantly complain that only apples that are uniform in size, shape and colour are acceptable to supermarket buyers, and this means that many traditional varieties are dying out. Tomatoes, too, have little or no flavour, but they are round, red, and the 'right' size.

These problems are exacerbated by year-round availability. Outside a few favoured climate zones, most fresh produce has seasons – but in a modern supermarket, almost everything is on the shelves twelve months a year. Buyers follow supply round the world, so fruit and vegetables may come from Europe, Africa, the Middle East, Australia and New Zealand, South or Central America, and so on. There are two problems with this: flavour, and environmental damage. On flavour, many out-of-season products may look good, but totally lack flavour, mainly because they have to be harvested unripe to survive the journey and repeated handling. The environment is harmed because of the 'food miles' that they travel, burning fossil fuels on the way. Have supermarkets responded to consumer demand in Europe and America for strawberries in December, or have they made us used to the fact that they are available? The stores make more profit this way than by selling only the produce that is locally in season – but we do not have to buy it.

This is not a new criticism. We find it expressed in a surprising source:

> The bourgeoisie has, through its exploitation of the world market, given a cosmopolitan character to production and consumption in every country. In place of the old wants, satisfied by the production of the country, we find new wants, requiring for their satisfaction the products of distant lands and climes. It creates a world after its own image ... constant revolutionising of production, uninterrupted disturbance of all social conditions, everlasting uncertainty and agitation distinguish the bourgeois epoch from all other ones. All fixed, fast-frozen relations are swept away. All new-formed ones become antiquated before they can ossify; all that is solid melted into air.'

Karl Marx wrote this in the Communist Manifesto in 1848; perhaps we are not as different as we think.

On the matter of healthy eating and obesity, we also have a balanced argument. There is no question about the scale of the problem. Obesity is a huge health issue in the USA, closely followed by Great Britain and other western countries. Even those areas of the developing world where a healthy diet traditionally prevailed show signs of following the trend, as soon as western foods become available there (Lang 2003). There are explanations for this apart from food: lack of exercise is the main culprit, but this may be due to safety fears (justified or not), the attractions of computer games and the Internet, the car culture, and schools cutting down on organised sport. On the intake side, some suggest that evolutionary pressures from our hunter-gatherer days make us inclined to consume large quantities of fat and sugar whenever they are available; manufacturers and supermarkets make sure that they are always available and prominently displayed.

Whatever the reasons, the western world has a problem with obesity, and it is exporting it to healthier cultures. Food manufacturers have come under attack, as it is they who mainly supply the processed foods rich in fat, sugar and salt that are the contemporary villains. Supermarkets, on the other hand, have a major say in what is produced, and total control of what is put on the shelves. In a typical British supermarket, a whole display will be devoted to crisps (potato chips). Not only that, the only size available is the giant multi-pack: if you want one or two bags of crisps, you have to buy the whole pack. Demand or supply?

Chilled, prepared food and 'meal solutions' have been one of the growth areas for supermarkets; led by Marks & Spencer and followed closely by British supermarkets, these developments are spreading rapidly to other countries. They meet a need, strongly felt by some sections of the population. They are profitable for the stores. What is the problem?

> Supermarkets have played a major role in this [the 'elimination of domestic cooking in Britain'], providing the means by which the UK has become a 'can't cook won't cook' nation whose idea of a gourmet night is eating a supermarket ready meal on a tray while watching a procession of celebrity chefs cook fantasy food on TV. (Blythman 2004 p. 52)

Many American readers will recognise the jibe, although there, much of the non-cooking is food bought in cheap restaurants and fast food outlets.

There is a paradox here. Never has so much information on healthy eating and the benefits of exercise been so ardently propagated by governments and the media. Supermarkets would argue that they make all the ingredients of a healthy diet easily available. Yet the problem persists, and supermarkets are blamed for contributing to it. The criticism is justified if the food sold is not only unhealthy, but its unhealthiness is also hidden from consumers. The difference between home-cooked and shop-bought food often comes down to additives, and the problem for consumers is deciphering what these actually are. The label must list ingredients, but a prepared meal may list between 20 and 30 of them, and many are called things like 'disodium diphosphate', or 'mono- and di-glycerides of fatty acids'. These may be healthy or unhealthy: we do not know. The fact that some of these dishes look and taste good does not necessarily mean that they deliver the same nutritional value as the home-cooked equivalent. The supermarkets must take responsibility for these products, because, although they do not make them, they decide on their exact specifications. In their competitive battle, the chains have tried to make the dishes more authentic, and they use endorsements from well-known chefs. But we suspect that considerations of shelf life are as important as quality of ingredients, and that too much effort is devoted to food-processing factors such as 'mouth-feel' and perceived flavour. We must acknowledge that safety is paramount, which accounts for the preservatives, but the products remain, in the end, artificial.

The free-market line is, of course, that it is up to consumers to choose: they can buy fresh, healthy food to cook for themselves, or prepared dishes, according to their needs and preferences. Supermarkets are neither charities nor healthcare organisations. If people want fatty, salty, sugary foods, they can buy them. If one supermarket chain did not stock them, their rivals would, so they all have to. As the obesity and healthy eating debate comes more to the fore, as it must, the stores may have to take a more careful line.

When it comes to the other side of the chain, the suppliers, supermarkets have also come in for some stick. Their model is based on economies of scale and bargaining power; naturally, they try to extract the best possible deal from all their suppliers, as any business does. The problem arises where industry concentration rises to such a level that just a few chains control the majority of the market. This is true of many countries in northern Europe, and others such as Australia; more countries seem likely to follow. The USA is much less concentrated at present, but that is changing as consolidation proceeds; there are also regional patterns of concentration.

We argued in our previous book (Seth and Randall 2001) that supermarkets in Britain constitute a complex oligopoly, and a similar oligopsony, that is they form the next best (or worst) thing to a monopoly as both buyers and sellers. This situation is reproduced in many countries. Consumers can buy from only a handful of chains; and suppliers can supply to only a few buyers. It is no exaggeration to say that any supplier wanting to reach a significant level of sales beyond the purely local has to sell to the supermarkets. We need to waste little sympathy on the huge multinationals – the Procter & Gambles, Nestlés and Unilevers of this world; they complain about their treatment at the hands of supermarkets (see Text Box 9.3), but they should be capable of looking after themselves. There is a possible danger that, because so much of brand owners' time and marketing budget is devoted to the retailers, investment in brands and innovation will suffer. There might then be a general loss to the public.

BOX 9.3

CAN THE BRAND SURVIVE?

There is much anxiety in the boardrooms of European marketing companies these days. For many years these leviathans, most of them internationally strong, and basing their business on fast-moving consumer goods (fmcg), have had things very much their own way. Most are household names – Procter & Gamble, Nestlé, Unilever, Heinz, General Foods – and all must sell their brands through the big supermarkets. That is the source of their single biggest collective problem, and resulting anxiety. The balance of power, which has long been shifting steadily against them in favour of the retailer, has now shifted gear and pace. The global coverage many retailers have has put new pressure into their cost/price negotiations – international pressure, the need to have a global brand's cost and prices comparable across national boundaries to satisfy the retailer's buying requirements. Since retailers themselves have to deal with internal pricing pressure – from hard discounters mostly – there is high tension in the entire system. This tension is hurting the European brand owner.

The same pressures now affect the USA, although at a less advanced stage since only Wal-Mart has effective national US coverage. American brand owners have therefore begun to take pre-emptive action, on a global basis, starting, unsurprisingly since they are the most international, with Procter & Gamble. Noting the rise of the discounter phenomenon in the US, primarily with Wal-Mart, and in Europe, with Aldi and Lidl most prominently, P&G decided to cut prices to the retail trade across its brand range. Its rationale was to inhibit the discounter's ability to grow share on the trade's own cheaper – discount – brands. P&G knows and well understands the significance of discounters from its US experience. It was probably first to appreciate the strength of an emerging Wal-Mart, and one of the earliest to locate its own supplier teams at Wal-Mart's Bentonville HQ. Relationships between Wal-Mart and P&G, while no doubt always tough and combative, resulted in both parties to the negotiations doing well over the long term. P&G now puts one third or more of its US brand volume through Wal-Mart, and their strong brands – Tide, Downy, Pampers – have maintained positive momentum there. The dramatic and unexpected announcement in February 2005 that P&G would take over Gillette underscored the central strategic importance of the supplier–retailer relationship. One of the major reasons for the merger is to give greater leverage in negotiating with the trade, notably Wal-Mart: the new entity will have 21 brands with global sales of over $1 billion. If these two giants of consumer goods feel the need to defend themselves against retailer power in this way, what must all the smaller companies be thinking?

Interestingly, however, the big losers from the P&G price changes have not (yet) been the targeted European discounters, but European brand competitors to P&G in its product markets. Unilever, who have for long funded a weak foods portfolio through a strong household and personal business, where it competed effectively with P&G, found its margins collapsing and this strategy increasingly unworkable. Colgate, after 23 years of unbroken profits growth, finally succumbed to a profits warning on its international business. Germany's Henkel made big workforce cuts, affected by the same margin decline in markets where it competes with P&G. Each of these companies now faces the twin problems of strong retail competition, alongside an international market leader in their branded market who is taking a decisive pricing and margin stance. It is an unhappy conjunction of events for all of them.

Hence the question – can the brand survive? The strongest brands will have nothing to fear. P&G accompanied its announcement of lower trade prices with an assurance that it planned increased brand investment on its key brand properties – in the US, Tide and Downy were mentioned. P&G know that without its key brands, it has no competitive advantage. Its brand competitors are in exactly the same boat. Many, particularly companies whose strength is primarily European, face huge dilemmas, since there the trade balance is fundamentally weighted against them, even before discounters began to win market share. In some product fields, brand manufacturers allow the trade to wrest innovation initiative away. Specifically in foods, retailers have big market shares, gained from branded foods companies who can be accused of inertia as they supinely allowed the brand development role to be taken over by hungrier retailers. Strategic change, psychological re-equipping on a major scale, is needed if these manufacturers are to re-acquire lost skills and survive what is now ruthless and international challenge to their expertise and will to live.

Retail power, coupled with a winnowing of branded competition – as P&G may now be engineering globally – are big issues for fmcg companies. Their job was, in any event, not easy, given the increased demands of consumers and governments for new levels of product delivery in advanced European markets – the UK, France and Germany. In the food markets for example, there is now major demand for healthier eating, which has revised brand portfolios substantially. Obesity has become a pressing government, as well as a consumer, concern. Ingredients are increasingly under scrutiny and require the fullest disclosure and manufacturer defence. Technology faces diminishing returns as a prime tool in R&D-based innovation. In any case, scientifically based progress can be rejected out of hand by consumer movements with powerful social agendas seeking new levels of individualist independence in decision making – GM foods would be one example that has made foods brand development a virtual minefield.

American companies should not think they are in the clear. Anti-American sentiment (noted earlier in this chapter) is growing and threatens some of the great global icons – Coca-Cola, for example, probably the world's most inclusive brand. McDonald's is heavily influenced by the consumerist and government pressures, noted above, on health and obesity. Long-run patterns of growth and expansion of these American powerhouses have been interrupted, some might say permanently and for the better. Certainly, these companies are making, and must persist with, big changes to product and presentation; such changes themselves generate more inherent risk to their established brands.

One thing is sure: the 21st century brand owner will not have an easy life!

The real issue is with smaller suppliers, who complain vociferously of a variety of bad practices. The difficulty is that these complaints are rarely or never voiced openly. Such is the chains' power – almost the power of commercial life or death – that no one dares to speak openly. The Competition Commission, in its very thorough investigation in Britain, mentioned a climate of fear. The Commission identified 27 practices of the chains that could operate against the public interest, and recommended a Code of Practice to regulate future dealings. The headings of the proposed code suggest clearly the nature of the hidden complaints (see Text Box 9.4). The code was drawn up, but the doubts of sceptics seemed to be confirmed when the Office of Fair Trading (OFT) felt the need to carry out a review of the operation of the code in 2003–4. Its conclusions demonstrate that, essentially, nothing has changed. There had been no formal complaint within the code, and no request for mediation. Many organisations approached by the OFT did not reply, and those that did were unwilling to provide any detailed evidence of breaches of the code. Those associations and firms that replied thought that the code had not brought about any change in the behaviour of supermarkets at all; some thought that the situation was worse. The OFT had encouraged trade associations to build up dossiers of alleged breaches of the code, but none had done so (Office of Fair Trading 2004).

BOX 9.4

COVERAGE OF THE PROPOSED CODE OF PRACTICE

(a) Retailers should ensure that the standard terms on which they do business are in writing and are made available to suppliers.

(b) If retailers wish to vary those terms, reasonable notice should be given to suppliers.

(c) Retailers should pay suppliers within the time specified in the agreement, and in any event within a reasonable time after the date of the invoice.

(d) Retailers should give suppliers reasonable notice of any intention to change a price previously agreed, and should not request retrospectively any form of discount or overrider, nor seek a change of price to match the price offered by a competing retailer.

(e) Retailers should not request suppliers to contribute to retailers' costs of buyers' visits, or to contribute to retailers' costs of artwork and packaging design, consumer or market research, to the costs of store refurbishment or opening, or to provide hospitality.

(f) Retailers should not seek any form of compensation for profits being less than expected, whether on a promotion or otherwise, or for product wastage.

(g) Where retailers change any volume ordered, or the specification of any goods, or introduce any changes to any supply chain procedure, they should give reasonable notice ... and should compensate suppliers for any costs or losses to them where reasonable notice is not given.

(h) Retailers should compensate suppliers for costs caused through the retailers' forecasting errors.

(i) Retailers should give suppliers reasonable notice of any intention to hold a promotion in relation to the suppliers' products where there is likely to be a significant impact on suppliers' costs; they should not over-order goods at a promotional price; and they should not require suppliers predominantly to fund promotions.

(j) Retailers should not seek payment or better terms as a condition of stocking or listing existing products, or for better positioning of any products within a store, or for increasing shelf space.

(k) Retailers should not charge suppliers in respect of consumer complaints unless the complaint has been verified as justified, and as being caused by the supplier, and the supplier has been notified of the outcome; charges should not exceed the purchase cost of the goods to the retailer.

(l) Retailers should not require suppliers to use particular third party suppliers of goods and services where the retailer receives a payment from that third party supplier in respect of that requirement.

Source: Competition Commission 2000

Overall, the report confirmed the finding of an earlier Competition Commission report, that 'there remained a fundamental imbalance of negotiating strength between supermarkets and most of their suppliers'.

Because of the climate of fear, the OFT recognised that no implementation of the code, or its enforcement, would be possible until suppliers were ready to give detailed, specific allegations that the supermarkets could have a chance to refute. As the OFT noted, with some apparent frustration, 'the ongoing climate of apprehension among suppliers would seem to preclude them as a source of the necessary information'. The OFT therefore decided to conduct its own audit directly on the supermarkets. The audit concentrated on the clauses of the code for which complaints are most frequent: payment times; retrospective reductions in price during the period of a contract; supplier contributions to marketing costs (whether or not ostensibly of the supplier's own volition); lump-sum payments as a condition of supply; payments in respect of consumer complaints; and tying of third party goods/services (this refers to the practice of insisting that the supplier uses, for example, a particular supplier of packaging, from whom the supermarket may expect a kickback).

The OFT finally reported in March 2005, some three months late. Its conclusions were that it could find no firm evidence of improper practices by the supermarkets, except a few minor examples. It recommended that suppliers insist on written contracts, and use the complaints procedures to produce real evidence if alleged breaches occurred. This seems naïve in the extreme: the whole problem is that suppliers feel powerless against the retailers' ability to de-list them.

The retailers' replies are bland: they 'have told us that they are committed to the code and that relations with their suppliers are generally good'. According to retail analyst Robert Clark, there is indeed some evidence that this is true, and that in practice, many small suppliers are perfectly happy with their relationship. There does seem to have been a change in the big retailers' behaviour, and the worst abuses may be in the past. Much of this is due to the retailers' need to differentiate themselves, and therefore to work closely with suppliers to develop a distinctive offer. There will, of course, always be tension and hard negotiation.

The fear of suppliers in the new countries into which the chains are spreading must be that the big retailers will bring their culture and tactics with them. The suppliers will mainly be local and relatively small, so they will eventually suffer the same fate as those in Britain when the supermarkets' power is sufficiently large, unless governments take action. The situation in Britain suggests that it is extremely hard to regulate such relationships. As long as the supermarkets can show that they are efficient, and provide a service that customers want at competitive prices, then they will be hard to challenge. That they will change their spots of their own volition seems doubtful.

To sum up the societal impact of the big international retailers is difficult, when the situation is complex and nuanced. Our subjects are impressive businesses of world class; they run very efficient operations, and provide a service that millions of consumers use and mainly appreciate. They are part of economic and social changes that have adverse impacts on society: destruction of small shops, hollowing out of town centres, reduction of choice, increase in consumption of fossil fuels. They use tactics in dealing with suppliers that are not acceptable as a responsible way of behaving. Unless firmly regulated, and that in itself is difficult, they will continue to behave in ways that deliver profitable growth to them, whomever else it harms.

10 Strategic Options for Local Retailers

Many successful food retailers have not ventured abroad. They may have made a conscious decision that this is the right strategy for them, or they may simply not have got round to it yet. In a large country such as the USA, it is possible to grow to a significant size within the boundaries of the country. In other, medium-sized countries, such as France, firms such as Leclerc can develop a strong domestic business. The question for all these is, how will they be able to compete against rivals who have international scale and learning?

Starting with the Americans, and their three significant, 'semi-national' competitors, all three would find themselves by size among the top ten retailers of food in the world, Kroger being nearest the top, ranking below Carrefour but above Tesco. This would imply that, collectively if not individually, they would have a great deal to say about the future of world retailing – but for the moment, they do not. Their problems with survival at home are demanding. 'Choosing a differentiated strategy is proving to be very difficult' said Deutsche Bank (March 2003); to a large extent they appear to be stuck in the middle between specialised stores, eating 'to go', and the rollercoaster discount phenomenon led by Wal-Mart, which has swallowed a big chunk of the supermarkets' profitability and all their current growth. There is little prospect of any of Kroger, Albertson or Safeway seriously considering international strategy in the near future – most of the traffic has indeed, with the exception of Wal-Mart, been in the other direction. Their shareholders would not stand for it, and the likely outcome would be a further weakening of the domestic business, leading then to questions of survival. There has been a pattern of US retail failures in recent years: Kmart (treated separately in Chapter 2) and Winn-Dixie, now slowly recovering, are two prominent examples. The US market is consolidating, but simultaneously, still fragmenting, the key influence being the ever-present threat from Wal-Mart's cost reduction and share growth – 'the Wal-Martisation of everything' was a recent *Financial Times* description. While these trends continue, which they should for some years ahead, we can afford to ignore any breakout by the US supermarket leaders into global trading. It is unusual to find a big global market much more susceptible to European influence than to the US, but here it is, and the trend should continue.

It is a paradox that the American market appears to be highly competitive – it is heavily over-shopped compared with most other countries – but most of the large chains have spent much of their life in rather cosy, regional near-monopolies. One Europe-based American analyst, in a private communication to the authors, commented that these retailers would not dare to venture abroad, as they would be eaten alive by the competition. Their challenge, one to be shared by many firms in other countries over the next few years, is how to live with Wal-Mart. The strikes in California, provoked by Safeway's and Kroger's attempts to cut labour costs to meet the threat of Wal-Mart's imminent entry, shows how they see the danger.

While it is clearly essential to lower costs where possible (but why had they not done so before?), that will never be enough. A strategy of taking on Wal-Mart on price is doomed to fail, as the giant will always be cheaper when it wants to be: given its scale and efficiency, its costs will be lower, and its whole promise is based on low price. Specialist retailers, such as bicycle shops, may be able to focus on the niche of enthusiasts, with wider and deeper ranges. This is harder for food retailers – and they are one of the types of stores to suffer most from the entry of Wal-Mart (Stone 1995).

However, Wal-Mart aims to have the lowest prices only on some 1200–1500 items (about one per cent of the total), and these are the known value items (KVIs). Rivals cannot and should not compete head-on with these, but should aim to stay within sight (say ten per cent). On other, less sensitive products, they may target selected items and promote lower-than-Wal-Mart prices.

Aside from pricing, firms must differentiate themselves in some way. This might include catering to local tastes better than the giant leader, or highlighting a high-quality fresh meat counter or delicatessen. An excellent example is H-E-B.

The Butt family business started in Texas in 1905 with one store. When Clarence's son Howard E took over, the company became HE Butt, and now trades as H-E-B. It is still a private company, and still run by a Butt. It has stayed almost entirely in Texas, with a step over the border to Mexico. Sales are over $10 billion from its 300 stores, and the company has won many awards, as a retailer and for its humanitarian efforts (HE Butt was a Baptist and a Mason, a strict teetotaller and non-smoker). H-E-B has managed to adapt to changing tastes and pressures, adopting new technology and new formats.

The firm competing across the board with Wal-Mart that has done best is Target. Where Kmart has comprehensively failed, Target has succeeded. Although a full-range discounter like Wal-Mart, it has differentiated itself as cheap but chic. Although the parent company is much older, the first Target store opened in 1962 (the *annus mirabilis* of retailing). It has always lived in the shadow of Wal-Mart, and saw that competing head-on was useless. It does compete on many prices, but adds to that appeal some fashionable ranges in clothing and home wares (some jokingly pronounce its name as if it were French – Tar-zhay). In an example of its marketing flair, it opened a temporary boutique showcasing the designer Isaac Mizrahi's collection in Manhattan: '*fashionistas* crammed the store for a chance to snatch up the affordable, trendy styles' (*Financial Times* 3 January 2005).

So successful is this strategy that the company has sold off its department store chains, to concentrate on Target alone. Although it may eventually look overseas, for the present it sees ample opportunities for expansion at home; Bob Ulrich, chairman and chief executive, thinks that Target can at least double sales in the US, and so has no international ambitions. This must be good news for local retailers in other countries, giving them scope to learn from and apply Target's lessons in their own territory before the original arrives to overwhelm them.

Another example, close to home, is Loblaws, the largest food retailer in Canada. Its best-known differentiator is President's Choice, a top-end own-label brand launched in the early 1990s. Mike Nichol, the president of Loblaws, had visited the UK with his wife, and had been impressed by the high-quality own-label lines developed by Marks & Spencer – a then-unusual example of retailing innovation crossing the Atlantic from east to west. President's Choice positioned itself as offering top quality at reasonable prices, and Mike Nichol personalised it by appearing in the advertising – a risky strategy, perhaps, but one that is harder for rivals to imitate.

Loblaws recognised that this was not enough, and copied Wal-Mart's determined focus on supply-chain efficiency as part of their three-part strategy of innovation, market domination and cost reduction. They also continued to expand their product range, and struck up strategic alliances with service companies such as coffee shops, fitness studios, photo marts and wine shops to offer one-stop shopping within a Loblaws' atmosphere (Moore and Caney 2003). The company had anticipated Wal-Mart's arrival in Canada, so were prepared for it in 1994. Loblaws' advantages were its identification as Canadian, and its differentiation (through its products, alliances, music, store design and general atmosphere). It has continued to try to differentiate itself through its unrivalled knowledge of its local market, enhanced by its use of customer data from its President's Choice Financial Credit Card which allows it to identify spending patterns, and product and price preferences (compare, say, Tesco).

On pricing, Loblaws uses a hybrid of EDLP on 500 or so frequently bought items, and high–low pricing on the rest. The use of relatively high-margin own-label products allows it to be very competitive on some lines without damaging its overall profitability. It knows it must carry on squeezing out costs from the supply chain, and continue to differentiate itself, but it has shown that these, based on a deep understanding of its customers, means that it can compete successfully even against the 'American behemoth' (Moore and Caney 2003). There are lessons here for retailers everywhere: be prepared, screw down costs where possible, know your local customers better than the competitors, and differentiate.

In the USA, the majors are getting their act together, but it is hard to be impressed with them so far. Although Wal-Mart has only some 8 per cent of total retail sales, it is still gigantic, and threatening. It feels it has plenty of room for manoeuvre in opening up new stores, and is confident of beating any existing competition – and with the few exceptions such as H-E-B, Wegmans, Hannafords, Stop 'n Shop and Cub Stores, they are right. The examples of H-E-B and Loblaws show what has to be done, and the Krogers, Albertsons and Safeways need to be single-minded in their determination to survive. Some further consolidation is likely, but a merger or acquisition will not solve any of the big three's strategic problems, and may distract them from the laser focus on essentials they need.

When we look at other countries, we know that Wal-Mart is present in some, but not yet dominant. We can distinguish between those in which large multiple retailers already control most of the market (such as Western Europe) and those where their shares are still fairly small (China and many emergent economies). The situation in France is almost a reversal of the small local versus the big international. The market is regarded as a protected one, as laws prevent many new large stores opening, and there has been a law controlling predatory pricing. The leader, and international pioneer Carrefour, seemed to have an unassailable position, but in fact this has come under attack in the last year from its domestic rivals. The nature of the attack is quite simple – price. Both its second-place competitor Leclerc, and hard discounters including Aldi and Casino's LeaderPrice have launched an all-out assault, and Carrefour has begun to look vulnerable. Its international spread has been of little help, and may even have been a hindrance if concentration on expansion overseas took its attention away from its home base.

Germany, too, has seen the big international operator struggling, in this case the mighty Wal-Mart itself. Again, with new store expansion difficult or impossible, a determined low-price attack is difficult to fight off. In this case, although Wal-Mart is itself a low-price operator, the hard discounters such as Aldi and Lidl undercut it, especially as it does not have sufficient scale and will find it hard to acquire it. Aldi, described elsewhere, is clearly happy with its successful formula, and will not need to change it to compete with new entrants.

The other big European market, Great Britain, is similar in some ways (dominance by a few chains, new store building hamstrung by regulations), but more typically British in others. The two leading supermarket firms, Tesco and Wal-Mart's Asda, are battling it out on a low-price, full-range platform, with Tesco increasing its lead. Waitrose and Marks & Spencer have claimed niche segments, offering perceptibly better quality at slightly higher prices. As long as Waitrose stay within their segment, they offer a model of how to compete with the biggest, but it is not a strategy that can be extended to a mass market. In every country, however, there will be a niche for a Waitrose-like operator, so there are opportunities waiting in many markets.

Finally Sainsbury's – another story of rapid and seemingly inexplicable decline. One of the earliest international players, the UK market-leading Sainsbury company, bought US Shaw's supermarkets in Connecticut in 1983. Shaw's, no longer owned by Sainsbury's, is still trading successfully, However Sainsbury's, for many years, the doyen of the UK market, started falling apart in the latter years of the 1980s, and fifteen years later has forfeited first and now second position in its home market to Tesco and Wal-Mart (Asda). It seems possible that Morrison may soon overtake, pushing

Sainsbury further back into fourth place. As a result of the decline, (see Text Boxes 4.1 and 4.2) it is simply not credible to regard Sainsbury as an international force ahead or a rival for the leaders at home. The ground to be recaptured is too much and the starting position – Sainsbury profits have collapsed in the year to May 2005 – far too precarious. This is a sad verdict on a once great company with major international aspirations. Even today, its size and occasionally strong operational characteristics – good store sites, high footfall, and worthwhile innovations, for example banking – might suggest that turnaround is feasible. But until the sales decline, share loss and poor store performance can be arrested, the company is best ignored, and the sensible verdict is that, whatever happens to the UK business, like Ahold, Sainsbury's days of local dominance and international aspiration are long gone. The lesson is the one that no business dare forget: 'the world changed, and we didn't'.

Japan is a special case among developed nations. Its leading manufacturers such as Toyota and Sony are world-beaters, super-efficient and innovative. The distribution system, on the other hand, is notoriously complex, expensive and difficult to penetrate. Consumers are famously demanding, seeking high quality and presentation, even at high prices. Many retail entrants have failed there, and Carrefour has recently admitted defeat, withdrawing after four years. Wal-Mart has entered the market, but slowly and cautiously through a stake in Seiyu. This was the fifth-largest supermarket chain, but had over-expanded in the 1980s, and was left with large debts and little free cash. Wal-Mart has experienced resistance from consumers to its early attempts to impose EDLP, since the consumers associate low prices with low quality. The American firm is clearly determined to learn, and to proceed step by step.

The most innovative and aggressive local retailer is Aeon (368 stores, $25.8 billion sales). Its reactions to the imminent and now present threat have been interesting. The first thing it did was to send what became hundreds of its staff to study Wal-Mart stores in the USA, Korea and China. It is open about being ready to learn from, even to copy, Wal-Mart techniques and formats. Its new Jusco stores look very like Wal-Mart supercenters, and borrow some of its display tricks, such as showing clothes on hangers instead of folded. It has opened three supercenters, and plans to open 27 more in the next three years. Aeon has also begun to move away from the complicated, multi-layered Japanese distribution by buying direct. It thinks that it can compete by beating Wal-Mart at its own game, by learning from it and adding its own local knowledge of customer tastes.

Ito-Yokado, the biggest supermarket chain, is taking the opposite tack. It believes that land prices in Japan are simply too high to make supercenters a feasible proposition. Instead, it is sticking to its principles, for example by maintaining high staff levels to keep shelves stocked and check-out queues short: 'Ito-Yokado isn't offering everyday low prices. It's offering higher quality' said Yoshinobu Naito, an Ito-Yokado board member (Fackler and Zimmerman 2003). One trick it has borrowed is to run a 'Made in Japan' campaign, as Wal-Mart ran a 'Buy American' drive.

There is no doubt that some aspects of Japan's retailing industry will have to change, notably its supply chain. Beyond that, it is hard to predict which of the two models of resistance, Aeon's or Ito-Yokado's, will prevail, or how much Wal-Mart will have to adapt its cookie-cutter approach.

Outside the very concentrated countries, most markets are fragmented. There is occasionally a dominant player – CBD in Brazil, E-Mart in South Korea – but otherwise a share of over 10 per cent is rare, and figures under 5 per cent more common. These markets remain to be organised, and at present, it is the foreign challengers who are most likely to do that, as Carrefour did in South America from the 1970s to the 90s. The international players have the know-how and skills, and, with local partners, can acquire local knowledge. One choice for the local incumbents, therefore, is to lie back and enjoy it: sell out to the invader. Proprietors can then decide whether to take the money and run, or join in to learn and help to apply the new knowledge. A joint venture may be an especially attractive option, as that gives the opportunity to learn, with a possible chance to take over the business if the foreign partner decides to exit. It is a well-established pattern in foreign alliances that one partner ends up dominating; if local conditions are difficult enough for the foreign entrant, the local may well win the endgame for control. China has seen many of these outcomes, although not yet in food retail.

Those opting to stay and fight as an independent need first to capitalise on their unique asset – local knowledge. Jollibee saw off the then all-conquering McDonald's in the Philippines using this strength, and grocers can do it too. They will, in addition, have to gain new skills to stay ahead of these new and different competitors. The resources of the mainly very small local companies may not be enough on their own, so some form of combination looks desirable. Voluntary symbol chains on the pattern of those in Western Europe could be attractive, but would almost certainly involve inviting in expertise from the existing symbol chains, as the locals would not possess it themselves. How acceptable and workable such an arrangement would be must depend on local culture: in many of the societies, businesses are strongly family-based, and family loyalties may prevent such close cooperation. Merger and acquisition are not well developed, but that is another obvious avenue to explore; the foreign entrants will be using that tool, so why not pre-empt them by doing it yourself?

Incumbents can gain knowledge in other ways. Study abroad is a traditional route. Sending bright young members of the family to work for a foreign company is one obvious method. The higher up the management ladder these emissaries can go, the better. While technical knowledge is essential, soft data on management culture, styles and tactics are also valuable – 'know your enemy'. Preparation is the key: knowing what new entrants are likely to try to do, what their strengths and weaknesses are – the weaknesses in particular. Then plan on how to survive and win.

Any local company has to use to the full its priceless local knowledge, not only of consumers, but also of suppliers, and other players such as banks and governments. These are the things that entrants find most difficult, and they make mistakes in their early days. No one can rely on that, though, and missteps should become less common, so the locals must decide on their strategy. Loblaws should be the model: prepare; build on your strengths; stress your localness; develop a point of differentiation; reduce costs. Above all, do not challenge the invader head-on unless you have very deep pockets and an impregnable defensive position: otherwise only disaster and defeat lie that way. Be better at something that your customers value: probably centring around local foods and dishes, but possibly also ways of packing and displaying products, and level, methods and tone of service. The smart entrants will try to look local, so the real natives must claim and show authenticity, as well as matching at least part of the foreign offer.

11 Strategic Options for International Retailers

While there has been rapid change in perceptions and behaviour by retailers over two decades, and the move to take international positions has accelerated significantly through the 1990s, the fact remains that today, and for that matter tomorrow, food retailing will remain a national, even local industry. It is estimated that under ten per cent of the world market is currently occupied by 'transnational' retailers – those selling outside their national boundaries. The movement to create global retailers has still a very long way to go.

Twenty years ago there had been few signs of movement. In the US, the major companies were beginning to emerge from the legal constraints which had actively set out to prevent companies from adopting even a national profile across the country. Today, no single player other than Wal-Mart has an effective coast-to-coast presence, and even in store-saturated America, Wal-Mart itself believes it has big new territories to occupy, for example in the cities, and is building new stores at an impressive rate, principally massive supercenters.

In Europe, there had been little determined expansion before the strategic change process which Carrefour initiated through the 1980s. With the exception of Carrefour – discussed below – such moves as were made were mostly small and experimental, modest forays, for example by German companies, to expand into Eastern Europe, and some limited position-taking in the Mediterranean by French leaders. Sainsbury's made an early sally into Connecticut with the Shaws acquisition in 1983. Tengelmann of Germany had owned the once-powerful A&P company in the eastern states of the US for some time past. Delhaize, Aldi and Ahold had all put down marker positions with local US acquisitions through the late 1970s – they still seemed principally like learning posts in the mid 1980s. However, Carrefour seemed to have had a coherent, bigger scale and more ambitious vision.

Carrefour, as France's leader, needed to move internationally in order to grow. It was a simple equation for Carrefour and one is tempted to conclude that the company, as well as the French nation, have both gained substantially from the market interference routinely enforced by the government. France retained a strong high street which has more than preserved its leading and high performing food culture. New potential international entrants were pointedly discouraged, as a standard feature of French industrial policy, from viewing France as fertile territory for invasion. Carrefour, well ahead of its competitors, needed to find the territories where it could grow its brand profitably. It was a simple equation for a company that wanted to grow.

Find them, eventually, it did, but not without several false and expensive starts. There were highly visible failures both in the USA, and in the UK, from which the company has retired, so far never to return. However, the leadership achieved far greater success in the apparently less competitive and developed markets of Southern Europe, Latin America, and even Asia. Carrefour spread its net widely and effectively and by the early 1990s had achieved a position where it was operating profitably in three continents, and was no doubt surprised still to have much of the global expansion to itself. But there had been a stirring in the retail dovecotes, and soon Carrefour was to find itself increasingly surrounded by ambitious and active global competitors from both sides of the Atlantic. The 1990s saw the first genuine recognition that food retailing could, perhaps, one day become a global market. Lots of companies, both food manufacturers like Unilever and Nestlé, and the majority of supermarket operators, resisted the process, but the more strategic and energetic performers had begun to think differently.

The case for change had become stronger, through high market concentration in many markets (notably Western Europe), accompanied by a slowing of food-sales growth and segmentation of the market, allowing both specialist retailers as well as the 'eating out' markets to grow strongly, often at the expense of major store food sales (USA and Europe). Legislation, initially confined to France and Germany, has spread and most European markets now have restrictions on sites and growth. In the US, Wal-Mart's expansion has been strongly resisted by individual states and communities, notably Vermont and, latterly, California. International expansion can therefore now be viewed as risk reduction – the capacity of successful but constrained companies to grow more quickly in newer, faster expanding parts of the world.

Through the 1990s a pattern has emerged in many developed markets for a truly dominant and apparently secure market leader to emerge. US Wal-Mart, Carrefour (France), Tesco (UK), Aldi (Germany), Delhaize (Belgium), and Ahold (Netherlands) all fit this bill. Most of these six do not look remotely likely to be dislodged in their respective national markets (except Carrefour, possibly). So strong are their domestic fortresses, that the weakest, Ahold, has held on to unchallenged supremacy in Holland through two years of painful and cataclysmic dismemberment of its global portfolio, unprofitable trading and a collapsed balance sheet. Most of Ahold's pre-crash business was international. Global expansion has in virtually all cases been spearheaded in the most recent period by companies who have been able to rely on a consistent and expanding domestic profits base to fund their global extensions. 'Win at home' is an invariable maxim for global success.

There are now visible positive factors beginning to operate which have accelerated the strategies of the successful players. The importance of scale and the economies it can generate is now significant. Procurement is a crucial area of advantage: Wal-Mart is now sourcing merchandise worth $15 billion from China; Tesco is now doing the same and pursuing differential pricing by manufacturing suppliers across markets in East and West Europe; Carrefour gains significant savings from central buying. This process is still in its early days – there is much more to come as processes are re-examined and cost opportunities recognised, and there will ultimately be just a few global (and retail) winners. Suppliers are treading with consummate delicacy, endeavouring to manage the cost and price changes confronting them, at a speed that preserves historic margins, and does not encourage the more investigative global retailers to move their supply category to the top of the list for harmonisation of cost and pricing. Category management, one of the attractive partnership philosophies of the 1990s has taken on an entirely novel meaning for some of the world's biggest brand supply companies and it is unsurprising that many of the biggest (Nestlé, Kraft, Unilever) have had continuous difficulty in holding brand margins, and maintaining brand support expenditures as these demands have become more insistent. True battle between these titans is now joined.

At the same time, there are other areas where global presence can create cost reduction and margin growth. Capital costs, service procurement, development costs, and finally the application of a coherent management process to companies physically a long way apart, are all legitimate opportunities. Naturally, with this scale of competitive advantage, a rapid recognition by a few strong domestic players of how much there is to go for, and, simultaneously, the 'freezing' of many weaker companies within their existing boundaries, the gap between weak and strong, loser and winner, is becoming more pronounced. International failures are still eminently possible – Ahold overall, Carrefour in the USA, Tesco in France, even the massive Wal-Mart in Germany – but what is more obvious is the total inability of the companies not making a move to create the funding or the strategy to become meaningful international competitors. It is always dangerous to say 'never' but today it is difficult to see many, if any, new global players emerging from the pack. China is big enough to change equations of course but it does look as if the maxim now is 'to them that hath shall be given'. It is a position that must make the leaders of the big three – Wal-Mart, Carrefour and Tesco – sleep better at night.

The size of the global prize is truly enormous. Wal-Mart, already the world's biggest business, has international retail turnover that still represents under 10 per cent of total revenues. What will happen when, instead of a series of halting and indifferent international moves, Wal-Mart collects its energies, applies an effective global strategy, and 'makes things work'? Of course, the conclusion is not inevitable, but the company has the strength, the funds and perhaps, given the stage the market has reached, even the time to get it right. Or take Tesco, who from a much smaller domestic base has successfully occupied a dozen markets, and has as much retail space abroad as it has at home, registering double digit growth both home and away. What happens when Tesco either secures a leading position in South-East Asia's burgeoning food markets, or finds a strategy to enter the US and/or

Western Europe? Or finally, Carrefour. Sitting on a well-protected (though threatened) French base, it too has the same chances beckoning as Tesco, and has time advantage on its side, as well as worthwhile positions in Europe, South America and Asia. The development opportunity is truly mouth-watering, assuming these companies can maintain effective strategies across several continents, and most significantly, deliver a distinctive brand appeal in very different world food markets. As the song says 'we've only just begun....'

The major oil companies operate in more than 150 countries, as does IBM. Unilever and P&G fly the flag in 90. The biggest retail player, Carrefour, today is in around 30, and all its competitors are in many fewer places. Truly, their international presence is still limited and, as their leaders recognise, they are late entrants who need to engage in a comprehensive learning process in order to move from successful national players to true global companies. The way Sam Walton and his successors talk about P&G, or the willingness of Terry Leahy to study Unilever's global management process, emphasises the understanding the best leaders have of their current embryonic place in global business development.

Who are the current winners? Looking at the very different policies adopted by the leading competitors, in sales terms, this is a relatively rich area of study. The recognised 'leading three' do not have much in common and of course, they come from different home bases. We start with Carrefour, who is accepted as the leading international retailer, not only because of its wide international presence, but because of its corporate strategy; it has willingly embraced and become driven by internationalisation over two decades. Undaunted by early failure in two big-scale markets (the US and UK), it pressed on, determined to raise standards and learn from mistakes. It was ready to take on high-risk markets with scale opportunity, and thus has entered Asia, including both Japan and mainland China – where it has been recognised as international leader – and Latin America, again in scale markets including Brazil. It has been flexible in approach, sometimes using acquisition to provide the base, but on other occasions, notably in Asia, setting up new Carrefour stores from scratch, strongly redolent of the home French model – the store in Shanghai's Pudong district looks to the untrained eye like a typical French hypermarket.

One has the impression that Carrefour trusts its model, feels it has stood the test of time, can cross boundaries and therefore that it prefers organic growth to acquisition. However, in Turkey or in Italy, for example, it was prepared to acquire, perhaps regarding this as a low-cost and low-risk move into a well-understood adjacent Mediterranean country, and it has done better than most competitors there. (In fact, there is no sign yet that any of the international players has understood how to extract scale and profits from the idiosyncratic Italian market – 'it may be close but boy is it distinctive', is what they must all be saying to themselves). Meanwhile, given its big unoccupied markets, Carrefour would have to rely on acquisition to enter the USA (many possible targets present themselves), the UK, and Germany (like Italy, next door but a distinctive challenge). It is unlikely to make any of these moves quickly, given its well-known problems at home. In fact, it seems most likely that its international expansion will be curtailed for several years.

Carrefour's early adoption of a global strategy has given it time to experiment and learn. It has been flexible with choice of format and, when it has seemed right, has used a discounter approach, rather than the hypermarket model that gave it home leadership. In some cases, supermarket models have replaced the hyper, but it is unsurprising where the Carrefour preference lies. The historic record is impressive, and Carrefour can list many significant markets where it leads. It entered China almost ten years ago, and so far Carrefour has managed to stay, just, ahead of competition. In Taiwan it has done well, but in South Korea is now being pressured by Tesco. It is not having its own way in Latin America. Its strategy is to move to the big cities where population densities are highest. It intends to lead where it enters a new market and, until the recent moves by Wal-Mart and Tesco, has been virtually unchallenged in this objective. Now its world might be changing, and not for the better – while there is room enough for many more than one global winner in say, China, or even Japan or South Korea, investors are looking carefully to see whose mix of strategy, brand, operating skills and local sensitivity will be the most powerful. Today, Carrefour's performance is under close examination virtually everywhere it is. It has continued to enter new markets, in Europe and Africa, and to increase stores in Asian markets where it is present. It seems to have digested the enormous French Promodès acquisition successfully, thus deepening domestic dominance and affording further margin improvement.

Its absence from America and the UK might, in the short term at least, be an advantage – its ability to grow profitably in places other than these two, where it would be starting for a second time and from scratch, must be greater.

However, in the medium term, and even sooner as the early skirmishes are beginning, particularly in Asia, Carrefour will need to take on the best and be seen to succeed. The present judgement must be that this is not yet proven. For too many years Carrefour has had markets to itself and has only had to take on local competitors, sometimes good ones, but companies without its experience or deep pockets. For a few years ahead, Wal-Mart's necessary preoccupation with US growth, and its apparent clumsiness in managing its entries into Asia, notably Japan, will give Carrefour much needed breathing space. So will the fact that Tesco is barely more than half Carrefour's size and is internationally a small and capital-constrained world retailer. There are however head-to-head confrontations beginning, and if domestic performance is anything to go by, which it must be, both Wal-Mart and Tesco can point to much more impressive recent growth and profit records. Both have global sourcing records and competences visibly better than Carrefour's – Wal-Mart is streets ahead. In some ways this ought to be a surprise, given Carrefour's long time advantage and its resource levels – its international operations at Les Ulis near Paris have more than 500 people managing international trading and marketing, and handling international supplier relationships. Many contracts have been running for more than five years. The Carrefour process is in place, the knowledge must be there, but it is difficult to see anything as dynamic or measurable as Wal-Mart's relentless pursuit of lower cost, notably for its US business, from wherever it comes. There are signs that this has been a complacent international company – something which can happen if one is left on one's own for too long. Carrefour has not made the most of the lead that it built up in the early years, and rivals are catching it up.

Inevitably perhaps, it is in China that Carrefour's future as a great international retailer will be played out. There is no question that apart from moving early (1995) it has taken the market seriously, and worked hard at creating a successful growth strategy in the world's ultimately biggest, but historically most impenetrable, market. Carrefour used local partnerships to create a base, and is therefore already in most of China's top twenty cities. Despite a severe set-back when Chinese authorities stopped the company in its tracks for opening stores without government consent, Carrefour worked to achieve consensus and, permission being granted, is again moving store openings ahead. Today it has 30 branches, still ahead of competition. It has launched a discount chain in Shanghai and other cities. Carrefour has stated ambitious expansion plans, but in truth nobody, so far, has done more than scratch the surface of this country with its huge potential. With both Wal-Mart and Tesco present, the former with a well built infrastructure, and others – Metro, Auchan, Ito-Yokado, Aldi – hungrily prospecting for growth, this is the key battleground. Carrefour has the equipment, the knowledge, and time advantage on its side. However, searching for some unique competitive advantage which Carrefour might possess, it is not immediately obvious where this lies. Time is one essential, but this lead is now rapidly disappearing as competitors start to chase down the same opportunities. Carrefour had ten to fifteen years of strategic advantage – that it used the time well to create a world platform and leadership in several developed markets is not in doubt. But it certainly has not laid down competitive positions, anywhere in the world, that are now viewed as unassailable; even in its home market, which is highly protected, it is threatened. The inescapable conclusion is that Carrefour is now, and for the first time, being tested in the fire, and if it can cope with Wal-Mart and Tesco, not to say half a dozen other future global players, it will have done well, and perhaps surprised itself in the process.

Wal-Mart's approach and model is fundamentally different. Today it is little more than 40 years old. It has become a national phenomenon in the USA, succeeding where all others have failed in creating a country-wide presence. It has been lucky to emerge at a time of steady US market growth, when economic development has been more predictable and linear than that in Western Europe or Asia-Pacific, the other significant triad markets. The US today accounts for around 20 per cent of the world food/grocery market, and it has given Wal-Mart a wonderfully secure growing home urban platform.

For most of 30 years there was simply no real need to think about an international strategy – Wal-Mart ought to have had its hands full, growing at a pace no other US retailer ever consistently matched. Yet founder Sam, and his successors, David Glass and Lee Scott, were clear that their formula had the potential, and indeed the right, to travel, and that it ought to work as well globally as it did in the US. Wal-Mart had lit upon the 'virtuous circle' which growing companies pray for – growing volume, producing reducing cost, reflected in lower and ultra-competitive pricing, resulting in even faster growing volume.

Walton, Glass and Scott were confident that the world would appreciate the inherent simplicity of their US model. Why wouldn't they? Wal-Mart started logically, where it felt comfortable, with the large NAFTA markets of Mexico and Canada, purchasing a significant company, Aurrera in Mexico, and rapidly achieving food market leadership. WalMex is now one of Mexico's very largest companies. Canada was initially slower to grow food share against very good local competitors such as Loblaws, but it also did well, primarily through discount stores and then clubs. Wal-Mart went on to buy 122 Canadian Woolco stores, bolstering its non-food share substantially. These two adjacent country moves afforded Wal-Mart the chance to see how its model would work in markets where consumer per capita spending was at 50 and 20 per cent of US levels, a sensible first step to scope a future world strategy. In both markets, Wal-Mart showed ambition and flexibility by introducing its range of formats quickly where it had the opportunity, and in Mexico, growth has been explosive, reflecting the penetration of the entire company range, including supercenters. Perhaps by the mid-1990s Sam's successors were beginning to think that international expansion was easy. If so, they were in for a surprise. Like many US companies, they found that Europe was not going to be a pushover.

Along the way, Wal-Mart had entered Indonesia – a huge emergent market – but it failed to make this work and retired quickly. Wal-Mart's next major moves were to tackle Western Europe and it made acquisitions in Germany in 1997 and the UK in 1999. Where possible, Wal-Mart was willing to buy as big as it could. Not for Wal-Mart a policy of hanging around the edges – even an acquisition as important as Asda UK, now number two in Britain, was a 'small change' purchase for the Bentonville company. The moves were significant, medium to high risk in size but Wal-Mart never hesitated – indeed had it been given the chance to buy bigger, there is no doubt it would have taken it. Its philosophy is utterly transparent – to be in the biggest markets and to be number one, and it wants this to happen as soon as possible. The company has been uncomplicated in choosing between central policy direction or local adaptation to its US model – wherever possible it has stood firmly behind the EDLP (every day low price) strategy, and has not been afraid to carry with it much concomitant American practice and behaviour. This has worked better in some places than others.

Specifically, Asda UK worked a whole lot better than the acquisitions of Wertkauf and Interspar in Germany. While Asda has continued to grow with the Wal-Mart acquisition, and has made profits progress, the reverse has been the case in Germany where, seven years after entry, the competition are openly dismissive of any strategic threat from the Wal-Mart arrival. Metro's CEO, acknowledging the Wal-Mart failure, attributed it to a profound misunderstanding of the German consumer and market practice. Aldi/Lidl do not disclose opinions, but have seen strong market share advances since Wal-mart's arrival. There is little doubt that Wal-Mart is targeting Western Europe as a primary growth opportunity, and would like to establish a position in France, Spain and/or Italy. It seems equally certain that its decision not to move over the seven years since it entered Germany, or the five since entering the UK, has been motivated significantly by the ignominy of public German failure, and the pressing need of turnaround in German performance. French Auchan would seem to be a likely, and conceivably available, target, with Casino as a good second bet – once requisite confidence exists. But German turnaround looks as far away as ever.

Meanwhile, however, the company has not stood still, and has turned its focus on Asian markets, which it views – alongside Western Europe – as the key strategic location. Wal-Mart opened in Japan (2002) with the purchase of Seiyu, and despite indifferent progress and some uncertainty about format development, has increased its stake in Seiyu since. Seiyu was number five in Japan, but Wal-Mart also evinced real interest in buying some or all of Daiei, universally regarded as a 'basket case' in Japan, indicating that Wal-Mart does not believe that Seiyu alone can generate sufficient share or drive Wal-Mart to leadership in this core market. The current position in Japan is therefore unsatisfactory and the forward strategy – partners, store format, immediate application of EDLP – are all business problems. In some ways, Japan has been as worrying for the company as Germany.

An even bigger priority is China, where Wal-Mart, like Carrefour, has a toehold. Wal-Mart has been operating in China for eight years, however, and has built a meaningful company infrastructure, which now constitutes a 'first mover' opportunity that could distance the company from international competitors – Carrefour, Metro and perhaps Tesco. Both in scale and strategic fit, China would appear to represent Wal-Mart's biggest chance to take a lead as an international retailer. Only Wal-Mart has the financial muscle to move quickly in a country as big and diverse as China, and only China, perhaps, can replicate the USA as a market where the Wal-Mart low cost/low price machine might render competition at the mid/low price end of this enormous market ineffective. China, therefore, would seem to represent Wal-Mart's biggest immediate opportunity, since its entry to Mexico, for international market dominance. The time it is taking, and the fear of failure – following German and Japanese results – shows that it remains cautious to throw the big dice, and it must know that, given its size, once it moves quickly, Armageddon might beckon here. There are good grounds for caution.

We have seen how Wal-Mart holds elements of unique competitive advantage in the contest to achieve and hold leadership of the global retail market. It also has constraints. First, its historic focus has been more on non-food, but given recent US progress this view is now changing. A bigger constraint has – so far – been its inability to translate the Wal-Mart approach and culture into overseas markets, particularly those which are not English speaking – Mexico is a lone exception. Far from receding in importance, this must now rank as a more sizeable problem for it. Alongside continuing consumer resistance to supercenter intrusiveness at home, a commercial backlash is in train, or waiting to happen, across the non US world, especially perhaps in developing countries, as a result of public reaction to US foreign policies during the last two US administrations. This is affecting, and will affect, all major US brands for some years ahead, and will help determine both national and local government reactions to Wal-Mart's arrival as well as to some degree conditioning consumer opinions. At worst, Wal-Mart will be seen as the archetypal 'ugly American', and the company strategy, removing the adjective, is directly congruent. Wal-Mart is archetypal middle-America, proud of its heritage and, one suspects, somewhat bemused that the international markets entered hitherto have not always seen its heritage as positive. In this context, evaluating Wal-Mart's international strategy for the future, this is a significant negative, which it possesses against all comers, and which will have to be eliminated. It may not be easy to do so, especially if, in its heart of hearts, the leadership has not taken the issue on board.

To summarise, Wal-Mart's capacity to win the leading position in food retailing ahead is simple to see. The economic factors all operate in its favour, and, as the market globalises, this advantage gains in significance – the cost and price gap will widen. Its strategy has the benefit of huge simplicity and abiding relevance for the majority, though not all, consumers. EDLP is best for customers and best for Wal-Mart's supply chain. A further sign of focus and simplicity is that Wal-Mart, by concentrating on the Triad, is heading for the big pickings. If one includes China, it is present in all five of the world's biggest economies – which no one else can claim. Its resources dwarf those its competitors can generate. Even with today's weak US dollar, it is four times bigger than number two (Carrefour) and six times bigger than Tesco, which is now perhaps becoming Wal-Mart's most worldly-wise competitor. Because of its scale, this huge gap is widening. By any standards, this constitutes market dominance. It is not easy to see how this will either reduce, or end, in years ahead. Despite the limitations noted above on future expansion, the strategy which Sam Walton prescribed, and which his successors are continuing, has been a phenomenal business achievement, and the presumption should be that it can persist, providing the company has the open-mindedness to understand that changes to the execution of international strategy will be needed, perhaps several times in different places. The change has to happen in the minds and comprehension of tomorrow's Wal-Mart leaders, and will require levels of global consumer understanding that have not so far been widely displayed.

Tesco rank miles behind Wal-Mart in scale, and is not much more than half Carrefour's size – though it is catching up fast. That it merits third place as a potential international retail leader may be surprising. It comes from a relatively small country, has operated internationally for a small fraction of the time Carrefour, and many others, have, and it has usually followed Wal-

Mart, although here the time gap has been less. It is the Johnny-come-lately of the international market, but the speed of its penetration since 1997 has been truly remarkable.

Initially, Tesco international strategy took an entirely false turn. Aware that others were already present in a range of developed markets and that its principal rival, Sainsbury's, had an American base (since sold) it decided the adjacent market of France might be a good place to start. Tesco purchased the northern French chain Catteau, small in size, not too successful, and, in France, thoroughly atypical in approach. Tesco quickly recognised that it was unable to create advantage from this base in what is one of Europe's most oligopolistic markets – the five leading chains are in secure positions, and are all French. Tesco, to its credit, beat a rapid retreat. It reviewed strategy, and decided on an approach which was very different. ('If the strategy fails, find a better one', was an early sign of Tesco's flexibility and humility.) Its decision was to apply the learning it had acquired in creating a strong British base, selling primarily to middle and lower income customers, by entering growing markets which had a similar consumer profile to that the UK might have had a decade or two earlier. It also took the decision to enter markets where the size and stage of development would allow it to learn and grow quickly, and to become a major force in the nation's economy, that is, not too big.

Tesco began in Central Europe, although consumer spending across these markets was low – ten markets in 2002 still accounted for just 2.7 per cent of world spending. It chose its time well: these new markets, having been starved of any investment prior to 1989, were becoming very interesting, and Tesco was among the first to spot this trend. It achieved very rapid sales growth, and within five years was able to claim market leadership in each of the four markets it entered (Poland, Hungary, Slovakia, Czech Republic), using the traditional European hypermarket format. This, too, represented an innovation for Tesco, since its development in the UK had excluded hypermarkets, which had been the preserve of Continental European retailers. However, as its Chairman stated, it had early and confident recognition that this was the formula that would work best in these markets and offer the best chance of growth and a leadership position.

Given success in Central Europe, Tesco then felt able to strike out further, and had established positions in six Asian markets by 2004. Once again, its approach would appear to have worked well. By now, the company had not only agreed on hypermarkets as the best point of entry, it had also determined on a policy of buying a stake in a competent, often small, local operator in the new market and then taking control, once it was clear that the strategy was working. (Note the difference of tactic from Wal-Mart's – perhaps a case of the rapier rather than the bludgeon.) Tesco has moved from the earlier and smaller markets (Thailand being a particularly successful early venture) to take positions in some larger Asian countries. South Korea has been highly successful and Tesco has extended its stake recently. Latterly it has moved to Japan, where it initially bought a convenience store company, but has since made a further acquisition. By 2004 it had established a position (Ting Hsin) in China – obviously the crucial strategic move in Tesco international expansion. Each of the three leading international companies, plus many others, is therefore now represented, albeit on a small scale, on the Chinese mainland. In making these moves at speed, and moving from a British base, to 11 international markets, Tesco has moved at a remarkable pace and with great sureness of touch to date. Today it has as much retail space internationally as it holds with its dominant position in the UK – where nevertheless it is extending rapidly with a big range of formats. It has been a terrific story, and the level of sales increase which Tesco is recording with its still relatively young strategy internationally, while relinquishing nothing to Asda/Wal-Mart and others at home, is a tribute not only to the clarity of the approach, but also to the sensitive and professional execution of strategy taking place in a brief seven-year period, across a range of quite different individual countries. Ignoring retailing comparisons, the Tesco bandwagon has rolled quickly and successfully across more national frontiers than most highly experienced corporate international companies in any sector, and bears comparison with the very best exponents for success achieved.

There is doubt about the level of return that many international retailers generate in the emerging development markets. A 'very crowded and costly place' is the way Deutsche Bank describe Poland, and similar descriptions have been applied to much of Central Europe. The increasing level of competition in Asia, means that the percentage growth increases being recorded in the early days of international penetration are no longer being achieved in today's more recessionary climate, with much more competition on the ground. However Tesco has done better than the average – its push to leadership in Poland and Hungary, for example, has been speedy and impressive. In Asia, while its record has not been uniformly so good – progress in Taiwan, for example, has been weak – it has still outperformed its major rivals who have been on the ground for longer (most notably, and in many places Carrefour, who claim that Tesco has overpaid for land and acquisition without realising it). Thailand and South Korea are markets where excellent progress has been made. Turkey is a further important new market of the future where Tesco has opened, and we must not ignore the successful early drive to number one position in Ireland. In total, Tesco now has 500 stores in the emergent markets of Europe and Asia. While it is true that the company has concentrated on smaller and medium size countries, where limited capital resources could create impact quicker – contrast Wal-Mart's focus on the biggest markets – the advantage has been that Tesco could apply lessons learned quickly, build up discrete but well-integrated local management teams, get to market leadership quickly in markets with the hypermarket formula, and thus gain confidence in extending further. It is, comparatively, a highly practical business approach and given the record it is hard to accuse Tesco of the over-investment its competitors sometimes claim to see.

Tesco does generate a large operating cash flow from the UK and the improvements it makes at home ('staggering' being a normal response to the year 2004, maintained in early 2005 increases) have created the platform for fast international expansion. The product diversification in the UK, taking Tesco well away from traditional food, and indeed manufactured consumer goods as categories, shows how hungry it is for cash increases further and faster to speed the pace of international expansion. Tesco leaders appear to know they are playing catch-up. On the record, and viewed as percentage turnover or market share increase, and speed to profitability, Tesco can claim to be best in class. It is a highly competent online grocery retailer – in this area, the world's largest. This will be a further confidence and business booster in years to come, across the world, as it can roll out British experience. Its problem will for some time remain, that as a global competitor, it started late. Carrefour is well entrenched as a leader in several markets, where Tesco will not be able to dislodge it quickly, while Wal-Mart has virtually limitless cash to fund its drive for the biggest central market positions. What this implies is that Tesco needs another five or even ten years of 'best in class' growth abroad, and a secure cash generation position in Britain, if it is seriously to aspire to lead in the end game internationally. At some stage, not too far ahead, Tesco will have to contemplate how it achieves entry into the developed markets of Western Europe – where there are acquisition opportunities, but where cost would inhibit a continuation of what has been hitherto a crystal-clear development strategy. The same applies, even more forcibly, to potential US entry. It is possible that partnership may open doors, and Tesco's technical capabilities make such prospects more genuine. Safeway Inc may need Tesco's IT knowledge more than Tesco relies on any reciprocal benefits, and from such relationships, bigger foundations can be created. Overall, Tesco firmly intends to be a significant global retailer in the long run, and overall it is hard to see a worldwide company better placed to achieve a leading position. Of the major global contenders, it may at the same time be both the most surprising, given its limited experience, but paradoxically, the most secure and confident.

We must now consider a group of potentially strong international performers who are in the second rank and seem unlikely, for various reasons, either to dominate proceedings or indeed, outside their national markets or specific niche territory, to exercise significant influence. There are ten that might have been thought to be possible contenders: Kroger, Albertsons, and Safeway from the US, Casino and Auchan, both French, Metro and Aldi in Germany, Ito-Yokado 7-Eleven from Japan, the Netherlands' Ahold, and Sainsbury's (UK). On the fringes of mainstream food retailing, there are Target and Kmart (US), Costco's warehouse clubs and, for different reasons, French Leclerc. We consider their international strategies, where discernible, their aspirations, and any likely effect on, and participation in, the global end-game.

Many of these we have already discussed and dismissed as international players of any consequence: the Americans, Ahold and Sainsbury. We do not need to spend any more time on them here.

Casino, Auchan and, theoretically, Leclerc are all major players in the French market and the first two have international aspirations, for much the same reasons that drove Carrefour to break out twenty years ago. Leclerc is a finely differentiated and powerful company with a long record, and a national market share close to Carrefour's in France. However, as a uniquely structured, 'individual branch' franchise operation, its objectives and outlook are strictly home-based. Casino and Auchan are smaller, but strong, players in an oligarchic market, used to stable trading and good margins deriving from legally controlled availability of trading space and a range of other statutory constraints on trading and pricing. Casino is strongest in the south, and is equal second to Carrefour in the Paris area. Casino, which owns Franprix/Leader, a hard discount chain, has grown sales and margins at home, and acquired the failing but important Dutch chain Laurus in 2003. It has a range of different international subsidiaries, some in Latin America, a cash-and-carry business in California, and limited positions in the emergent European and some Asian markets. The best summary of Casino might be that it has strong international aspirations, a good recent trading record, and is well diversified, by format and country. However, it is prepared, on the record and given its size, to be a follower rather than a leader, and to be tactical rather than strategic in acquiring new positions. It seems happy to operate in Carrefour's long and omnipresent shadow and to slipstream Carrefour's expansion strategy.

Auchan is a brand-centric business, with a low level of own-brand development, strongest in the Lille–Strasbourg corridor, adjacent to Germany and Belgium. It is second but equal to Casino in Paris. It acquired, and has integrated, the important Docks de France chain into its portfolio. Internationally it has seen some big increases in sales in recent years, is now in 15 countries and about one third of its sales are outside France. Its approach has often been to generate organic growth which has built good shares in Italy and Spain. However, it has made acquisitions – in Poland, Spain and Portugal – and has small joint (50 per cent) ventures in Italy and, latterly, China. Auchan appears (post 2001) to have changed tack and now to be registering international growth as crucial to future strategy and group expansion, allocating further responsibility for this goal to local company teams. It has joined Casino in establishing a joint international sourcing company. Its aspirations appear to have taken a more adventurous international turn and, given its Southern Europe prominence, it should now gain in influence. However, at best it ranks in the top 20 international food companies, which means it has a long way to go if it is to become a significant world player. A partnership – with Tesco for example – might be an attractive move for it, and perhaps for Tesco, providing the latter could continue to call the international shots. There are better synergies with Tesco than perhaps with any other of the internationally competent majors, but Wal-Mart too would be an eager buyer of Anchan's established position in France, where it has a good reputation among consumers.

Germany is an unorthodox, but huge, European market. It now resembles the US in nature, given the dominance and continuing growth of discounters – hence perhaps Wal-Mart's early entry. High-labour and low-capital costs characterise this market, and it has become increasingly problematic for the conventional big chains to prosper – again we may liken it to the USA. Metro, the biggest and longest established chain, has found life particularly difficult. Profits in the conventional sector are reputed overall to be negative, and Metro's domestic strategy has been unclear for some time. Lower German prices, increasingly dominant small-range discounters, and non-branded competition are leaving the company with few apparent answers. However, it is about to become the world's third biggest chain – overtaking Ahold – and international sales now outstrip German, in recent periods reaching annual growth levels of eight per cent, while German sales have been flat. Metro's Real and Extra supermarkets are now experiencing nega-tive year-on-year sales. However China, and a distinct cash-and-carry posi-tion, are producing better figures, and Metro has announced a further 12 stores to add to the 21 it now has. The focus on hotels and restaurants appears, for the time being, as a strength.

Metro and its CEO Hans-Joachim Koerber are in truth a conundrum. It is represented in a wide range of geographic markets, probably second only to Carrefour in numbers, albeit often with a mere handful of outlets. However, there is little strategic pattern to the moves, outside of the cash-and-carry focus. It is especially prominent in Europe, and partnered Dutch Makro into many markets in the three decades of successful expansion. Cash and carry has low capital requirements, and this enables the company to produce good returns quickly. It is, in strategic terms, perhaps best seen as a distinct but strong player, with a unique format niche guaranteeing good growth and margins. It can grow further, at least through the early years of market development. However, it is hard to see the company making a meaningful entry into the key consumer markets of the world – the scale of Metro's Chinese success will be the best guide to this.

Aldi is a different kettle of fish. Profoundly secretive and deeply deter-mined, it was an early part of the German post-war recovery, owned by two brothers, Theo and Karl Albrecht. Their limited-range, low marker-price strategy has been enormously successful, first at home, where Aldi is the undisputed German leader. Recently, Aldi growth has powered ahead, driven by a deep and lasting domestic recession. However, Aldi is much more than a German phenomenon. It has good positions, using an identical approach to its German base, across Europe, notably in France, the UK, Benelux and Austria. While weak in the UK, it is preparing a major new assault on Britain. More surprisingly, it has penetrated the US with great success, acquiring Trader Joe's, growing its own fascia and even taking a small percentage holding in Albertsons. The differentiated low-cost, limited-assortment (1,250 units versus 40,000 in a big self-service store), discounter format has not only held on, but grown share across the US, where Aldi's holding is now well across the East and mid-West. In the US, its store holding approaches 1,000. Aldi is likely to be one of the most profitable store oper-ations in the world, and *Forbes* magazine has rated the brothers as the wealthiest family in Europe. Its capacity to expand further is considerable. Apart from Europe and the US, it has a position in Australia but has stayed away, perhaps sensibly, from joining the battle for mainstream Asia.

Although still small, and with sales of $23 billion, not yet even near the top ten retailers, the distinct nature of Aldi's appeal, together with its management controls and capacity to win in difficult markets (the US and Germany are good examples) suggest that, outside the big three, this is the company best positioned to make competitive gains in the future. It is unquestionably a force to be reckoned with, not yet close to the big three in size, but most likely of the remainder to 'make a run on the rails'.

Geographically, Japan's Ito-Yokado is one of the most diversified international retailers, present in more than 20 countries, usually through licensing arrangements. Superstores form a major element in the company's domestic portfolio, but the sluggish Japanese economy has slowed growth badly over many years. Not so in the convenience store market, where the company has a powerful and growing presence, based on its well-recognised 7-Eleven brand. The Dallas-based 7-Eleven company is the premier name and the largest chain in the convenience retailing industry and has stood up well to increased US big-store and discounter competition. Ito-Yokado has therefore highly complementary strengths and in two big and very different markets. First, it owns the leading convenience store brand in the US, backed by steady if undramatic expansion into a range of European and Asian markets with this format. Around a quarter of Ito-Yokado's growth has come from the US and related market convenience stores. The majority of revenue is, however, in Japan, and here the company, as the incumbent player, has the full range of trading formats and a good own-brand presence. Responding to increased international competition in Japan, and cheap food imports coming across the border from China, Ito-Yokado has introduced the concept of 'Everyday Fair Prices', a description which indicates that the company knows from whence its key future challenge will emanate. It has divested its discount portfolio and strengthened superstores, and the home base will be crucial to company long-term success. In summary, we can say that Ito-Yokado is a significant long-term international player because of its successful convenience store brand and policy, married to a big country Japanese base. For it to become a leading overall competitor ahead, it needs to sustain its leading position in Japan, and hope for better domestic economic trading conditions. It resembles German Metro, although much smaller. They both operate in a becalmed domestic base, but with historic strength, bolstered by command of a growing minor segment (Cash and carry for Metro, convenience stores for Ito-Yokado). Each represents an interesting strategic position as mainstream competition intensifies.

One final company of potential international significance, however, is Costco, which has hitherto confined its aspirations to the NAFTA area, where virtually all its sales are located as a warehouse club operator. As such, it is selling primarily to professional customers, but there is major overlap in the drive for shared customers, and food is a key component of Costco business.

Recently, Costco has begun to venture internationally and, apart from Canada, where it is important, and the UK, it has established initial positions in several Asian countries. It is showing interest in doing the same in Continental Europe. Costco is single-mindedly a club operator, with considerable focus, an excellent sales and profits record and confidence in its trading mission – 'we run a tight operation ... eliminating virtually all the frills and costs historically associated with conventional wholesalers and retailers ... with extremely low overhead which enables us to pass on dramatic savings to our members' is the summary in its Annual Report. Until 2002, growth in revenues and profits had been strong, but since then it seems that club store saturation may be becoming a feature of the US market. This has no doubt accelerated global aspirations. Costco's strong trading record, its unique position outside the US, and its global aspiration are points in its favour against which must be weighed US store saturation and Costco's unenviable role as probably Wal-Mart's most frontal competitor – Wal-Mart owns Sam's, Costco's US main rival. Although a big company, and close to being a top ten world player, it seems Costco globally starts from too far back, and lacks the international resource and know-how to be a significant global player in the immediate future.

Conclusion

We have considered the gamut of international aspirants and are now in a position to reach conclusions on which strategies have worked, and may work best ahead; which companies are already in the frame as global companies today, and which others may reach this level in the near future.

▶ The first category is those whose strategies are too limited to have future global influence, unless circumstances change dramatically in their home market trading.
  Non-participators: The three US chains – Kroger, Albertsons and Safeway Inc. – and Sainsbury's.

▶ The second category comprises companies with significant current global presence, a trading record, and apparent global aspirations. There are many companies who have these qualifications including some we have not had space to consider here, for example Delhaize, Tengelmann and Lidl. Our verdict is that these companies may have an international role to play but it is likely, given their strategic goals and record, to be at best a supporting one, or one dependent on alliance/partnership with another, probably bigger, company.
  Supporting Cast: Casino, Auchan (France), Ahold (Holland).

▶ The third category summarises companies who have niche market strength, a position in a discrete market segment which they can dominate, and strategic focus to control and grow this position. Sometimes such companies also have general market positions to defend, such as Metro's German supermarkets, or Ito-Yokado's Japanese supercenters. Only Costco seems truly to 'stick to its last' strategically, that is, focus on the warehouse club. This may ultimately represent strategic strength, providing clubs can be made to grow globally, something of an unknown today. **Niche Commanders:** Metro (Germany) cash and carry; Ito-Yokado (Japan) 7-Eleven convenience stores; and Costco (USA) warehouse clubs.

▶ Finally, we reach the small group of companies who have a combination of established trading performance, recognisable global aspiration, and clear market-driven strategies to drive future leading international performance. German Aldi is an impressive discounter with strategic focus and a unique low-cost, limited-assortment vehicle working consistently well on both sides of the Atlantic. It is constrained only by a limited-appeal trading format and lack of Asian presence. Tesco is working at pace and has the best recent trading record, after Catteau, and a highly confident expansion strategy in Europe and Asia. It is entering some of the biggest markets only now. Can it win in China? How and when will it compete in the US and Western Europe? Carrefour is number two in the world market, a 'first mover' with over two decades of global trading and knowledge of European, Asian and Latin-American markets. But it failed in the US and the UK. Its capability to grow now that Asia has become a battle-field is unproven, and focus in its international business and brand strategy remains unclear; its powerful home base is under threat. Wal-Mart is a dominant US and world leader, today's unquestioned number one. Global leadership is Wal-Mart's to lose or retain. Its economic dominance is undoubted, its US growth achievement compelling. It has performed indifferently in some key overseas markets. It has made big mistakes in Indonesia, Germany and Japan. It has, however, so far, stuck firmly to a successful 'full frontal' US-driven global strategy: grown as a discounter in non-foods and foods simultaneously, driven cost and price advantage single-mindedly against all comers, and built the biggest stores as part of a full trading format, in the world's biggest countries.
World Leaders: Aldi (Germany); Tesco (UK); Carrefour (France); Wal-Mart (US).

If a rank order is required, this list is in ascending order of global leadership potential. However, Tesco may begin to over-take Carrefour in the future.

12 The Future: Where, How, Who?

In this final chapter, we look first at the countries of the world that offer most promise for food retailers. We then draw some conclusions about what those retailers will have to do well to succeed, and finally offer our views on the strengths and weaknesses, and prospects, of the main contenders.

Which countries?

As we noted at the beginning of this book, no food retailer will be aiming to enter every country in the world over the next decade or two. They need to make choices and identify priorities within a rapidly changing competitive scene.

The USA is – and will remain for many years – by far the biggest single market. Whatever the government in power, the economy will continue to grow, although one must enter a caveat about the budget and current account deficits: if these are not brought under control, the consequences could be dire.

For other businesses, it has been the common view for some time that, to achieve what counts as global coverage, you need to be in the triad areas: North America, Japan and South-East Asia, and Europe. Is the same true for food retailing, or is the American market simply too difficult for outsiders to crack? That has certainly been the experience of many Europeans trying to cross the Atlantic: many have failed, or have limped along, just staying alive but making little progress. Sainsburys, for example, owned Shaws for many years, but seemed to gain little from it.

Ahold, on the other hand, showed that it could be done. Until it imploded after massive fraud at one of its American businesses (but foodservice, not retail), it had reached fourth place among US supermarkets, and even won an award. It did so by buying good businesses, and leaving them to carry on as they were, while trying to wring efficiency gains from the back office systems. That may offer one option for others, though any acquisition will not come cheap. The big players such as Kroger or Albertson are too big for most, except possibly Carrefour; for reasons outlined in Chapter 3, Carrefour will probably not be in a position to contemplate such an acquisition for some years. Other smaller chains might be potential targets at some stage, though an acquirer would have to balance the cost and risk against alternatives such as further expansion in China. The opportunity to take part in the consolidation of the industry that must happen is tempting, but will need nerves of steel and deep pockets.

Other developed countries are similar, in that they will continue to be rich, attractive markets, though growing more slowly than the USA. Again, acquisition is, in most cases, the only feasible way in. Italy is a possible exception, in that it is the least consolidated market in Western Europe, but any entrant would probably want to start with a local partner. Despite a great deal of talk, there have been remarkably few cross-border deals in Europe in recent years, and many commentators think that is likely to continue. Wal-Mart has the depth of pocket to allow it to consider acquisitions, but having burned its fingers in Germany, may be cautious for a while. Shareholders may not be willing to fund speculative acquisitions, as they have seen too much value destroyed by such deals in the past; often, the only gainers are the shareholders of the company acquired.

Another cautionary note is that in all these markets, food is essentially not a growing market, for the reasons outlined earlier. The chains have to look for growth in non-food and services, a strategy which will serve them well for a while, but does not have unlimited potential. Added to this are the current deflationary trend in food prices, and a widespread increase in consumer price consciousness. This is visible in several countries, and whether it is a reaction to discounters' actions, or a symptom of a deeper social change, is less relevant than the fact of its existence.

Finally, the level of concentration in many countries is such that there may come a time when consumers start to react negatively to the sheer size and dominance of the leaders. In the frequently mentioned statistic, one pound in every eight spent in all shops in Great Britain is spent in Tesco. Even the mighty Wal-Mart pulls in only one dollar in twelve in America. At present, only a few middle-class activists are complaining, and it is certainly an argument that most people may not like the dominating chains too much, but they love the convenience and the prices, so they will carry on shopping there. This may change.

If we add to this the effect of online shopping, which is certain to take a growing share, then overall we must conclude that developed countries are not growth markets – but they are, of course, large.

The CEE countries should grow rapidly, depending on their politics. The more advanced have already been the destination for FDI (foreign direct investment) from the west, and some, such as Poland, are already over-shopped. The less developed tend to be small, and may be unstable – as of course may be the large, such as Russia.

One country that, like Brazil, has been the country of the future for some time without ever quite living up to its promise, is Turkey. It now seems stable, and is actively modernising to try to join the EU. With a population of 69 million (and growing), and the economy also growing, this must be an attractive target. Carrefour, Tesco, Metro and 7-Eleven are already there, and Wal-Mart has recently (end 2004) been in talks with Koc Holdings, which owns supermarkets. Prospects look good.

Japan is a notoriously difficult and complicated market, as Carrefour found before withdrawing. Any entry is likely to be with a local partner, as Wal-Mart is doing. As a very large and wealthy market, it is bound to be on the radar, but may not be a high priority, given the challenges it presents. Of the other countries in the area, South Korea, Thailand and Taiwan have entrenched competitors, and it may be hard to dislodge them. Many of the others are subject to the sort of political/economic problems we have seen elsewhere: Malaysia, Indonesia and the Philippines must be on many lists, but the latter two remain difficult and risky markets.

Latin America has many possibilities, though like the CEE countries, much will depend on the political and economic stability that successive governments can achieve. As we saw from our earlier discussion of Brazil, it can be a rollercoaster ride. The experience of Carrefour in the region in the 1970s and 80s seems unlikely to be repeated: wherever an attractive and stable market develops, competition from both local and international players will be intense. If the countries can regain a stable growth path, they must be attractive markets.

Africa is the focus of much of the world's attention from time to time, but sadly, because of the seemingly endemic problems there, it seems unlikely to offer major opportunities in the near future. South Africa is a transitional economy, and, given the right policies, should grow and become wealthier. It is a substantial market (42 million people) but not large, and most other countries of the sub-Saharan region are too poor to rank high on any list of priorities for expansion. The big countries such as Nigeria (137 million people) will present opportunities when they finally get their politics right, and others will, we hope, follow. There are some chains, such as Shoprite, operating in several countries; it seems likely that this will remain a distinct regional market for some time. In North Africa, the bigger countries such as Egypt (76 million people) and Ethiopia (68 million) may enter the reckoning.

Let us then turn to the BRICs discussed in Chapter 1. On some forecasts, the BRICs' economies could be over half the size of the G6 by 2025 in US dollar terms, and larger than them by 2040 (Wilson and Purushothaman 2003). If we take purchasing power parity (PPP), then China's GDP could overtake the USA before 2020 (though GDP per head would remain lower) (*The Economist* 2 October 2004c). Some think that the forecasts in the first study are too conservative, as other fast-growing economies in the past have sustained high growth rates for decades. In that case, China will overtake the big Western European countries in a few years.

All such forecasts are based on assumptions about growth in employment, capital stock and total factor productivity (technical progress). They have to make heroic assumptions about political stability: we know that in these countries and many others, growth has varied enormously because of government policies. There are also such external factors as recession or financial crises elsewhere, oil shocks, and natural disasters such as the SARS outbreak, or the appalling earthquake and tsunami damage in South-East Asia in late 2004. Any of these can upset an economy for a short time. Polit-

ical or social unrest could cause more permanent harm. Although economists argue about it, there is some consensus around the need for four
conditions for growth:

▶ Macro stability (of prices, government debt, exchange rate and so on)
▶ Sound institutions (legal and financial systems, markets, government)
▶ Openness (to trade with other countries)
▶ Education.

(Wilson and Purushothaman 2003)

At present, all the BRICs fall somewhat short on institutions, all are
improving on openness (though China leads and India lags), and India falls
short on education. On macro stability, all have suffered in the past, and
Brazil does not look out of the woods yet. On all, the jury must be out.

Accepting all these caveats, it seems very likely that all will achieve good-
to-excellent growth for at least a decade, and probably longer. They will
therefore be large and important economies, and worthy of serious consideration by any international retailer. They all, of course, carry some level of
risk. Brazil has been very unstable, and may revert to political type. Russia
seems a matter of taste: some commentators are very favourably inclined,
and think it the best opportunity in Europe, while others – with exactly the
same information – find it still too chancy. India will certainly grow, but it
may be worth waiting a little before committing funds. It is opening up, but
starts from a long way back. China is risky too, and might fall prey to social
unrest or even break-up – but on balance most will probably feel that the
huge opportunities are worth the gamble.

How: what will be needed to win?

From this consideration of the opportunity markets, it is easy to see how
much is still to play for. Wal-Mart, the most committed major market
entrant, has a toehold in China, little more in Brazil as yet, and nothing in
Russia or India. Carrefour, long-term internationalist, is comparably placed.
Tesco with a briefer but high quality record is just beginning in China, while
the others with established global performance pedigrees are some way
behind (Aldi, Metro) or frankly, nowhere.

We now propose to review the criteria that we judge to be critical to
future global performance. Any such exercise involves considerable speculation, and the priority weightings of individual performance criteria is a
further area where personal judgment must be exercised. Then, in the final
section of this chapter, we will consider the record and potential of the key
entrants who should be among tomorrow's global leaders, at the same time
considering where those who once had a chance to lead, fell away and why
this happened.

There are perhaps four groups of performance characteristics that will be
critical to long-term global success. They can be summarised as:

▶ Strategic
▶ Operational
▶ Customer marketing
▶ Human performance.

We will itemise and review these in sequence.

Strategic

1. *The company must have a clear, tested strategy for international growth.*
   Does the company have a clear and winning strategy? Does it stick to it through all its locations and trading formats? Is it, however, sufficiently flexible and aware of market development, to modify strategy when it has to, to maintain advantage? Can its global strategy work across different markets and can it stand up, that is, will the business still grow when facing up to the best international and local competition?
2. *Winning global retailers focus on the store as the key to performance.*
   Has the company a dedicated store focus? Is its decision making process driven by a persistent search for long-term customer advantage – loyalty – manifested in the store? Does the company treat its store managers as leaders and innovators, not merely as executors of the agreed business plan? Is the company committed to, and proud of, the way in which its stores present to the customer? Are the company's stores truly differentiated from competition?
3. *The company must deliver the three things customers need from a store.*
   There is general agreement that there are three on-going elements that all customers need in some measure from all their shopping. These are, in no priority order, quality, service and price. Does the company have a clear notion how it will compete, globally, on each of these three dimensions, and what their relative priority within the strategy will be in future? A strategy which is wholly uncompetitive on one dimension is unlikely to succeed in the long run, unless it has a very big lead on one or both of the remaining requirements.

Operational

1. *The company must deliver a successful track record wherever it goes.*
   Operating credibility internationally depends on the maintenance of a winning track record. If companies falter when tackling new challenges, they will be increasingly vulnerable not just to other global competitors, but in the big markets to powerful local players. Demanding a 100 per cent success record may be too stringent as the pace of global entries accelerates, but the need to maintain consistent success and to avoid painful mistakes (see below) is paramount.
2. *The company must avoid big and damaging mistakes.*
   Avoiding all mistakes sets an impossible standard. However, it is important to avoid big and public errors that can not only damage profitability

but, more significantly, hurt the company's reputation, not just in the market where it happens but globally. This is one reason why small-scale experimentation can be sensible in limiting uncertainty. A crucial element under mistake avoidance is to repair the damage effectively and quickly. A continuing 'sore' is damaging.

3. *The company needs an innovative competitive approach to store formats.*
Trading formats vary widely and there is certainly no likelihood, ever, of one format becoming universally more successful than others. Winning companies review format options, searching for competitive solutions for the specific market. Where appropriate, they look for effective format extensions to the company's brand that can attract a wider customer base. The best approach ensures that the company uses one brand name, or one closely related to the parent brand.

4. *The company needs to establish and maintain supply chain pre-eminence.*
Supply chain performance is a requirement to compete effectively. Hitherto, delivery of distribution and supply chain advantage has been achieved principally on a national rather than international basis. However, there are signs that this is changing, and the need to command resources internationally will sort out future global winners and losers. Scale economies will need to be derived on a global basis in the years ahead, so numerically there will be fewer winners.

Customer marketing

1. *The company needs a differentiated, recognised customer brand proposition.*
Retail brands have been developed on a national basis, but increasingly there is awareness of the need for global brand perceptions to be recognised. Winning companies will determine brand presentations that can cross national boundaries, and will find an effective marriage of local accept ability and international reputation that will carry maximum credibility in global markets. High sensitivity to local response will be required, especially from the most powerful global entrants.

2. *The company must have good and easily interrogated customer information.*
Aggregated information on customer requirements and responses are valuable. However, it is specific and detailed customer information, capable of being probed regularly by company management, so as to determine future actions, that represents major strategic advantage for the retail owner. So far, not many of the global players have sought for advantage from this area.

Human performance

1. *The company needs exceptional, consistent strategic leadership.*
Successful national retailers have always needed to have strong, visionary and committed leaders. The requirement on a global basis is greater, since the leader's task is infinitely more demanding. Winning companies seem to have the knack of attracting high quality individuals, and then of

keeping them and their successors in place, so that a consistent ethic and style are built up. Durability of leadership style and message is invaluable.

2. *The company needs humility as a permanent belief.*
   Most companies are able to cultivate humility when they start out, and many can still generate it as they grow. Once they achieve leadership, or, a fortiori, market dominance, the chances that arrogance may emerge is greater. The damage that complacency can wreak in successful retailers is well documented (think of Kmart, Marks & Spencer, and Sainsbury's). The advantage that truly humble yet committed companies will create for themselves is significant.

3. *The company needs a high performance ethic in its entire team.*
   Companies adopt divergent approaches to team motivation and control. Some successful companies have adopted strongly communicated 'top down' approaches that have secured long-term business advantage. The best companies in the global market of the future will create an innovative 'can do' ethic that can drive business forward in very different local markets. The capacity to marry local and team-based initiatives with responsiveness to global strategy will be a determining characteristic of future global success.

Who will be the winners?

In this final section, we examine the credentials of the key global players, considering who may be best placed for future global success, and conversely who might, through their actions to date, have missed future international opportunity. We will review performance dealing with the four principal headings under which the detailed criteria for success were grouped. These were:

▶ Strategic
▶ Operational
▶ Customer marketing
▶ Human performance.

Clearly, there is a large amount of overlap and duplication between these four areas.

Of the leading contenders, it was the case until recently that Carrefour led the field in possessing a clear and tested strategy for international growth that had stood the test of time. Perhaps Carrefour still leads, but there have been signs that its supremacy is no longer so clear. In some markets, Carrefour has not dealt adequately with competitive entries. There are signs of uncertainty in Carrefour itself on the content of its approach – what importance should it place on a separate discounter brand to survive? Finally, it is under major threat in its home market, and this seems certain to curtail its international ambitions for some time. Given these reservations, it seems right to say that Wal-Mart's strategy is now at least clearer than Carrefour's and that Tesco, albeit with limited big country experience, has been able to take on Carrefour and win.

If compelled to pick one winner now it would have to be Wal-Mart despite some mistakes, discussed below.

Ahold is an example of what happens when a major global player ventures far and wide and takes on the biggest challenges without proper strategy or experience. The overstretch in Ahold's product range, and its inability to integrate its acquisitions, meant it was exposed quickly, despite some years of excellent growth.

Store focus as a determinant of success probably favours Wal-Mart, committed to pushing its supercenters round the major markets with as much speed and determination as possible. Wal-Mart has intrinsic superstore advantage against all comers, if only because of its massive scale and experience. Some might feel Tesco's store focus is so well developed, and central to its strategy, that it is already an effective competitor, despite Wal-Mart's scale advantage. Time will tell, but there is no question that Tesco has marshalled its resources around the store and its management in a far-seeing way. The remainder of the global leaders would seem to be behind on this parameter.

Kmart's blindness to store performance allowed Wal-Mart to pick up what was a US Kmart store innovation, tackle it comprehensively and with detailed attention, producing competitive advantage. Wal-Mart beat Kmart in the store.

The third basic element of strategy is the delivery requirement on the three 'no brainers' of retailing – quality, service and price. The generalists of food retailing all claim to do this, and Tesco, notably in its home market, has achieved this balance splendidly, taking away Sainsbury's clothes and taking on Asda/Wal-Mart successfully as it did so. Carrefour reigned supreme in more than twenty markets round the world, setting standards. Latterly, it has not found its offer as competitive as it ought to be, raising questions regarding future success.

There is another way of tackling the three key customer dimensions, and that is to over-deliver so compellingly in one area that the market settles for moderate under-achievement elsewhere. Aldi and Lidl do this in Europe with hugely discounted prices, a not dissimilar approach from US Wal-Mart's. So far, no competitor has achieved global recognition by overdelivering quality or service and being uncompetitive on price. Will anyone ever manage this?

It is worth noting that losing market position and a customer reputation on one key dimension often means losing it not too much later on all three. This happened to Sainsbury's in Britain. Having steadily forfeited its food quality reputation, it lost ground on service, and as a result of lost volume and higher costs, its prices became uncompetitive: an irresistible circle of business uncompetitiveness.

Moving to operating parameters, the global track records of the aspirant global players need consideration. Carrefour led for two decades, and only in the past few years has its unique and enviable record of international growth and expansion over three continents been challenged. Now, however, it has been, and there are remarkably few markets where Carrefour's early entry has offered it dominance. The record now looks patchy. Wal-Mart has a US money machine, and several big international winners, but again its record – Germany and Japan – is by no means perfect. Tesco, apart from one brief nugatory foray in France, has an excellent, but still short-lived, record. Perhaps, in summary, there is as yet no obvious overall global winner.

Aldi and Lidl, whose secrecy can conceal some elements of their failures, have impressive international business expansion records, using their particular format. Finally, under this heading, it is right to observe that time is needed to evaluate the strength of a trading track record. When we wrote *The Grocers* in 1999, Ahold looked to all the world like a blue chip global player, and the US food industry voted the same company 'Retailer of the Year' in 2000.

Next on the operating list is the criterion 'avoid big damaging mistakes'.

Wal-Mart's appallingly managed entry into Germany comes into this category. Only as large and profitable a US company as it is could have withstood such a series of errors without it affecting its global result. German Wal-Mart offers another insight on mistakes – once you have made one, resolve it as quickly as possible to ensure your international reputation is unaffected. Wal-Mart has not done this either. Carrefour made a big error in its China strategy when it chose to ignore government regulations on opening new stores. It has however resolved the issue quickly, and is once again on the front foot in China.

Mistakes can 'floor' a business, as Ahold is learning, if they are big and serious enough. Sometimes, a series of big mistakes, simply reflecting weak trading and management over years, produces the same outcome – Sainsbury's and Kmart's problems arrived in this way.

An important differentiating element is trading format. Can successful companies manage the challenge of new format requirements well across many markets? Tesco's adoption of the hypermarket for its Asian and European ventures, when it had no experience of them in its home market, has been courageous and, on its record so far, inspired. Wal-Mart tends to adopt a saturation approach, using any format where it can get its low-price message across. Carrefour is now placing as much emphasis on the discounter brand and format as it has done traditionally with hypermarkets. Is this a sign of strength or weakness?

Meanwhile, there are winning, albeit smaller, global retailers who can adopt specific, sometimes niche, formats which they dominate, and which allow them high measures of control over the risk and cost of expansion. Metro's cash-and-carry approach fits this model, as do Ito-Yokado's convenience stores. The hard discounters have been able to drive their small-store, limited-range approach single-mindedly and are winning handsomely, even, in Aldi's case, a long way from home (USA and Australia, for example). The warehouse club (Costco) has so far not travelled far internationally. No doubt in due course it can.

The final operating characteristic that offers clear winners is supply chain pre-eminence, or even effectiveness. In this we include sourcing as well as logistics. There is only one global winner and that is Wal-Mart, supported by its US volume, but also by committed global logistics policies that have already created scale advantage. Carrefour, despite years of international learning, has not moved at anything like Wal-Mart's heady pace of expansion. Tesco is moving but on this dimension is well behind – in the UK it recently claimed £2 billion of global cost savings, which compares with Wal-Mart's existing level of $15 billion sourcing savings from China. These are the supply chain leaders, although everyone is chasing down the same global cost advantage.

Marketing is the third key dimension. Global winners will need a recognised and well differentiated consumer brand to march behind. Wal-Mart's is certainly this, but it has not always made comparable appeal in its international markets. Carrefour has a clear, recognisable presence wherever it is – in Pudong, Shanghai, for example, the store fascias could be anywhere in France. Tesco has a less pronounced belief in the need for its brand proposition from home ('Every little helps') to travel, but has been a first-class exponent of local presentation in ways that generate a positive response to the Tesco arrival. The hard discounters have an immediately identifiable appearance wherever they are.

Wal-Mart is unmatched for brand clarity and awareness, but there may be others whose understanding and ability to deal with local customer requirements might win in the long run.

Customer information and insights will provide significant advantage for global retail entrants. Particularly on an international basis, this criterion is still in its infancy: there are no competitors yet who possess meaningful systems comparing customer attitudes and behaviour across national boundaries. (Some international brand manufacturing companies have made good progress, on which they need to capitalise if they want to stay ahead!)

There is one winner here and it is Tesco, who has a substantial capacity to address its customer database in ways that provide strategic as well as operational answers. So well is Tesco's lead appreciated in the market that it has been able to provide customer-information systems assistance to competitors – some of the principal American supermarket companies – for which the latter have been prepared to pay. It is a surprising position, viewed from the supplier or buyer angle.

Wal-Mart has adopted a different approach, basing its information on the store and the supply chain. It is oversimplistic to say that one approach is always better than the other, but it is likely that Tesco will be able to create a more differentiated set of customer strategies internationally, if it can translate its UK advantage into a world lead without anyone else catching up. Apart from the reticent Aldi, reputed to have a powerful customer database, at least in Germany, it seems nobody else has made progress here.

On the critical human performance dimensions, it is not difficult to discriminate. Exceptional and consistent leadership is what Wal-Mart has enjoyed through all its 42 years. Sam, while unorthodox, was a phenomenon, whose record cannot be faulted. David Glass and Lee Scott have not faltered in maintaining momentum. Wal-Mart scores on calibre and consistency. Carrefour has emerged from an era of family policy direction and it is to Daniel Bernard's enormous credit that it now enjoys an increasingly normal free-market decision structure. However, the transition, in protected France, is not complete, and Bernard's operating record came under assault. His leadership was vulnerable, and in February 2005 he and his ally Joel Saveuse were forced to resign (see Chapter 3). Jose Luis Duran, the highly regarded CFO, has taken over as chief executive, with Vandevelde as non-executive chairman. It is expected that Duran will open up the management structure; the relationship between the chairman and chief executive will determine who really has the power. Finally of the big three, there is Tesco, which, after chaotic beginnings, had 15 coherent years under MacLaurin. He then handed over the CEO's job to a young, apparently untried, Terry Leahy. The performance of this company under Leahy's guidance has been nothing short of remarkable, and puts his company in the best world class for consistent, winning leadership.

Less obviously, the two brothers Albrecht have quietly pioneered German Aldi through a half century of expansion. Dieter Schwarz is getting fine European results from Lidl. Hans-Joachim Koerber has clear strategic views of what Metro can do, but, like Carrefour's Bernard, some results from his diversified company have not been good.

There have been big and visible losses. Cees van der Hoeven has attracted personal blame for Ahold's collapse and is being pursued in the courts. Sainsbury's had several top leader failures, culminating in the acrimonious and highly publicised departure of Sir Peter Davis. Chuck Conaway's strategic mismanagement at Kmart resulted in his very rapid departure.

A critical component of retailer success seems to be the ability of companies to remain humble in the face of high prosperity. This may prove an issue for Wal-Mart, whose mid-western 'hunter' origins are not conducive to generating humbleness. As it expands, management will need to nurture unaccustomed behaviour, and the need for humility will test them. Comparing two British companies, Tesco and Sainsbury's, is instructive. Tesco, from buccaneering insouciance, gradually matured, and while its ethic is driving and purposeful, there is no hint of arrogance, despite great performance. Sainsbury's was the best in Britain for a century, but fell victim to complacency and arrogance, which was its undoing. These examples may be extreme. Nonetheless, to compete long term as a global retailer, it will be crucial to maintain attitudes of realism and humility, even in times of high achievement.

Finally, the ability to drive high performance from the entire team is an issue where practice has varied significantly. Some discounters would not recognise this as a requirement. Their goal has been to ensure labour costs are kept to a minimum, seeing this as the root of advantage. Lidl are one clear exponent, while Wal-Mart practice has been equivocal – determinedly cutting labour costs, but simultaneously using techniques to encourage workforce morale. It is questionable whether this paradox can endure on an international basis. Carrefour's profile on workforce commitment is unclear and, notably in France, its behaviour seems institutionalised and somewhat distant. Finally Tesco, who through a series of learning behaviours, practised regularly, and on a store-by-store basis, looks the leader on this dimension.

Let us try to summarise. Logically, given its economic prowess and scale advantage, the big global winner should be Wal-Mart. Yet, it has the capacity to deliver poorer than anticipated performance on some key characteristics and in some locations. The current top contender is Tesco, with a high record of achievement across most performance attributes, moving at speed and with confidence, but starting a long way back. Carrefour is slipping, from a position where it had a clear time and scale lead in international operations. It is still a big and important player, and has positions of strength, but it needs to up its game at home and globally if it is not to lose further ground.

The discounters are clearly profiled and have a winning platform. They will probably gain internationally. Aldi and Lidl, if it can operate outside Europe, will be big winners. Metro's cash-and-carry business will allow it to grow for several years, but it does not look a strong business. Ito-Yokado, with strength in Japan and a convenience profile, can also grow. The others look also-rans.

A look ahead

Finally, what are the effects of the continuing growth of international food retailers that we foresee? We believe that a small group of companies will lead the pack, and will come to dominate in many countries around the world as they have in Europe and, to a lesser extent so far, in the USA. There will be strong local competitors in some places, and some regional players who may also be powerful. Will this be good for shoppers and consumers, or bad?

We saw in Chapter 9 that there have been vociferous critics of western supermarkets, but that the majority of consumers generally like the convenience and range they offer. The multiples certainly exert a strong influence on what people buy and eat, although they of course would argue that they sell only what shoppers will buy. They have great power over suppliers, particularly smaller farmers, and their tactics in dealing with them have been severely criticised, by government bodies among others. They have put many small shops out of business, and have been accused of destroying town centres, and so on.

The other side of the coin is that they are superbly run, world-class businesses. They are extremely efficient, and help to keep the cost of food and supplies down. They are generally clean and hygienic. The range of products and services they offer is truly staggering. For those unable or unwilling to drive to them, they offer online ordering and home delivery. What's to dislike?

How the scenarios play out in the transitional and developing countries that we have discussed is a fascinating question, to which we have no easy answers. We do not see any dramatic new ways of shopping that could destroy the existing models (though there will be innovations to reflect changing consumer tastes – see Text Box 12.1). Online food shopping, with the added attraction of many other products from the same source, will grow, but will never be more than a minority of total supermarket revenues. One pattern could be that the boring and bulky goods – the chore aspect of shopping – will be ordered online, leaving consumers to spend time on the more interesting products. This will leave empty space in the stores, but the retailers are confident that they can fill it. Such a development would also open up new opportunities to specialists. As these scenarios develop in the richer nations, they will follow, probably at a rather faster pace, in the transitional economies.

Modern retailing, with efficient supply chains and a range of formats in the outlets, will gradually take over from traditional shops and retailers in all markets. Much will depend on how the different governments react. They have the advantage of seeing what has happened in developed economies, and can take a view of how they want their country to end up. If they have a strong food culture, some may wish to legislate to defend traditional markets and specialist retailers; we know that it is possible, and can disagree about how desirable it is. Others may take a free-market, liberal stance and let the market decide. What we would like to see is a real choice for consumers that they can exercise with full knowledge.

BOX 12.1

A GLIMPSE OF THE FUTURE?

Food retailing will continue to change in reaction to changes in the environment, and consumer tastes and preferences. Currently, healthy eating is a preoccupation, at least for some segments of society. In Europe, there has been a reaction against genetically modified organisms, and an unwillingness to try the resulting 'Frankenfoods'. Part of this general trend is an increasing interest in organic produce, and in natural rather than processed food.

Add to this the need to get away from food shopping as a chore, and the desire to inject some element of entertainment, and you get Whole Foods USA. Its new 80,000sq.ft. store in Austin, Texas, is a shining example of how to profit from change, and differentiate yourself from competition. Some features of the store are:

▶ The seafood team tossing whole Yakatuk salmon back and forth
▶ Pastry chefs rolling out huge squares of dough, next to displays of artisan bread
▶ Dining opportunities such as an oyster counter (with wine)

► Choice of live fish and shellfish in tanks
► Live mushrooms growing in the middle of the produce display
► An outdoor market hall that aims to recapture the authentic atmosphere of the traditional market
► The chance to grind your own flour.

As many of the store's products, such as deli meats and smoked foods, are prepared on the premises, usually in clearly visible areas, the shop smells like a food store, and is miles away from the efficient but antiseptic supermarket image. Organic cotton fabrics add to the natural theme.

Whole Foods has expanded from a small health-food store, and now has 169 branches in the USA, Canada and Britain; its aim is to reach 300 stores and turnover of $10 billion by 2010. As Mark Dixon, southwest regional manager for Whole Foods says: 'Either we want the cheapest groceries in town or we want the best'. 'The standard, conventional grocery market – their days are numbered.'

Little of this is spectacularly new, but the combination and presentation are unique. The challenge for the big supermarket chains will be to match some of this appeal within their overriding need for cost efficiency.

Source: 'The Aisles Have It!' by Amy Culbertson, Knight Ridder Newspapers, www.MontereyHerald.com, March 2005.

References and Further Reading

AGSM (2000), *Carrefour vs. Wal-Mart: The Battle for Global Retail Dominance*, Australian Graduate School of Management

Asia Times (2004), 'Prices Going up in China Across the Board', 5 November

Aslund A (1999), *Why Has Russia's Economic Transformation Been So Arduous?* Paper presented at the World Bank's Annual Bank Conference on Development Economics, Washington

Basker E (2005), 'Job Creation or Destruction? Labor Market Effects of Wal-Mart Expansion', *Review of Economics and Statistics*, MIT Press 87(1): 174–83

Berner R (2004), 'Meet the Sage of Connecticut', *Independent on Sunday*, 21 November

Bloomberg (2004), *Price Reductions Restrain UK Inflation*, 15 November

Bloomberg (2004), *Tesco Shares Climb to Highest*, 25 November

Blythman J (2004), *Shopped: The Shocking Power of British Supermarkets*, Fourth Estate

Bordier A, Gunz J, Meldrum F and Webb S (2002), *Global Retailing 2003*, IGD Business Publications, Watford

Clissold T (2004), *Mr China*, Constable and Robinson

Competition Commission (2000), *Supermarkets: A Report on the Supply of Groceries from Multiple Stores in the UK*, Cm4842

Deloitte (2005), *2004 Global Powers of Retailing*, Deloitte with *Stores* magazine

Democratic Staff of the House Committee on Education and the Workforce (2004), *Everyday Low Wages: The Hidden Price We All Pay for Wal-Mart*

De Nunzio T (2004), 'Wal-Mart in UK: Five Years on', unpublished

DETR (1998), *The Impact of Large Food Stores on Market Towns and District Centres*, The Stationery Office

Dixon J (2004), 'K-Mart's Guru Seeks Turnaround Recipe', *Detroit Free Press*, 23 October

Dornbusch R (1997), 'Brazil's Incomplete Stabilization and Reform', *Brookings Papers on Economic Activity*, (1): 367–74

EBRD (2004), *Russia Strategy Overview*, European Bank for Reconstruction and Development, 6 November

Economist, The (2003a), 'Vlad the Impaler', 30 October

Economist, The (2003b), 'And the Owner Is?' 6 November

Economist, The (2003c), Reinventing the store, special report on 'The Future of Retailing', London, November

Economist, The (2004a), 'Turning Japanese', 28 August

Economist, The (2004b), 'Face Value: The Everyday Price Cutter – Lee Scott', 11 September

Economist, The (2004c), 'The Dragon and the Eagle: A Survey of the World Economy', 2 October

Economist, The (2005a), 'The Struggle of Champions', Special Report: China's Champions, 8 January

Economist, The (2005b), 'Shoprite: Africa's Wal-Mart Heads East', 15 January

Economist.com (2004a), 'Russia's Economy', 28 May

Economist.com (2004b), 'Russia: Forecast', 25 October

Economist Intelligence Unit (2004), 'Brazil Country Profile: Economic Structure', 6 April

Emling S (2004), 'Early Signs of a Blue Christmas', *International Herald Tribune*, 20 November

Euromonitor (2004), 'Retailing in Russia'

European Bank for Reconstruction and Development (2004), *Country Strategies: Russia*

Fackler M and Zimmerman A (2003), 'Store Wars: Wal-Mart Takes On Japan', *Far Eastern Economic Review*, 25 September

Flanagan M (2004), 'King Has His Work Cut Out at Sainsbury', *The Scotsman*, 16 October

Fletcher R (2004), 'Tesco Flexes its Muscles with the Big Suppliers', *Sunday Times*, 26 September

Forbes Global (2004), 'Giant Slayer Wal-Mart's No. 1 Enemy', 6 September

Gilmour B and Gale F (2002), 'A Maturing Retail Sector: Wider Channels for Food Imports? In *China's Food and Agriculture: Issues for the 21st Century/AIB-775*, Economic Research Service/USDA

Hall J (2004), 'Hampton's Shopping List', *Daily Telegraph*, 31 October

Harichandan AA (2003), 'MNCs v Kirana Shop Owners', *The Hindu Times*, 7 December

Hays C (2004a), 'Fast Foods Executive Appointed Chief of Kmart', *New York Times*, 19 October

Hays C (2004b), 'American Retail Formula Lost in Translation', *New York Times*, 16 December

Head S (2004), 'Inside the Leviathan', *New York Review of Books*, **51**(20)

Herz, R (2001), *The Silent Takeover: Global Capitalism and the Death of Democracy*, Heinemann

Hilton A (2004), 'Is it Enough to Save Sainsbury?', *Evening Standard*, 20 October

Hjeldt P (2004), 'The Fortune Global 500', *Fortune*, 26 July

Humby C and Hunt T with Phillips T (2003), *Scoring Points: How Tesco is Winning Customer Loyalty*, Kogan Page

IGD (2004), *The Carrefour Report*, Institute of Grocery Distribution

Iyengar J (2004), 'China, India Confront the Wal-Marts', www.atimes.com

Iyengar J (2004), 'China's Retail Market: Distribution the Key', www.atimes.com

Jay (2004), 'Shelf Life of a Victorian Pioneer', *Guardian*, 19 October

Jiang J (2004), 'Tesco Makes Foray into China Market', www.chinadaily.com.cn

Johnson AH (2002), 'A New Supply Chain Forged: Wal-Mart Put Intelligence in its Inventory and Recognized the Value of Data', www.computerworld.com

Jones C (2004), 'Sainsbury Continues its Convenience Store Push', *Food and Drink Europe*, 1 December

Jones DT and Clarke P (2002), 'Creating a Customer-driven Supply Chain' *ECR Journal* 2(1) Winter

Kiss TS (2004), 'Lidl Stores Finally Open', *Budapest Sun*, 4 November

Klein N (2000), *No Logo*, Flamingo

Lang T (2003), *Changing Food Lifestyles: Challenges and Opportunities for the Food Economy*, OECD Conference on Changing Dimensions of the Food Economy: Exploring the Policy Issues

Lee T (2004), 'Wal-Mart Expansion Might Fade Rainbow', *Star-Tribune*, Minneapolis

Lichtenstein N (2005), *Wal-Mart: Template for 21st Century Capitalism?* Proceedings of a conference at University of California, Santa Barbara, New Press, forthcoming

Lorentz H (2004), *The Q4/03 State of Food Retail Industry in Russia*, Turku School of Economics and Business Administration

Lukas P (2004), 'Our Malls Ourselves', *Fortune Magazine*, 18 October

McCarthy D (2004), *Competing with Tesco and Wal-Mart*, Citigroup Smith Barney

McKinsey (1998), *Driving Productivity and Growth in the UK Economy*, McKinsey Global Insitute

McKinsey (2001), *US Productivity Growth 1995–2000, Section VI: Retail Trade*, McKinsey Global Institute

Moore K and Caney S (2003), 'The Battle with Wal-Mart: May the Best Grocer Win', *European Retail Digest*

Nevill-Rolfe L (2005), 'Every Little Helps', unpublished

O'Brien L (2004), 'Technology Creates Trouble in Store', *Supply Management*, 4 November

OFT (2004), *The Supermarkets' Code of Practice*, Office of Fair Trading

Ortega B (1999), *In Sam We Trust*, Kogan Page, London

Panagariya A (2004), *India in the 1980s and 1990s: A Triumph of Reforms*, IMF Working Paper 04/43

Prasad A ed. (2004), *China's Growth and Integration into the World's Economy: Prospects and Challenges*, International Monetary Fund

PriceWaterhouseCoopers (2004), *From Beijing to Budapest: 2004/2005 Global Retail and Consumer Study*

Rabattu D and Botteri X (2003), *Eat Cheese or Surrender: Global Food Retail*, Deutsche Bank, 18 March

Rajshekar M (2004), 'Gentlemen, Fasten your Seatbelts', 'Charging Full Steam Ahead', 'Testing the waters', 'Economies of Sale', Retail Survey 1–4, *Businessworldindia.com*, 16 February

Raman M (2004), *India Still Has a Long Way to Go*, Rediff Interview, Michael Porter, www.rediff.com

Reuters (2004), 'Grocer Ahold Posts 3rd Quarter Loss', Reuters Research, 24 November

Reutter H (2004), 'Speaker Offers Strategies that have Worked for Competing with Wal-Mart', *TheIndependent.com*, 23 April

Reynolds J and Cuthbertson C (2004), *Retail Strategy: The View from the Bridge*, Elsevier Butterworth Heinemann

Riera J (2004), 'Tesco Sets $2 Billion Sourcing Target', *Retail Week*, 12 November

Rumbaugh T and Blancher N (2004), 'International Trade and the Challenge of WTO Accession' in Prasad A (ed.), *China's Growth and Integration into the World's Economy: Prospects and Challenges*, International Monetary Fund

Ryle S (2004), 'The Only Game in Town', *Observer*, 5 December

Sabnavis N (2004), *India Powers Ahead on Retail Boom*, www.rediff.com/ /money/ 2004/dec03

Serwer A (2004), 'The Wal-Mart Fortune', *Fortune Magazine*, 15 November

Seth A and Randall G (2001), *The Grocers: The Rise and Rise of the Supermarket Chains*, 2nd edn, Kogan Page, London

Schafer S (2004), 'A Welcome to Wal-Mart', *Newsweek International*, 17 December

Siegle L (2004), 'Off Your Trolley', *Observer Magazine*, 5 September

Silverstein M and Fiske N (2003), *Trading Up: the New American Luxury*, Portfolio

Singhal A (2004), *The Retailing Boom*, www.rediff.com//money/ 2004/feb07

Stalk G and Lachenauer R (2004), 'Hardball: Five Killer Strategies for Trouncing the Competition', *Harvard Business Review*, April

Stiglitz J (2002), *Globalisation and its Discontents*, WW Norton

Stone K (1995), 'Impact of Wal-Mart Stores and Other Mass Merchandisers in Iowa 1983–1993', *Economic Development Review* Spring

Sunday Times (2004), 'Business Focus: Family Takes Stock', 30 October

Supervalu (2004), 'Supervalu Reports Record 2nd Quarter Earnings', 14 October

Tdctrade.com (2001), *Metro, Auchan and Carrefour Openings 'Challenged' by Russians*, 7 November

Transparency International (2004), *Corruption Perceptions Index*, www.transparency.org

Troy M (2004), 'In South America, Ahold's Loss is Wal-Mart's Gain', *DSN*

Retailing Today, 2 March

Turner G (2003a), 'An American Odyssey', *Daily Telegraph*, 18 June

Turner ML (2003), *Kmart's 10 Deadly Sins*, Wiley

Usborne D (2002), 'Wal-Mart Shrugs off Downturn', *The Independent*, 22 February

Walton S with Huey J (1993), *Made in America: My Story*, Bantam Books

Watts C (2004a), 'All About Asda', unpublished

Watts C (2004b), 'Wal-Mart International Data Sheets', unpublished

Wilson D and Purushothaman R (2003), *Dreaming with BRICs: The Path to 2050*, Global Economics Paper No: 99: Goldman Sachs

Wolf M (2004), *Why Globalization Works*, Yale University Press

Womack JP, Jones DT and Roos J (1990), *The Machine that Changed the World*, Rawson Associates

Womack JP and Jones DT (1996), *Lean Thinking: Banish Waste and Create Wealth in Your Corporation*, Simon & Schuster

Workday Minnesota (2005), *Wal-Mart Elected Grinch of the Year*, Minnesota AFL-CIO

Yueh L (2003), *China's Economic Growth with WTO Accession: Is It Sustainable?* Asia Programme Working Paper No 1, Royal Institute of International Affairs

Yueh L (2004), 'Russia' in *The New Economic Powers: Brazil, Russia, India and China*, www.alllearn.org

Index